3.8

3.50

A

DuBose Heyward

READER

The Publications of the Southern Texts Society

Michael O'Brien, Series Editor

University of Cambridge

A
DuBose Heyward
READER

Edited and with an Introduction by

JAMES M. HUTCHISSON

The University of Georgia Press
Athens and London

© 2003 by the University of Georgia Press
Athens, Georgia 30602
All rights reserved
Designed by Sandra Strother Hudson
Set in 11.5/14 Centaur by Graphic Composition
Printed and bound by Thomson-Shore
The illustration used on the title page and part titles is by Theodore Nadejen. It is from
a 1925 edition of *Porgy* published by the George H. Doran Company.
The photograph (p. xvi) of DuBose Heyward, circa 1929, by Doris Ullman,
is courtesy of the South Carolina Historical Society.
The paper in this book meets the guidelines for permanence and durability of the
Committee on Production Guidelines for Book Longevity of the Council on
Library Resources.

Printed in the United States of America
07 06 05 04 03 C 5 4 3 2 1
07 06 05 04 03 P 5 4 3 2 1

Library of Congress Cataloging-in-Publication Data
Heyward, DuBose, 1885–1940.
A DuBose Heyward reader / edited and with an introduction by James M. Hutchisson.
p. cm. — (The publications of the Southern Texts Society)
Includes bibliographical references (p.) and index.
ISBN 0-8203-2468-x (alk. paper) — ISBN 0-8203-2485-x (pbk. : alk. paper)
1. Southern States—Literary collections. 2. American literature—Southern States—
History and criticism. 3. Charleston (S.C.)—Literary collections. 4. African Americans—
Literary collections. 5. Southern States—Intellectual life. 6. Southern States—In literature.
7. African Americans in literature. 8. Southern States—Civilization.
I. Hutchisson, James M. II. Title. III. Series.
PS3515.E98 A6 2003
818′.5209—dc21   2002010199

British Library Cataloging-in-Publication Data available

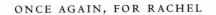

ONCE AGAIN, FOR RACHEL

Contents

Acknowledgments

THANKS ARE DUE first to my research assistants, Cathy Hamann and Heather Crosby, for their help in annotating the texts. Clay Hasty assisted with typing. Colleagues in Charleston and elsewhere offered advice, critiques, and information on the occasional point of southern arcana that seemed unannotatable: I sincerely thank David Weaver for his knowledge of black American theater; Wayne Shirley for his expertise on the musical score of *Porgy and Bess*; Martha Severens for her research on visual artists of the Charleston Renaissance; and Harlan Greene for his willingness to share the stupendous mental archive of all things Charlestonian that he has developed these many years of reading, writing, and lecturing on Charleston writers.

Michael O'Brien must be singled out for his useful suggestions on reading the first draft of the manuscript.

Equally important was the institutional support offered by The Citadel and its academic officers—notably English Department Head James S. Leonard, Provost Harry S. Carter, and past Dean of the College of Graduate and Professional Studies David Reilly. A sabbatical in 1996–97 supplied some of the time for work on this book. Fellow Americanist Tony Redd shared his knowledge of southern literature with me, as did David Shields, who suggested that I do this project for the Southern Texts Society.

Albert J. Cardinali, executor of the estate of DuBose and Dorothy Heyward, gave permission to reprint Heyward's writings, and in part made possible the publication of this volume through a subsidy by the Heyward Memorial Foundation.

The staff of the South Carolina Historical Society in Charleston once again made my research a smooth and pleasurable task. The willingness of its staff to answer any question, photocopy any document, or search back in the recesses of the formidable building that houses the Heyward Collection was inexhaustible. Thank you, Peter Wilkerson, Daisy Bigda, Eric Emerson,

Karen Stokes, Pete Rerig, Pat Hash, Steve Hoffeius, and the numerous interns and runners who helped out while I worked on this book.

The following institutions supplied photocopies and/or gave permission to quote from their collections: College of William and Mary, Rollins College, University of Mississippi, University of Pittsburgh, University of Georgia, University of South Carolina. In addition, the following individuals answered queries: Phillip Banks, North Carolina Room, East Asheville Branch, Asheville-Buncombe County Library System; Eugene Waddell, College of Charleston Special Collections, Charleston, South Carolina; Vivian Fisher, African American/Special Collections Department, Enoch Pratt Free Library, Baltimore, Maryland; Joan A. Pickett, Archives, Jacksonville Historical Society, Jacksonville, Florida; and Kay Bost, University Archives, Southern Methodist University, Dallas, Texas. As they have in the past, Debbe Causey and Kathleen Turner of the Daniel Library at The Citadel uncomplainingly filled my many interlibrary loan requests, for which I am grateful.

My wife, Rachel, deserves special mention. Since I first started writing about literary Charleston several years ago, it has seemed almost as if the ghosts of DuBose Heyward and of the city's past have taken up permanent residence in our lives. I hope that, like me, she's found it to be a happy haunting.

J. H.

Abbreviations Used in the Text

DBH   DuBose Heyward
DKH   Dorothy Kuhns Heyward
JB   John Bennett
JSH   Jane Screven Heyward
SCHS   South Carolina Historical Society

Introduction

IN 1924 DuBOSE HEYWARD was an insurance agent working in his native city of Charleston, South Carolina. One year later he was world famous as the author of *Porgy*, a major novel by a white southerner that depicted African Americans with realism instead of condescension. In just three years, the slim book that began to change national perceptions of race would be adapted for the New York stage by Heyward and his dramatist wife, Dorothy, and would create new opportunities for African American actors. Eight years later, Heyward would collaborate with George Gershwin on transforming his story into the folk opera *Porgy and Bess*, a masterwork that would become one of the crown jewels of America's musical heritage and one of the most enduring cultural icons of the American South.

DuBose Heyward was inextricably a part of Charleston, both its past and its present. Forever associated with secessionist politics and the romantic glamour of the antebellum South, Charleston in the 1920s was only just beginning to take its first halting steps toward scrutinizing—not yet embracing—the modern temper in art. Herein lay Heyward's—and Charleston's—great interest for intellectual historians and literary analysts of the South. For in both the author and the city can be seen a contradictory impulse—the attempt to create change while at the same time lamenting it, battling the encroachment of modernity, and clinging self-consciously to the past. Nowhere among Charleston's writers and other artists is this bifurcation better seen than in Heyward, who would become Charleston's most visible cultural ambassador. The sampling of his writings in this volume illustrates the pulls and tensions that defined his art.

Race was the crucible in which his writings were forged. Heyward was drawn to the world of the Charleston blacks—especially the world of the sea-island Gullah—for he saw the Gullah people as a noble, vast, and essentially unexplored subject for art. Initially he depicted them with sympathy and understanding, but still as an "exotic," alien subspecies. Eventually, however, as he matured as a writer, his social thinking deepened and broadened—never completely, perhaps, but significantly. He moved from a staunch social conservatism to a liberal, although nonrevolutionary, advocacy of black rights.

Heyward was neither an apologist for the Old South nor a propagandist for the New South. As part of the modern southern cultural scene, he was both an anomaly and a trademark. This makes for a rich dynamic in his writings, which are collected here for the first time. Through his poetry, his fiction, and his critical articles, we can see the evolution of this southerner's social conscience. This volume should introduce new readers to Heyward, reacquaint familiar ones with his work, and expand everyone's understanding of this unusual writer's contributions to modern southern literature.

HEYWARD'S PERSONAL HISTORY is compelling dramatic material, for his early life was one peculiarly unsuited to writing about African Americans without hewing to the cultural stereotypes then imprinted on much of the southern consciousness. He was descended from the choicest South Carolina stock.[1] Heywards had been instrumental in the founding of the colony of Charles Towne; the author's great-great-great-grandfather was a signer of the Declaration of Independence. When through the cotton trade in the nineteenth century Charleston became the queen city of the South, several of Heyward's ancestors played roles in quelling slave rebellions, particularly the Denmark Vesey revolt of 1822.

Heyward took more than an amateur interest in his family's history; late in life he went to considerable trouble trying to pinpoint whose sympathies lay where during the American Revolution (a question he was never able to answer to his satisfaction). In print, he surveyed episodes in Charleston's history several times ("The Negro in the Low-Country," "Dock Street Theatre," and "Charleston: Where Mellow Past and Present Meet") but came closest to penetrating the tightly woven scrim with which the first families of the city protected themselves in *Peter Ashley*, the historical novel he set in Charleston on the eve of secession.

After the war, of course, the social fabric of white elite Charleston was so torn asunder that its many peculiar institutions—not just slavery but the pursuit of the arts and leisure in myriad forms—were lost. Heywards, Manigaults, Rutledges, all alike were left with little money to trade on; their names sustained them—creating jobs where there were technically no vacancies, opening doors, as always, to business opportunities and social functions, and helping to maintain status and privilege. There was, nonetheless, a sense of privation, of something lost that could never be regained. And it was through this imaginative leap of fellow feeling that Heyward may well have made his first emotional connections with Charleston's African Americans, who had always known privation—in a much deeper, more immediate, and more tangible sense than did Charleston's old white society. Then there was the peculiar geography of the city. Its prewar integration had been by quirk of fate preserved so that black and white lived mixed together, affording someone like Heyward as close to a dual existence as could be had in that time and place—as he observed the unique culture of the African Americans who surrounded him.

Certainly Heyward's mother, Jane, was touched by African American culture. Janie, as she was called, had had her prospects twice reduced: once when her family's plantations failed after the war and again when her young husband, Ned—who had been reduced to working as a wage laborer in a rice mill—died in a job-related accident. The young DuBose was not quite three at the time; his sister, Jeannie, was two. Janie was devastated: she recorded in her journal dire predictions for the young family's future—"I pray there will not be another grave [in the churchyard] next year," she worried—and could not overcome her previous dependence on her husband.[2]

Janie found strength through contact with the Gullah world—those servants, primarily female, who had raised her and who also raised DuBose (his first language may well have been Gullah). Janie began to try her hand at writing, and this career soon blossomed. She became a leading "dialect recitalist"—giving oral interpretations of Gullah folktales and stories she drew from the lives of the Gullah women she knew. These sketches she later collected and published in two volumes, *Songs of the Charleston Darkey* (1912) and *Brown Jackets* (1923). By the early 1920s, Janie was famous throughout the East as audiences, particularly northern ones, were curious about southern culture and wanted to see something of the life they had glimpsed during the war.

Janie exposed DuBose to this Gullah world. African Americans were part of many of his formative experiences. One summer he worked in the cotton warehouse at the port, watching laborers; another summer he supervised farmworkers on his aunt's plantation; as a youth he worked for an insurance company and collected "burial money" in black neighborhoods; then during World War I he gave speeches at rallies in the black neighborhoods, selling liberty bonds. As these experiences accumulated, Heyward moved from being an interested but detached observer to someone genuinely curious about the life he saw unfolding about him to, finally, an inchoate artist unconsciously absorbing the customs and rhythms of this life.

Heyward's attraction to this "alien" subculture became irresistible: in the introduction to the play version of *Porgy* ("The American Negro in Art"), Heyward was later to write, "What was this life . . . going on within our own, yet was apart from it?" It possessed a certain "indefinable quality" that remained with whites "only in a . . . vestigial state, and at times seemed to have departed altogether. . . . From admiration of the manifestations of this secret law my feeling grew to one of envy." In his youth that curiosity had to remain unsatisfied, but soon thereafter it found magnificent expression.

HEYWARD WANTED to be a writer but he ended up being an insurance agent. As a young man—primarily during a series of convalescences from illnesses (diphtheria, typhoid, and polio) that seemed to wrack him with deliberate fury—Heyward dabbled in all kinds of art forms. After painting for a bit he tried drawing, then etching; he acted in amateur drama productions and tried set designing; he wrote plays, poems, short fiction, and even a screenplay.[3] But like so many southern gentlemen in the postwar years, Heyward still very much thought of writing as an avocation rather than a profession. He had to do something "proper" with his life, because he was, after all, a Charlestonian, a Heyward. So he partnered with a family friend and entered the life-insurance business. He found he had a natural flair for entrepreneurship, and the business flourished. Still yearning to inhabit the world of art, however, in 1920 Heyward cofounded the Poetry Society of South Carolina, the first regional poetry circle in America. This organization, some would say, was also the early prime mover behind the great Southern Renaissance of the late 1920s and 1930s.[4]

The Poetry Society evolved from the groundswell of artistic activity that had been taking shape in Charleston just after World War I. The watercolorist Alice Ravenel Huger Smith, for example, brought fame to Charleston with her romanticized scenes of the low-country plantations, as did the etcher Elizabeth O'Neill Verner, whose starker, more realistic black-and-white cityscapes were likewise drawn from the city's rich Gullah culture.[5] Under the influence of two visitors, Gabrielle Clements and Ellen Day Hale, the Charleston Etchers Club was formed, and soon thereafter the noted printmaker Alfred Hutty came to Charleston in search of a winter retreat, only to become a permanent resident. Entranced by the low country, artists from other regions were drawn to the city—Edward Hopper and Childe Hassam, for example, stayed for a while; others, like Anna Heyward Taylor and James Fowler Cooper, founded their careers on studies of local subjects. Theater groups sprang up, and the Charleston Museum hired a female director, Laura Bragg, who became the doyenne of cultural education in the city.

Women, in fact, dominated this surge in the arts, for in addition to Smith, Verner, and others, many of the fledgling writers in the city were women, among them Josephine Pinckney, a descendant of Eliza Lucas Pinckney, the colonial author and symbol of the self-reliant woman. Pinckney would go on to write *Three o'Clock Dinner*, arguably the quintessential Charleston novel, and a bestseller of 1945. Advancing the empowerment of women in politics and the professions became almost an outreach mission of the city's cultural movement. Anita Pollitzer, a Jewish woman, would lead the National Woman's party, just as Laura Bragg, as the first female director of a scientific museum in North America, would initiate trends soon to be taken up by museum educators nationally. Susan Pringle Frost, who established the Society for the Preservation of Historic Dwellings, was a businesswoman and suffragette; through her work the city went on to create the first zoning preservation laws in the country. And other glimmers of a more dynamic, changing horizon were appearing: Charleston also launched the first serious Zionist in America, Ludwig Lewisohn, first a novelist and then a critic, who was praised by Sigmund Freud and Thomas Mann.[6]

To what degree was the Poetry Society a facilitator of change? Although most commentators have pigeonholed it (and demeaned it) for a lukewarm aesthetic sensitivity, it defies easy categorization. Certainly it was evangelistic—two of its manifestos, which appeared as forewords to the society's yearbooks and which Heyward authored, were among the most prominent examples of the Charleston art scene's cultural imperatives, although its bred-in-the-bone gentility probably impeded its progress as an agent of cultural change. At the suggestion of the children's book author and illustrator John Bennett, a native Ohioan who had moved to the city when he married a woman from a prominent Charleston family, Heyward and Hervey Allen (later to be famous as the author of *Anthony Adverse*, a best-selling historical novel of 1933) began an informal writers' discussion group that met on Wednesday evenings in Bennett's home. Here Bennett would critique the younger men's works in progress and offer literary guidance. From these meetings the Poetry Society developed, and it became the catalyst of Heyward's career.

Unique among its approximate counterparts in Richmond, Chapel Hill, and Nashville, the Poetry Society was a social organization that was also devoted to poetry. The cofounders got the names of the charter members from the city blue book. Then they set dues at a rather high rate so that people would know it was upper-crust, and very quickly there was a waiting list to get in. But Heyward took his work seriously. He developed a network of contacts with the literary world—people who came to Charleston to speak, like Carl Sandburg and Amy Lowell. And his early efforts paid off: a poetry collection coauthored with Hervey Allen, *Carolina Chansons,* was published by Macmillan—a major trade publisher.

At about the same time, Heyward and Allen were invited by Harriet Monroe to guest edit the April 1922 issue of *Poetry,* a special number dedicated to southern verse. In their introductory essay, "Poetry South," one of the earliest documents of the nascent Southern Renaissance, they surveyed the state of poetry in the region and made some predictions about its future. The essay well illustrates the paradox of the Charleston Renaissance. Artistic conservatism undergirds virtually every idea in the piece—Negro folk material, racial themes, and poetic experimentalism are all interesting but untested and should thus be used with caution—yet Heyward in particular wanted to be in the vanguard of the literary arts. One therefore finds an impulse toward compromise, or sometimes outright equivocation, in the essay: "We will accept with modern spirit the new forms in verse," they write, "but accept them as being valuable for their loosening effect upon the old rather than being all satisfactory in themselves." Such a highly qualified statement may help explain some omissions in the editors' selections of verse in the issue, notably the work of John Crowe Ransom and the other Fugitive poets.

In like manner, the preface to *Carolina Chansons* sounds like an exercise in prudence, especially in Heyward's urging "restraint" with the use of African American materials in verse. In both pieces Heyward is also alert to the dangers of local color, which possesses "the fatal tendency to remain local," but it would not be until the publication of *Porgy* in 1925 that Heyward would attempt to resolve the aesthetic conflict of using local-color material while at the same time trying to transcend it—in the ways that he several times suggested Robert Frost and E. A. Robinson had been able to do.

This early phase of Heyward's career shows the paradox of past and present, innovation and retreat, that tugged at Charleston, as it did at America
nationally, in the interwar years. Heyward's poetry was traditional—sedate
and somewhat Georgian in character, and it emphasized local color not as a
launching point for further aesthetic variation but simply as the subject matter of the poem, thus limiting its life span in the evolution of poetic modernism. In the *Carolina Chansons* preface, Heyward and Allen assert the pri-
macy of regionalism but also see a future in unconventional topics like "the
burning racial problem" and the use of the jazz idiom in southern verse. In
similar fashion earlier that year, Heyward had published in *Contemporary Verse*
one of his earliest notable poems, "Gamesters All," in which there is a view
of the human dignity of all races that anticipates much that is great in *Porgy
and Bess.* Typical of Heyward's position, the poem does not rail against racial
inequality, but it does implicitly condemn the white man's often callous dis-
regard for human rights.

The Poetry Society's speakers tended to be traditionalists in the world of
letters, but the organization also invited such "bohemians" as Gertrude Stein,
Edna St. Vincent Millay, and others. In like manner, the Gibbes Art Museum
hosted the first exhibit of Solomon Guggenheim's collection of nonobjective
art in the country. A city like Charleston could thus produce at the same time
a figure such as Herbert Ravenel Sass, a charter member of the Poetry Society
who made a career as an Old South apologist and later a staunch segregation-
ist, and Waties Waring, a federal judge whose rulings opened up the Demo-
cratic party to African Americans and helped end segregation. The same contradictory pull can be seen in Heyward: *Porgy* conveyed a new, sympathetic
view of African Americans, yet Heyward was also a founding member of
the Society for the Preservation of Negro Spirituals, whose white members
dressed up in authentic antebellum costume and, on stage sets meant to evoke
the plantation ideal, sang authentic work songs of southern blacks.

HEYWARD WAS NEVER comfortable as a businessman and a fixture in social circles. But, true to form, neither did he possess the daring that would
make him shed the role altogether. Two events in the early 1920s, however,
encouraged him to break with tradition and find his own way. One was
his gaining entrée to the famous MacDowell Colony for artists, located in
bucolic New Hampshire, where he began to stay every summer.[7] Here he
met E. A. Robinson and Elinor Wylie and others—figures even the most

bohemian people in his circle of acquaintanceship could not start to approach in terms of heterodoxy. The gulf, then, widened. He began to see what vast distance lay between the world of art as evidenced in Charleston in the Poetry Society and the more tangible, visible energies that thrummed through the MacDowell Colony each day as novels were written, canvases painted, and symphonies composed.

Heyward was thus primed for change when at the Colony he met his future wife, Dorothy Hartzell Kuhns—a woman much ahead of her time who was to influence Heyward greatly, in his artistic abilities and his social sympathies. They were similar—both sickly and fragile, both from families with a history of tragedy and loss. They even looked alike: "Hansel and Gretel lost in a wood," a journalist once wrote, "perhaps of their own making."[8] Both had a dreamy-eyed wonderment to them, a lack of self-confidence and of physical intensity. Dorothy had fled her conservative upbringing in Ohio, where her family had expected her to be a good little housewife, and broke into acting and playwriting. She graduated the star student of George Pierce Baker's famous playwriting workshop at Harvard. Thomas Wolfe was a classmate; a famous recent alumnus was Eugene O'Neill.

Dorothy helped Heyward realize what he'd been coming to think all along: the chasm between the world of art and the world of Charleston commerce and society. "The Colony was grand," he wrote her upon leaving, "and it is very hard to come back to this world of human business machines."[9] Encouraged by Dorothy, Heyward gave up his business and devoted himself full-time to writing. He had had the idea for *Porgy*, about a crippled black beggar and the woman he comes to love and to lose, for some time. His mother's writings had also inspired him, as had John Bennett, who had done extensive research and writing on Gullah culture. When Farrar and Rinehart accepted the novel, Heyward was stunned (he was typically self-effacing, modest to a fault): "God knows how I happened to do it," he told Hervey Allen. "I don't."[10]

Porgy was a watershed moment in southern literature because it depicted blacks in a straightforward rather than condescending manner. One New York reviewer said he was "fully prepared for another one of those novels about kindly black mammies" and was stunned by what he got. Back in Charleston, people were either perplexed or hostile: one wanted to know why he hadn't written about "white folks"; another said the book was "filthy" and "not worth the paper it was printed on."[11]

But to what degree was the dreamy-eyed Charlestonian desiring that the African American race be recognized and advance? Certainly *Porgy* is fearless in its straightforward, if implied, view of the black man as "merely a human being" and not some clownish misrepresentation. Yet in the same breath, Heyward could disavow any political intent, as he wrote to Herschel Brickell in 1928:

> Why, in Heaven's name must the writer have motives and "messages" wished on him? If I have discovered anything about the Southern Negro at all it is simply that, because he is still at heart a primitive, and has resisted American standardization, and has retained a native delight in color and song, he is a more fruitful subject for art than his conventionalized white neighbor. Beyond this I have tried to show him simply and honestly as I see him. That is all. I have no motive except the always forlorn hope of approximating on a printed page my own particular ideal of beauty.[12]

Whatever his motives, Heyward achieved fame quickly and almost as quickly began to distance himself from the Poetry Society and from Charleston. "I can't earn a living out of literature in Charleston," he told John Bennett.[13] But he was also sad to see that part of his life ending. He privately confided to another friend, "What will become of the old Poetry Society?" and quoted a Negro spiritual, "mudderless children have a hard time when mother is dead."[14] In fact, Heyward, along with Hervey Allen and Josephine Pinckney, were jumping ship at their first opportunities to pursue their own careers, in New York and elsewhere. The Poetry Society would very soon be eclipsed, primarily by the Fugitive/Agrarians, whose aesthetic imperatives would prove to be more global and whose verse would prove to possess more artistic staying power.[15]

Much can be learned by comparing the two groups' theory and practice of poetry. Both groups sought to identify elements that were traditionally theirs as Southerners, and both sought to preserve them. Both groups wrote as a corrective to contemporary cultural fragmentation. And both groups protested the abandonment of a social ideal in which, as Ransom wrote, man and nature "seem to live on terms of mutual respect and amity." The work of the Fugitives has come to represent the essence of poetic modernism; that of the Charlestonians seems antiquated, impermanent, merely "popular."

Yet in "Poetry South," Heyward and Allen spoke stirringly of the modern's "loosening effect upon the old," and they saw themselves as being in (uncritical) revolt against a lyric South of the former century, satisfied with the way things were. It may be that the peculiar social orientation of the Charlestonians in part explains their role in the currents of modernism. The Fugitives, for example, produced intellectualized, specialized writing for what was at least initially a very small audience. The Charlestonians adopted an expansive mode of writing that could best be described as pre-Raphaelite or late Ruskinian. They thought it essential to remain connected to the culture that produced them, and that only through participation in the culture that created them could they develop a sensitive awareness of the past and create a feeling of stability and permanence in the flux of an ever-changing world. Their activities were thus directed at enfranchising a wide community of readers as well as participants or collaborators in the creation of art.

In their efforts to celebrate and preserve a way of life that might be lost because of industrialization, they resembled the Fugitives. But in their attempts at preservation, they privileged a much different audience, the Gullah blacks. In founding a poetry society, Heyward and the others were practicing a kind of poetic imperialism. They thought that being "communal" should be an interest that appeals to a large majority of citizens representing all walks of life. The society's *Year Book* made available to the *public* a record of the poetic achievements of the year.

Heyward largely forsook these objectives once he had separated from Charleston and the Poetry Society. He began to see the trajectory of his career in much different terms as he lived part of the year in New York and part in the North Carolina mountains, near Asheville. His forays into New York in the mid- to late 1920s formed the next part of his unplanned artistic education, for little did he know what type of world he was stepping into: a world where white artists and intellectuals were positively obsessed with African American culture—the Harlem nightclubs, the all-Negro revues, and primitivism in the form of Josephine Baker's "Revue Negre."

HEYWARD'S ADMISSION TICKET to this ongoing cultural carnival came when *Porgy* was made into a nonmusical play. He recounts the experience in "The American Negro in Art." Dorothy was responsible for this success. She thought *Porgy* would make a great play, but she couldn't convince her husband. So in secret she drafted a script, telling the naturally conservative Du-Bose that she was working on a mystery novel. When he read it he realized his mistake. Then they refined the script together, and three producers immediately wanted to buy it.

The show premiered in October 1927 and initially got lukewarm reviews. The Heywards (who were never wildly self-confident) thought they had bungled it. So to atone for their mistakes, they locked themselves in their hotel room for three days rewriting the play. Then on the fourth day it was pouring down rain. They walked down to the theater and thought it odd that there was a long line snaking down the street and around the building. People were standing in the rain. They went in the stage door, found the producer, and told him what they'd been doing; the producer said to them, "You're crazy. We're a hit." Word-of-mouth publicity and better second-day reviews had made *Porgy* the hottest ticket in town. It was standing room only. In his essay Heyward gives a firsthand account of the difficulties of staging *Porgy*, then a revolutionary presentation of the life of African Americans in the South. Heyward shows how the intent of the play ran counter to the prevailing ethos in New York theatrical circles: that African American material was suitable only for vaudevillian treatment rather than a sober, realistic rendering.

In adapting *Porgy* for the stage, Heyward learned how to be a playwright. But he learned much more—about how African Americans were perceived in the north versus in Charleston. He met James Weldon Johnson and Nella Larsen and other leaders of the Harlem Renaissance—all of them applauded *Porgy*. At a rehearsal one day, he wrote his mother, "I wonder what my friends back in Charleston would think seeing me here addressing these people as Mister and Miss."[16] But Heyward had always had the seeds of liberal-mindedness in him: for example, he and Dorothy insisted that the cast be made up of professional black actors (of whom there weren't many in 1927) rather than whites in blackface, as was the custom of the time. *Porgy* helped advance the nascent black theater movement; after it, more leading roles were awarded to black actors.

The experience of Charles Gilpin, the award-winning star of O'Neill's *The Emperor Jones* in the 1919–20 season, is representative. Gilpin was dropped from the London run of *The Emperor Jones* for changing some of the play's more racist lines and epithets. In 1927 he was fired from a Hollywood production of *Uncle Tom's Cabin* because he refused to play Tom as a stupid darkey. No further film roles came his way. Thus, after reaching the peak of achievement

by a black performer, Gilpin reportedly had to go back to work running
elevators when the show ended its run. He explained to a friend how hard
it was "to get a chance to play even Negro parts in regular companies":
"I played such a part in one company, and some of the actors used to stand
outside my dressing-room and talk about me, evidently intending me to over-
hear them. 'Why did they get a nigger for that part?' they would say. 'A white
man could play it better than any nigger that was ever born!'"[17] In subsequent
years, the number of black performers awarded starring or significant roles in
Broadway productions rose steadily. James Weldon Johnson would later
state that "in *Porgy* the Negro removed all doubts as to his ability to do acting that requires thoughtful interpretation and intelligent skill."

The success of the stage version of *Porgy* also shows how much popular
culture—or the mass arts—depended on co-opting African American art
forms. As Constance Rourke, Gilbert Seldes (both friends of Heyward from
the MacDowell Colony), and others have explained, since folk culture is pre-
media and pre-literate, it depends on communal traditions of storytelling and
live performance.[18] After World War I, as Americans became fascinated with
their own cultural resources and gave up English and European traditions,
many like Heyward discovered that the deepest roots of American culture lay
in the blacks' endlessly exploited and long unacknowledged "gift of story and
song," as W. E. B. Du Bois proclaimed in a key essay in *The Crisis*. The newly
named Harlem "nation" of Aframerica (unhyphenated) suggested that blacks'
and whites' collaborative participation in art was inseparably intertwined;
black and white collaborative energy crested in the New York stage world.
One need only note that "The Charleston" was a black American dance form
that debuted in New York in 1923 in a black musical revue called *Runnin' Wild*.

This charged collaboration was essential to America's dawning global
hegemony in the fast-growing field of popular culture. Like other southerners (Ellen Glasgow, Paul Green), Heyward thus saw the highest trajectory for
his star as extending out of the South and into the cosmopolite society of
Manhattan. And like other whites showcasing black artistic work, Heyward's
small body of film and theater writing (see below) was part of the Negroiza-
tion of American culture—as was O'Neill's giving Paul Robeson the starring role in *All God's Chillun* and Charles Gilpin in *The Emperor Jones* (for which
Heyward later wrote the screenplay); Paul Green's writing *Green Pastures*, a
dramatic fable based on Negro folklore; even H. L. Mencken's urging Knopf
to publish Walter White's *The Fire in the Flint*.

Black actors and playwrights began to receive critical and financial support from such wealthy white artists. Later in the decade, for example, a literary contest for black writers was sponsored by the white establishment. The judges were Van Wyck Brooks, Eugene O'Neill, James Weldon Johnson, and Alain Locke. Langston Hughes and Zora Neale Hurston won prizes that helped further their careers. Black organizations such as the National Association for the Advancement of Colored People and the Urban League promoted artistic excellence among blacks, and white foundations like the Rosenwald Fund also awarded grants to subsidize the black arts movement.

Yet the situation of *Porgy* on stage also reflects the ambivalence, conflict, and compromise that black artists of the 1920s underwent. Most African Americans were pleased that attention was being brought to black artists and hoped that race relations might thereby improve. But many also recognized that the "New Negro" was merely a jazz-age version of the old plantation darkey, almost a pet rather than a person.

Some black intellectuals and artists were wary of this fascination by whites with black culture. It gave rise to unending debates over whether these explicitly sympathetic portrayals marked any real improvement over the racist caricatures that had previously dominated America's cultural landscape. The so-called "talented tenth" felt that African Americans should show that, given the right conditions, they could be as respectable as whites. On the other hand, black artists like Claude McKay and Langston Hughes thought that this was precisely what black artists should *not* do: imitate whites. Rather, they thought that black art should celebrate blacks' own special qualities and cultural gifts.

African American novelists like McKay in *Home to Harlem* and Jean Toomer in *Cane* wrote of black life in ways that appeared to reinforce the essentialist assumptions of what Zora Neale Hurston later named "Negrotarian" fiction. It is logical, then, that these African Americans should have been among Heyward's staunchest allies. However, others such as Walter White, Jessie Fauset, Langston Hughes, and Nella Larsen questioned the basis of racial identity and asserted the inseparability of economic, social, and cultural processes.

THE STAGE VERSION of *Porgy* was a chrysalis out of which Heyward emerged to shed his social conservatism. His progressive-mindeness then grew, and he used his writing to become more openly a social reformer and to adopt a more critical view of race and class in the South. In fact, in the late

1920s and early 1930s Heyward openly aligned himself with several liberal re-
formers who had gravitated to the University of North Carolina at Chapel
Hill, such as Howard W. Odum, a professor there who had founded *The Journal of Social Forces*. Heyward seems to have read this journal with some regu-
larity. He also was good friends with the dramatist Paul Green (who taught
at UNC) and with the Greensboro-based journalist Gerald W. Johnson (who
also taught at UNC, briefly, from 1924 to 1926). All of these outspoken figures
publicly applauded Heyward's moderately heterodox social views, as Heyward did their more extreme views. The University of North Carolina practically became Heyward's institutional champion, giving him an honorary
degree in 1928, publishing his writings in the *Reviewer* (which had relocated
there from Richmond, although it would fold after only a year or so), and
inviting him to speak at university-sponsored writers' gatherings.

The decade of the 1930s, then, became Heyward's most "liberal" period.
After deploring social uplift in early essays like "And Once Again—the Negro," Heyward wrote *Porgy*, which signaled a new thinking about human
rights. After the stage success of *Porgy*, Heyward openly shifted to encouragement of African Americans' aspirations in a remarkable novel—probably
his most effective work of fiction—*Mamba's Daughters* (1929). Taking his cue
in part from late Victorian novels of manners, notably the twin plots of mas-
ter/upstairs versus servants/downstairs, Heyward constructed a somewhat
creaky but socially enlightened novel of black and white society in Charleston. It is the story of three generations of Gullah women. Mamba, the grandmother, is an aged crone but possessed of the tactical instincts of a brilliant
field marshal. She insinuates herself into the home of a white family in Charleston, elevating her status from a "waterfront nigger" (the type Heyward observed as a youth in the seedy Bay Street district) to that of a "white folks'
nigger"—a household servant. With the income Mamba is better able to pro-
vide for her daughter, Hagar, an illiterate mother-of-the-earth, and her grand-
daughter, Lissa, who is raised to aspire higher than her destiny might seem
to allow her to go.

In the novel Heyward also interweaves a less convincing white subplot
that focuses on the autobiographical Saint Wentworth, male heir to a dis-
possessed Charleston family. (Dorothy even turns up in the novel, although
in reverse fashion—as Valerie Land, a northerner who visits the city, meets
Saint, and convinces him to throw over his moon-calf image and become a
serious citizen.) Saint and Mamba are friends, and it is Saint who intercedes

for Lissa in New York at the end of the novel when she arrives there to make her fortune as an opera singer. The finale of the book is eerily predictive of Heyward's intentions with *Porgy and Bess* six years later, as Lissa is recognized not as a black singer but an American singer, in whose voice the audience discerns a new cultural melody:

> "Good God, where'd she come from?" some one queried. "What's it anyway, a play—an opera—a pageant?" And the rejoinder, "For Heaven's sake, don't label it. That's the trouble with us. What we can't label we damn. Can't you see it's new—different? Can't you feel that it's something of our own— American. . . . It's native from the dirt up—it's art—and it's ours." "Ours?" a voice inquired. "Do you mean negro?" "Negro, if you will, yes, but first, American."

Heyward possessed neither a Jamesian talent for understatement nor a Flaubertian sense of detachment. Such "defects" were, for the time, splendid gifts; his unabashed sympathy for the plight of the African American woman is more than simply notable. Certainly, too, the shafts of criticism that Heyward shot in the book did not miss their mark, for when the book was published many Charlestonians balked at a scene in which Saint carries Lissa's suitcase. Heyward was mildly ostracized for this—more so than he had been for *Porgy.* In 1939 the Heywards dramatized the novel for the stage in response to a request by Ethel Waters—then just making a name for herself—who thought the soul of the plot relied more on Hagar, the daughter, than on Mamba or Lissa. The play in fact made a star out of Waters, whom critics universally applauded for limning a profound emotional experience.

Thus if in *Porgy* Heyward's vision of race relations was somewhat idealized, his depiction of Charleston society tinged by a nostalgia for a chimerical era that existed more in imagination than in fact, by the time he wrote *Mamba's Daughters* he had traded this vision of race relations for a more realistic, even sociological view of class and color issues that sometimes approaches the work of southern proletarian authors. Although Heyward's post-*Porgy* fiction is not specifically committed to a revolutionary social vision like that of Olive Tilford Dargan or Grace Lumpkin, it does transmute the old agrarian themes into reformist ones, especially the plight of blacks in the South. Although not a militantly antiracist novel, *Mamba's Daughters* is similar to Lillian Smith's *Strange Fruit* (1944) in its treatment of a black woman and a white man innocent of the world's meanness. Like *Strange Fruit, Mamba* effectively presents the social, ethical, and economic impact of white on black, black on white. To Heyward, the issue of race relations was the donnée of the socially committed writer.

Heyward even tried to write a novel with a specifically proletarian thesis. This uncompleted novel, which Heyward tentatively entitled "Merryvale," dramatized the much-publicized 1929 textile workers' strike in Gastonia, North Carolina.[19] Its main character, a single mother, is dehumanized by the cruel working conditions in the mill, preyed upon sexually by one of the managers, and punished for her outspoken condemnation of the factory's labor policies. Parts of the fragmentary novel are quite bold by prevailing southern standards of 1930–31, when Heyward seems to have worked on it; this element of the novel somewhat anticipates Caldwell's unrestrained method in *Tobacco Road* and *God's Little Acre.*

By targeting class relations in "Merryvale," Heyward showed he could embrace left-leaning social attitudes, although he would never commit himself to a revolutionary social program. What he usually did was redirect these tendencies into a type of fiction in which he could be critical of Charleston institutions without openly lambasting them. He found the guise of the historical novelist perfectly suited to this purpose in *Peter Ashley* (1932), in which he condemned the power of conformity (particularly the pressure of a monolithic community) to stifle free thought. Thus in the novel, set on the eve of South Carolina's secession, his hero—once again a thinly disguised version of his questioning, youthful self—debates the relative merits of rebelling (doing what he feels in his heart is the right thing to do by challenging prevailing political thought) versus belonging (and thus remaining part of a community—without which he might be permanently dislocated and thus in danger of losing his identity). Readers have discerned that this paradigm in the novel is a neat emblem of exactly how Heyward himself felt in his career, as on the one hand he inveighed against social injustice and tilted with the city's leaders over the treatment of African Americans and on the other acceded to the demands of his class and race and did not openly subscribe to liberal thinking.[20]

Thus the paradox of DuBose Heyward and, in parallel fashion, of the art of the Charleston Renaissance. Reading the stirring tribute to the Gullah women of his youth in *Mamba's Daughters* alongside some of the articles Heyward wrote on Charleston history is unsettling. Hitting the peak of his fame abroad when *Porgy* had its stage run in London, Heyward commented in a

London newspaper interview that while African Americans' "school and college facilities are still inferior to the White, and that [their] 'Jim-crow' cars are often overcrowded and dirty," they nevertheless know "that the enlightened element in the South is now awake to [their] needs."[21] Northerners, Heyward contended, "for years have protested the Negro's right to be there," yet "the resulting experience has been a disillusioning one for the Negro who has taken the altruistic protestations at their face value. The actual truth is that when confronted by the Negro in the mass Northern white men are no more anxious to fill their schools, colleges, churches, and theaters with them than are Southerners." In "The Negro in the Low-Country" Heyward conceded that during slavery there were "individual instances of injustice," but he also denied that stocks were bred up by forced mating and argued that the development of the family was the invariable law, citing evidence from slave registers from his mother's family's plantation. Again, slaves were punished, but during the period of slavery the cat-o-nine-tails was used in the United States Navy, and in the City of Charleston, as well as in New England, the public whipping post was "commonly employed . . . for petty white offenders."

The perceived amicable relationship between master and servant was a stereotype that Jane Heyward used to great emotional advantage in her writings. Heyward could demolish it in his own writings ("it has been sentimentalized and utilized *ad nauseam* in writing of the slave period"), yet, in typically ambivalent fashion, he elsewhere indicated that such was a valid cultural measure of antebellum life. Was this the contradiction that one friend observed in Heyward when she told a correspondent she had not read any of his work because she could not "reconcile the way his hands feel when you shake hands with him and the things he writes about the colored brother embracing of the sister"?[22]

To understand Heyward's thinking one must keep in mind the limitations of southern liberalism in his day, which carried with its commitment to racial justice a good deal of ambiguity. Heyward's views on race, reform, and history were complex, bound up as they were in personal history and regional mythology. Southern liberalism was not the same thing as the national racial liberalism of the Radical Republicans during Reconstruction nor the anti–Jim Crow protests of the twentieth century.[23] Southern liberals like Howard Odum and Gerald Johnson, for example, could see down the road that the South would eventually take to more openness and enfranchisement of its minorities, but how far they thought that road would stretch is another matter. By the end of his life, Heyward had a remarkable measure of social openness toward African Americans, but he also retained a romantic sense of their primitivism and a partly unreconstructed view of Southern history. Like other spokesmen for a better South, Heyward's voice was one of caution and equivocation.

IT IS ODD that, as the Great Depression created social dislocation and most American authors gravitated toward themes of social protest, the major figures of the Southern Renaissance as it emerged in full flower at this time— Faulkner, Wolfe, Tate, and others—tended not to use their fiction didactically. Thus in the literature of social commitment in the South at the time, Heyward's work belongs more with that of Harry Harrison Kroll, T. S. Stribling, Lillian Smith, and Erskine Caldwell. Like these authors, Heyward became increasingly concerned with agrarian reform, industrial change, social deracination, and, most of all, race relations. Like many of these writers, too, distancing himself from his own region allowed Heyward to see Charleston and its culture with a more critical eye.

Most of his later works could be said to belong to this literature of social commitment. In an aesthetically flawed but socially daring play entitled *Brass Ankle,* Heyward censured prejudice against the mulatto, a subject treated by black writers since the early novels and slave narratives of pre–Civil War times that reached its peak with Harlem Renaissance artists but was only lightly touched upon by white writers. Paul Green's *White Dresses* employed the topic, but mostly for melodramatic purposes. We must remember that in the 1920s and 1930s the idea of romantic interracial unions was thought of as a colossal cultural transgression. The producers of O'Neill's 1924 drama of miscegenation, *All God's Chillun Got Wings,* had to avert a riot when the playwright cast the white actress Mary Blair opposite Paul Robeson and word got out that Blair was to kiss the black man's hand in the play. Groups lobbied to close down the show before it even premiered. O'Neill had to make his white heroine go crazy before she kissed the black character's hand, thus making the scene palatable to white theatergoers.

In the 1930s this moderate dose of fame—along with a small link in the public mind with social causes, particularly race relations—got Heyward enlisted in various charities on behalf of African Americans. He accepted a position on the advisory board of the Association of Negro Writers and was also elected to the Writer's League Against Lynching. He was more than ever in demand as a speaker, yet his natural self-effacement, combined with an almost pathological lack of confidence, held him back.[24] Five years after its original publication, *Porgy* continued to sell well, spurred on by the success of *Mamba's Daughters.* The former novel was released in Swedish, and a new translation in Japanese was being undertaken. *Porgy* was now in five languages. In addition, *Mamba's Daughters* was appearing in translation serially in the Paris newspapers, as *Porgy* had before it.

Honors seemed to be bestowed upon Heyward virtually everywhere he went. In November 1930 *Vanity Fair* magazine nominated Heyward for its "hall of fame," not just on the basis of his recent successful books and plays but because he was "one of the most important figures in the literary renaissance of the South." Back home, he was made an honorary Phi Beta Kappa of the local chapter at the University of South Carolina. Sometimes, however, the old lack of confidence surfaced. The following year the University of the South in Sewanee, Tennessee, asked Heyward to give the commencement address, but he politely refused. Famous or not, Heyward still felt insecure around "superior" intellects, such as he expected to find at the college, and he did not want to draw attention to his own lack of formal education. "It was simply out of my depth," he told his mother. He did, however, accept the College of Charleston's offer of an honorary Doctor of Letters at their commencement exercises on 14 May 1931. A hometown degree was perhaps easier for Heyward to accept—a local boy who had made good.

By the time *Porgy and Bess* was staged in 1935, Heyward had evolved into a significant man of letters. He traveled abroad and was frequently in and out of New York, going to cocktail parties attended by the literati and the glitterati (though he was never fully comfortable with such fame). He did organize the first major gatherings of southern writers in the early 1930s— the first at the University of Virginia, the second (less well known) in Charleston. In an interview at the time he confessed his desire to abolish the isolation that characterized southern, as opposed to northern, writers.[25] But in truth he was not at all a writer's writer. He was distinctly unliterary in his habits and attitudes, regularly shunning the spotlight of publicity, begging off speaking at writers' conferences on often the flimsiest of pretexts, never arrogating to himself the privilege of pronouncement. When Hervey Allen sent him a prospectus for a writers' conference that Allen was organizing, Heyward wrote back to say: "[It] scared me to death. I have practically nothing to carry to such a meeting, . . . no project, no theory to defend."[26] This is one reason why his output of critical writing was comparatively small. "Realizing my limitations," he wrote in the same letter, "and that story-telling ability has really damn little to do with good criticism, I have adopted a policy of refusing all of the many kind and flattering offers from my friends . . . to do reviewing. It has always struck me as somewhat amusing that because someone does a successful story, he or she immediately becomes a critic . . . and is promptly given the books of other writers to be solemn and authoritative about. It results, not in criticism, but rather into a competition for good-sportsmanship, especially so as the author-critic is always sent books in his own field of writing." He never felt a bit "like a crusador [sic] who must get into a tin suit and save the day for American Criticism."[27] Heyward's belletristic output wasn't very large, either. He seems to have felt that he had but a limited store of words and ideas in his writer's warehouse. To dip into it was to make sure that he used what he had withdrawn wisely and well.

Heyward did occasionally take up with the Poetry Society again, to bring in famous people to speak. But here too his lack of professional savvy revealed itself. When he managed to engage Gertrude Stein to speak in Charleston, the latter gave her audience a typically fragmented, Byzantine lecture that no could one follow. But Heyward, her host, was always the gentleman. He later wrote her, "We loved you in Charleston. Even if we did not understand you."[28]

Just as Heyward was not always comfortable among the literati, he also made little of his two sojourns in the world of movie-making, the new industry to which writers flocked by the hundreds. Heyward was a skilled screenwriter, however, and the one screenplay for which he was sole author, *The Emperor Jones,* was a solid piece of writing. The film later became a landmark in movie depictions of African Americans.

Heyward found the moviemaking experience (the film was shot on Long Island) exasperating, tiring, and the final product rather a compromise with his and O'Neill's intentions. After Heyward had finished his script, others tinkered with it—the end product was flashier and more action-oriented than what Heyward had originally written. It is interesting for the framework that Heyward constructed of Jones's life before arriving on the island and installing himself as dictator there. "By throwing this character into contact with the disintegrating power of our white civilization," Heyward wrote, he "broke Jones down from the rather simple Southern Negro to the shrewd, grafting Negro of the play."[29]

In Heyward's version of Jones's early life, we meet him first as a pleasure-seeking party-goer in Harlem, who one night steals his friend Jeff's sweetheart. We then learn that, through a combination of Machiavellian determination and obsequiousness (a mimicry of whites and a playing up to their stereotyped conceptions of blacks), he has risen in the ranks of Pullman porters to the President's private car, thus gaining an advantage over Jeff. Always listening for important intelligence that might be discussed by his white employers, Jones learns of a forthcoming financial merger and is able to invest his meager savings in a scheme that yields considerable profits. When his new girlfriend mocks his ambitions, he abruptly abandons her. She then sees him at a cabaret in the company of another woman and stirs up trouble by goading Jeff into challenging Jones. Jones ducks out of the ensuing fight, but some time later encounters Jeff again in a gambling house in Savannah, where Jeff cheats him with loaded dice and then tries to kill him. Jones, however, overpowers his former friend and kills him in self-defense.

Jones is sentenced to prison for ten years. He eventually becomes a trusty, but when he refuses a guard's order to whip a Negro boy who has fallen over from heat stroke, Jones revolts, killing the guard and taking refuge in the stokehold of a boat bound for the West Indies. En route he jumps ship and swims to a nearby island, where he is able to outwit the tribal chief and become "emperor" of the land. From there, Heyward followed the original play. The first half of the film thus appears to be all Heyward, the second half largely O'Neill. Heyward's parts of the story recall elements of both *Porgy* and *Mamba's Daughters:* the gambling-inspired knife fights, the unjust working conditions for black laborers, and the questionable morality of killing in retribution.

Heyward's screenplay is most interesting as a continuation of his increasingly ironic, critical, and even jaundiced view of whites. Heyward's point here is the same as that in his earlier novella, *The Half Pint Flask:* the narrator of that story, a white resident of one of the Carolina sea islands, entertains a scientist-friend who, over the narrator's protests, violates a local taboo by taking a valuable old flask from a Negro grave. Destructive supernatural forces begin to erupt on the island, and the two men just barely escape by returning the relic to its original resting place. In the story, Heyward's theme is the destruction of a "pure" civilization by the corrupt machinations of white society. In *The Emperor Jones*, however, the point is made more emphatic by racial role reversal, as William Slavick has noted.[30] Jones is a black Horatio Alger figure, an embodiment of the "virtues" of white society that, in the end, become vices, which he exports to an untainted community: gambling, drinking, and, most important, the abuse of power by one class in control of the other. Heyward later said that the most enjoyable part of his task was making Jones "a black counterpart of our own big business pirate." The significance of Heyward's sardonic views was not unnoticed by his fellow Charlestonians. When Heyward suggested that the filming be done on nearby Folly Island, the residents there threatened to leave en masse.

One year later, Heyward accepted another screenwriting assignment, this time in Hollywood, on the MGM production of Pearl Buck's *The Good Earth*. The Depression had cut into authors' royalties severely, and many publishing houses could no longer even offer their writers advances. In contrast, by the 1930s moviemaking had become one of the ten leading American industries; writers thus thought of Hollywood as a promised land, a mecca of economic prosperity and artistic potential.

Heyward found the scene to be full of comic-opera material. His hopes for a truly meaningful story line were dashed by studio chief Irving Thalberg (and the some twenty other writers who followed Heyward on the project, butchering his original intentions), and he could not "network" with the other artists who worked there—further evidence of his discomfort in the world of letters and perhaps another reason why his fame has never been that large.[31] Installed in a penthouse suite at the Beverly Hills Hotel, Heyward also found distasteful the chasm that existed between the decadence and extravagance of the filmmakers and the rest of the community, which lived in a series of shanties and homeless camps.

His experience in Hollywood, then, was quite unlike that of other southern writers like Lillian Hellman, William Faulkner, and Erskine Caldwell, who successfully adapted their talents to the new industry. Heyward was bothered by the cog-in-the-wheel environment; he felt he was but a tiny part of a huge process that ground on ceaselessly, indifferent to him and his ideas. Further, there was no stability; the people he met at MGM seemed unreliable and capricious. There was endless socializing, but Heyward could not fall in with the crowd of self-consciously intellectual, voluble writers; they seemed to belong to one big country club at which he was merely a guest.

HEYWARD'S GREATEST achievement, of course, was *Porgy and Bess*. Gershwin had been interested in the project since the novel came out in 1925 and he had stayed up all night reading it. But it wasn't until the summer of 1934, when Gershwin came down to Heyward's place on Folly Beach, that work really progressed. Heyward tells the full story, with only a few romanticized touches, in "Porgy and Bess Return on Wings of Song." On several occasions Heyward took Gershwin out to Negro churches in the country to witness the "shouting" during services; Gershwin jumped right in and started "shouting" himself after a while.

Something of Heyward's personality uncharacteristically shows through in this essay, as well. One senses the pride with which he regarded his accomplishments, but often in the same sentence one detects his inbred need to restrain himself from trumpeting his successes too loudly—quite in contrast to Gershwin, whom Heyward correctly portrays in the article as possessed of a talent that needed no apologies.

Few realize the extent of Heyward's involvement in *Porgy and Bess*. He wrote the libretto single-handedly; he co-authored the lyrics to at least half of the songs and was single author for "A Woman Is a Sometime Thing," "Summertime," and "My Man's Gone Now"; and he assisted in many other ways. He was a full collaborative partner.

A good example is the song "I Got Plenty of Nuttin'." Heyward and Ira Gershwin were in the workroom of George Gershwin's house in New York. George felt there was a spot where Porgy might sing something lighter than what he had been singing, so he went to the piano and began to improvise; after a while there was this cheerful melody. Ira and Heyward both said: "That's it! Don't look any further." Then, a title popped into Ira's head. "I got plenty o' nuttin'," he said tentatively. Heyward and Gershwin liked the title, so Ira said he'd get to work on it "later."

Heyward then asked Ira if he'd mind if he tried his hand at it. He said, "So far, everything I've done has been set by George and I've never written words to music." "I'd like to take the tune along with me to Charleston." Two weeks later, Heyward sent him a completed lyric, which Ira then polished into the final product.

When *Porgy and Bess* premiered in 1935, it was a relative failure, critically and financially. The critics carped at it because it was a hybrid form: part Broadway show, part "serious" opera. Heyward and both Gershwins lost their financial investments in the show. Heyward was stung by the critical indifference to the work that he had put so much effort into—the work he had seen as developing new opportunities and new standards for African Americans in art. Heyward's keen awareness of popular culture makes it possible today to make a finer distinction about *Porgy and Bess:* it represents that moment in America when the popular arts rose to prominence and such a "crowd pleaser" as *Porgy and Bess* could be regarded as high art. That the opera was a major production featuring black performers also makes it a milestone in the democratization of art in America.

The astonishing vitality that we associate with American culture during the 1920s sprang primarily from the popular arts. Mass culture began to emerge in the 1920s and accelerated in the 1930s with the advent of radio, which had evolved from a mysterious curiosity to a universally accepted instrument of entertainment, business, learning, and mass communication, with few counterparts in American social history. In "Porgy and Bess Return," Heyward astutely observes that radio was the first truly mass medium and had the potential to democratize culture, both in terms of distribution as well as participation.

Radio was only one facet of the vast democratization of the arts in America in the 1930s, as preferences for all things European—the rage in the 1920s—gave way to new definitions of art, which now included popular or mass culture. The fine arts had become increasingly remote to average Americans, particularly in the economic hard times of the 1930s. Gilbert Seldes recognized this emerging transformation of culture in his 1924 book, *The Seven Lively Arts*. The title referred to those arts that were created to satisfy mass-entertainment demands—such things as slapstick movie comedies, comic strips, revues, musical comedies, newspaper columns, slang humor, popular songs, and vaudeville. Eventually he and such other critics as George Jean Nathan, James Gibbons Hunecker, Matthew Josephson, and Marsden Hartley would expand the boundaries even more to include such arts as industrial design, wpa theatrical productions, Bristol-Myers's roadside jingles, and the type of "Broadway opera" inaugurated by *Porgy and Bess*. It might be said that popular opera offered a new form of culturally accessible art.

Heyward had always been interested in the nexus between art and commerce; its unification seemed confirmed in this Broadway opera and its mass-culture cousins, a point made in jingoistic fashion by Seldes in a 1936 essay, which proclaimed that commerce and art had been irrevocably united in American culture: "When Bing Crosby spoke the name of Marcel Proust into the microphone . . . more or less in honor of Miracle Whip, the long uneasy, half-scandalous affair between commerce and the arts was at last acknowledged."[32] A necessary part of a program to democratize culture, of course, meant enfranchising African Americans in creating and presenting art, something that *Porgy and Bess* did in superior fashion.

AFTER CRITICAL INDIFFERENCE to the work became evident, however, Heyward tired and grew depressed. He had always lived with the sense that his stardom was some odd fluke, or even a cosmic irony, and that, like Porgy, he awaited the moment when the gods would call him down. So he beat a hasty retreat from the big-city world of celebrity. In 1936 Heyward resettled in Charleston and put his flagging energy into the Dock Street Theatre, where he was resident playwright. The theater, one of the country's earliest, had been restored as part of a WPA project. Upon completion, it became the locus of a movement to launch southern drama, drawing on native or regional materials. The introspection that marked Charleston in Heyward's heyday, the 1920s, brought it to an awareness of its architectural treasures and stimulated a great interest in historic preservation. Advocates of preservation felt the city was under a concerted attack almost the equal of the Union bombardment—this time by museum directors and collectors who were buying up houses, in part or in whole, and stripping them of their mantels, moldings, and other valuable parts. In 1920 Susan Frost and Mr. and Mrs. Ernest Pringle founded the Society for the Preservation of Old Dwellings, of which Heyward was a charter member, and the city became the leader of the preservation movement in the United States. Under Charleston's Old and Historic District Ordinance (enforced today with even stricter—some would say impractical—respect for standards) any exterior architectural changes to buildings had to pass the inspection of a Board of Architectural Review.

The Dock Street, which originally opened on 12 February 1736, had been the first building in America used for theatrical purposes. Later destroyed by fire, it was replaced with another playhouse, then turned into a series of residences. In the early nineteenth century these in turn had been converted into the elegant Planter's Hotel, which fell into disrepair after the Civil War. Hey-

ward officiated at the opening-night ceremonies on 26 November 1937, recit-
ing a newly composed prologue to George Farquhar's bawdy comedy, *The Recruiting Officer*. The city's interest in the stage was reinvigorated by the theater,
which infused new life into local repertory troupes like The Footlight Players, still in existence today. For Heyward, the new Dock Street Theatre provided a venue in which he could help young playwrights shape native folk
material into drama. With funds from a Rockefeller grant, Heyward was
later appointed the theater's resident dramatist. Just as Heyward had been
tutored by John Bennett when he began writing in the 1920s, now Heyward
mentored aspiring writers. In the wake of *Porgy and Bess*'s disappointing debut, this process became his most gratifying artistic experience.

The only notable success of Heyward's last years was the stage version of
Mamba's Daughters, which did far more for Ethel Waters than it did for Heyward. He also published a children's book (the only one of Heyward's works
to remain consistently in print) entitled *The Country Bunny and the Little Gold
Shoes*, which originated as a bedtime story for his young daughter, Jenifer. It is
sometimes hard to believe that this gem of a feminist parable was written in
1939, for in the story of the cottontail bunny who grows up to become the
Easter Bunny, Heyward wanted to show young women, as he had (in a sense)
shown African Americans, that they could move past social expectations,
past people who weren't necessarily cheering them on, and follow their destiny—if they trusted themselves enough to persist against the odds, as Heyward himself had done.

A notable failure was Heyward's last novel, with the unfortunate title of
Star Spangled Virgin, originally envisioned as another opera with George Gershwin. The book derives its title from the locale—the American Virgin Islands. Heyward visited them on a yachting cruise in the spring of 1937 and
discerned in the culture there the last bastion of unrestrained primitivism.
The novel concerns the foul-ups that ensue when the U.S. government tries
to "civilize" the inhabitants with New Deal initiatives. In its sometimes disturbing view of African Americans as happy in their isolation and ignorance,
the book bears a resemblance to Heyward's early work, in which he had not
yet begun to champion the social aspirations of American blacks. Heyward
seems not to have been able to choose between serious social criticism and
light-opera comedy, so this might be a reason for the jarring shifts in his treatment of the material. Gershwin suffered a fatal stroke in 1937, and Heyward

could not find another collaborator, so he compromised in publishing the book under circumstances that were probably ill-advised.

IT IS UNFORTUNATE that *Star Spangled Virgin* was Heyward's last public word and more unfortunate still that he died thinking that the one work in which he had invested the most time and energy, *Porgy and Bess*, was a failure. His mother's death in June 1939 depressed him further, as they had been so close. Then by bizarre coincidence, one year and one week later, Heyward suffered a heart attack and passed away within a matter of hours. His wife Dorothy survived him by twenty-one years, and she was in large part responsible for sustaining the opera's posthumous existence. She had to fight many battles: guaranteeing DuBose's claim to equal billing with Gershwin, for example; then civil rights activists in the 1950s opposed the show, saying that its portrayal of black people was demeaning. But history has vindicated Heyward's socially enlightened intentions. And *Porgy and Bess* has gone on to become a sort of Everyman opera: archetypal in its story and transcendent in its themes.

Heyward's life and career were fascinating. He emerged from a social environment that was rooted in the past, and he learned to look to the future. His early life was haunted by loss and by social sterility, yet he immersed himself in a world marked by vitality and celebration. He moved from the elite white world of Charleston into the world of the Charleston Gullah, then into the world of art and celebrity, and finally into the world of the New Negro. And all along the way his social conscience deepened and broadened. He was a man who developed his social views through developing as a writer.

Visiting Charleston in 1905, Henry James pronounced it "a flower-crowned waste." Did it take a provincial's eyes to see the tragic beauty in aging gentility and the ennobling tragedy of a race proudly demanding to be recognized? Heyward's—and Charleston's—varied, multitextured, and multilayered responses to these fascinating twin cultures would seem to answer "yes."

Critical Writings

Poetry South

IT IS A TRUISM that creative art from its very nature must be original, the peculiarly different and unexpected reaction of the artist to his environment. This is especially true of poetry, the least concrete of the arts; and it is this very quality of unexpectedness in the poet, constituting as it does so much of the charm of poetry, that makes an attempt to forecast the reactions of any group or school of poets a task which calls for the prophetic rather than for the merely constructive critic.

Nevertheless, poets as a rule are so profoundly affected by their environment that by understanding it, if we cannot precisely predict their reactions, we can at least say within limits what they will not write about, and perhaps even be able to forecast the general tendencies of a school or group in its day and place. If, in addition to the physical environment, we have also some grasp of the historical and ethnic background from which poets speak, some comprehension of the immediate social and local problems which surround them—in short, some knowledge of the poets themselves—we shall be able, to a large extent, to tell not only what subjects they will be most likely to select, but also, in a more limited sense, in what mood they will approach their theme; and from mood their style, for it is mood that dictates style.

It is from this standpoint of physical and spiritual environment, from the historical background, and from a survey of the tendencies evident in the verse being written by southern poets today, that this cursory presentation of the condition of poetry in the South is attempted. In so brief a space its statements must be rather general, with all the many exceptions implied.

Despite some vigorous assertions to the contrary, it seems as if southern poetry were going to be decidedly regional in spirit, with a quick human appeal but strongly local in tone—poetry of and about places. Much of

SOURCE: DuBose Heyward and Hervey Allen, "Poetry South," *Poetry* 20 (April 1922), 35–48.

3

American verse is city poetry. It is the similarity of our city life perhaps which has given to a great deal of American verse a note of sameness that is too often mistaken for a universal realistic appeal. The city, too, has given American poetry a tendency to mirror back the drab, and accentuated an almost morbid desire for self-expression which the crowd begets. There has been, to be sure, a gain in thought content and sophistication, but the spontaneous and simple have been sacrificed, while the constant search for the "new" has brought about a ceaseless experiment with alien forms. It seems probable that poetry written from the South will be, in nearly all these respects, the opposite of what has rather arbitrarily been called "city-verse," for the South is still predominantly agricultural. Although industrialism, under the spur of northern capital, has ridden in ruthlessly here and there, the plantation of one kind or another is still the economic, vital unit; and it may be expected that when the plantation poet speaks, it will not be from the necessity of introspectively asserting his existence as an individual apart from the crowd, but of objectively reflecting in simple measures the patriarchal life remnant about him. In this he will very likely be profoundly impressed by his sub-tropical or mountain landscapes, and reflect the spontaneously lyrical and primarily rhythmic melodies of the Negro. Indeed, the effect of the Negro on southern poetry demands a treatment by itself.

It is significant that the syncopation of the Negro, which has found its way into "jazz" music and verse, has seldom been adopted by southern poets. This is partly due to a "subconscious-intellectual" color-line, for strong social and racial prejudices are carried over into art; but to a still greater extent the omission of "jazz" in southern poetry is due to the fact that the short, choppy effects of syncopated rhythms do not lend themselves to the intimate mood of memory and contemplation which the South has to express. Therefore, the more obvious employment of Negro rhythms, and the attempts to gain the ear by poems in unauthentic dialect must not be overestimated. Due credit must be given, however, to the Valentine Museum of Richmond for its publication of authentic Negro dialect-poetry, and its experiments in recording for phonographic reproduction the exact sound of the passing speech of the old Negro. Thomas Nelson Page of Virginia, Harry Stillwell Edwards and Joel Chandler Harris of Georgia, and Janie Screven Heyward of the South Carolina coast country, together with a few others, are deserving of mention for having created literature which correctly records the Negro dialect of their own localities.[1]

The southern muse must be careful how she handles the tar-baby; but the weird, the bizarre and the grotesque in Negro life and story, and the tone of the "spiritual" will have to be reckoned with—indeed, they have already made themselves felt. With the Negro, poetry, music and the dance are still closely associated, as in all primitive races, and in the recognition and perpetuation of this condition lies a great opportunity for American art in the South. It is much to be desired that the southern group may recognize this immense fund of rich material for poetry which Negro music, legends and folk-lore hold in trust, and that the time may rapidly come when there will be Negro poets who can use adequately the artistic values inherent in their own race, and produce something worthy. Unfortunately Paul Laurence Dunbar stands almost alone; his was a unique contribution to literature, as Tanner's has been to painting.[2]

The Negro, however, is not the only source of folk-lore in the South. Even richer in poetic material is the lofty back-country of the Appalachians. The rush of American civilization has thus far touched only the fringes of this rugged land. Today one may take a trail from one of the mountain towns, and by traveling horseback for fifty miles in from the railroad he will discover for himself an eighteenth-century pioneer settlement; provided he is not mistaken for a revenue officer, and his route subjected to an immediate change of destination.

The mountains of the Carolinas and Kentucky were settled in the days of Daniel Boone and earlier by sturdy Scotch-Irish and English pioneers who built their isolated settlements behind the ramparts of rock. There, sequestered from the flow and change of civilization, they have continued to live the life of the pioneer. There are certain remote districts in the Black and Great Smoky ranges where life has remained absolutely static for a century and a half. There it is still possible to hear old English ballads and folk-tales which passed from current use generations ago; and one still encounters Elizabethan words. Certainly nowhere else in the America of today can one find conditions so favorable to the development of genuine folk-expression; with the background of an old, but still remembered civilization, and an absolute isolation which encourages the crystallization, by word of mouth, of the idea into the story.[3]

The mountaineer responds but little to beauty. In his great tumble of hills, which contains forty-six peaks of over six thousand feet, including the highest point east of the Rocky Mountains, amid a flora that is bewildering in its pageantry of color, he is stubborn, vindictive in anger, elemental as a child in his amusements, shrewd, silent, and unerring in his estimate of the "furreners" he may chance to meet. It should be added here, by way of extension, that the mountaineer is naturally on the defensive. Living as he does by a code of ethics and morals out of the past, he finds himself contending with the incursions of the present, and he knows instinctively that he is at a disadvantage.

But it is among the mountain women that one finds the pathos and tragedy of these isolated people. Burden-bearers, tillers of the soil, the women are old at thirty. Their faces tell nothing of their thoughts, but there is always a characteristic quality to the speaking voice: the tone is low, soft and drawling, invariably dropping to a lower key at the end of every remark, with an effect of hopelessness and infinite sadness.

The only emotional outlet for the mountaineer is the religious revival, and the occasional neighborhood dance. To both of these forms of entertainment he responds with the greatest gusto, and the extreme revivalist sects, such as the "Holiness" and the "Holy Rollers," have made many profitable excursions into his fastnesses. But such outbursts can not long combat the native reticence of the people, and they soon become self-conscious and indifferent.[4]

In spite of the fact that the southern mountaineer is probably the most interesting and least known figure in our national life, it will be many years before he will write his own story, if ever. The lack of schools, and his rooted indifference to educational advantages, will keep him much as he is, but he should be transcribed through the medium of some art before he passes: for there is nothing else quite like him on the continent.

The statement has been made earlier that southern poetry may be largely of and about places. If environment is going to affect our southern poets, if they are going to be at all objective, this will necessarily follow, for there is no other portion of the country so districted—i.e., where sections differ so one from the other as in the South. To pass from the country of the mountain-whites to the Carolina Low Country, for example, is to pass from one world to another, one with a different fauna and flora and a different ethnic background. Here the poets may tell of the sea-islands, with tidal lagoons where the wild fowl, ducks, marsh-hens, and strange gawky heron feed, and the migrating song-birds pass through each year like a recurring flame. They may speak of magnolia and azalea gardens, oriental in a polychromatic spring; of swamps and eerie live-oak forests where the Spanish moss hangs like stalactites in twilit caverns; of the mile of deserted rice-fields where turbaned blacks walk ruined dykes; and of the ancient baronies and manors, each with its legend, where the deer feed around the stately columned houses—shells of a life and an epoch which have passed away.

But if the past does not call the southern poet, the thrusting of industrialism into the Piedmont cotton and tobacco regions, with the rise of the factory system, child-labor, and a burning racial problem, offer a tremendous theme and a possible chance of legitimate propaganda for the present. Then in Florida, at such towns as Miami, a frontier is being peacefully settled, and dotted with villas Roman in their scale and magnificence; while from the Everglades the firelight of the stone-age Seminole glows in the midnight sky when he holds his secret corn-dances. Southward stretch the coral keys, haunted by huge sea-turtles, that crawl out to hide their eggs where pirates once hid gold; and even today the eagle boat of the whiskey-runner shelters there, making for Nassau or Bimini. Then there are the plains of Texas rich with the dusty-golden dreams of Spanish empire, with enchanted mesas, pueblos, Indian stories and cow-boy songs; or the cane-brakes of Louisiana, and faded Creole New Orleans of the old river days.

How absurd to say the South has nothing but genealogy! Who will sing of them, these cities—of Santa Fe or El Paso, San Antonio or St. Augustine, and of old Charleston with her three hundred years of memories? Who is going to write the epos of Coronado, of the lost Fountain of Youth, of De Soto, of the pirates, of Africa transplanted, of the outlandish voodoo that still lingers, and of the strange new Christ the Negroes worship? Is there no one who will tell over again from the clearer light of a better time how the awful, keen sword of civil war struck down these states, how the slave and freedman passed, and how through bitterness they have come to a saner, sweeter life again? Here is a challenge to the American renascence. It is ardently to be hoped that the South will continue to reply to it as she has begun to do, and that she will give us largely of her rich landscapes and historical material, and speak of and from the life of her memory and of her present. And it is also to be hoped that the cleverly inane, or the small accidental dream-life of the individual, so seldom worth uttering—tiny loves and smaller hates, and the baldly phrased usual; above all, the banal echo and the purely sentimental—will be left unsaid.

Faked sympathy, and crocodile tears for the past, are the stops which the southern poets must most carefully avoid. Unfortunately, the *vox humana*, pulled out full, is still good for a round of applause almost anywhere, but in the South there is an inherited bias in its favor.

In colonial times no other section of the country was so much affected by the eighteenth-century classical school as the South, particularly the Carolinas and Virginia. New England seems to have preserved and perpetuated, almost down to modern times, the spirit of the Puritan seventeenth-century literature, but in the South your Cavalier gentleman imported his advance leaves of the "latest books published in the United Kingdom," had them specially bound, added his book-mark; and read his Pope, his Johnson, and his Goldsmith, not always his Burke, with complete satisfaction. Education and plantation tutoring were largely in the dead languages; and in South Carolina the old Huguenot French stock read the French Bible, Voltaire or Rousseau according to their generation. Nowhere was the effect upon originality of style more blighting. Almost until the civil war the couplet of Pope held full sway—the English romantic movement seems to have had little effect upon it; verse remained an accomplishment of the idle and the polite, extremely sentimental and absolutely eighteenth-century in style.[5] Even today the old idea that there is a distinct poetic jargon persists in the South, and realism in poetry shocks the academic sense, while in files of old newspapers and privately printed books that throng second-hand book-stalls these old voices still tinkle from the dust in their endless couplets. In the aggregate an astonishing amount of such verse was written. Take General Albert Pike's *Hymns to the Gods*, for instance;[6] and William Gilmore Simms, who heads the list with eighteen volumes. How many single poems survive today?

Poe stands out from this crowd of gentlemen poetasters as the great exception. He actually developed his own forms, not turning to new forms but improving on the old. He reflected the life about him; for his poems are much more biographical than is generally suspected, and most of his verse shows strong southern influence in landscape and rhythms. Nevertheless, he also did not escape tradition entirely, and partly for that reason he seems more European now than American, but none the less great for that.

It took the civil war to goad southern poets into an authentic local utterance, although there were a few years, just before 1861, when it seemed as if the Charleston group—Hayne, Timrod, Simms, and some others—would make that city a southern literary capital. A magazine, *Russell's*, was started there under much the same kind of impulse as the *Atlantic Monthly*; but Sumter was fired on, and the war put a period to all such activity.[7] Both Hayne and Timrod dealt with landscapes and nature, but they are chiefly remembered for their war poems, and because, with a very few others, they were the only voices which to any degree adequately phrased the despair of reconstruction. Timrod once wrote to Hayne: "I can embody it all in a few words—beggary, starvation, death, bitter grief, utter want of hope."[8] It is impossible to judge men writing under such conditions by the ordinary standards of criticism. The wonder that they wrote at all is only transcended by the miracle that they also achieved some memorable lines.

Art, as it is the finest expression of the life of a people, is the last thing to recover from the ravages of war. Reconstruction, with its spiritual and economic despair, put a gag in the mouths of singers; the few voices that did speak were more like croaks than songs. However, one ludicrous little man by the name of Coogler, in Columbia, S.C., conferred five volumes upon a faintly amused world:

> Maude—for her gentle name was Maude—
> Wore many smiles, and they were sad;
> A thousand virtues she possessed,
> Many of which I never had.[9]

This, in its own way, is really great, and the last two lines could have stood truthfully for the relation of the southern poet of that time to his muse; for these were the days when prejudices, and the heritage of war, were too strong to permit of literature being written. Shakespeare himself would have been taboo on account of the Dark Lady of the Sonnets. That Sidney Lanier should have spoken out of this environment is all the more wonderful. He was indeed a protest against his age north and south:

> O Trade! O Trade! would thou wert dead!
> The time needs heart—'tis tired of head.[10]

Like Poe he developed his own style and theory of verse, and was not content simply to use the old forms as Hayne and Timrod had done. His knowledge of the two arts of music and verse largely made this possible. Lanier was too modern in one sense for his time, and too conservative for the moderns. He worked against frightful physical and spiritual odds, in the seventies and eighties, and despite it all at times achieved great beauty. He and Poe are, of course, the great names the South has to offer to American poetry. Madison

Cawein should not be forgotten.[11] These men overcame literary taboos and traditions, and dared to have personality; with them poetry was not simply polite.

The last few years have brought a new spirit into the South. With the recovery of her economic life has come the possibility of renewing old culture, and an opportunity for a leisure not due to apathy and despair. The great war has also stirred and disturbed her subtly and immeasurably, till a vast territory which has for a while lain poetically fallow is now awakening, and from here and there voices, small and inadequate perhaps, but nevertheless earnest and distinctive voices, are giving it utterance.

It is their desire that the rest of the country know and recognize this; for while these voices may utter with a *timbre* peculiarly their own, it is because they are moved, not by a provincial pride, but by the renascence of poetry throughout America; and being so moved by this spirit, they claim to be of it. The South will never express itself in constricted forms; mood, inclination, and tradition forbid, nor does it feel the urge completely to slough the old. Here, where the tides of immigration have brought no alien tongues, the grand tradition of English poetry still lingers strongly in an old culture which has survived the wrack of civil war and of reconstruction—a European culture, planted by a strong stock in colonial times; and it is from this tradition and from the descendants of that stock that the southern poetical renascence must come. It will accept with modern spirit the new forms in verse, but accept them as being valuable for their loosening effect upon the old rather than as being all satisfactory in themselves; and it brings to American poetry a little known but tropically rich store of material, an unurbanized beauty, the possibility of legend, folksong, romance, historical narrative, glorious landscape, and an untired mood; in short, a content which will save it from that sure sign of literary inadequacy, a too nice preoccupation with form.

PREFACE TO
Carolina Chansons

IN A CONTINENT but recently settled, many parts of which have as yet little historical or cultural background, the material for this volume has been gathered from a section that was one of the first to be colonized. Here the Frenchman, Spaniard, and Englishman all passed, leaving each his legend; and a brilliant and more or less feudal civilization with its aristocracy and slaves has departed with the economic system upon which it rested.

From this medley of early colonial discovery and romance, from the memories of war and reconstruction, it has been as difficult to choose coherently as to maintain restraint in selection among the many grotesque negro legends and superstitions so rich in imagery and music. Coupled with this there has been another task; that of keeping these legends and stories in their natural matrix, the semi-tropical landscape of the *Low Country*, which somehow lends them all a pensively melancholy yet fitting background. Not to have so portrayed them, would have been to sacrifice their essentially local tang. To the reader unfamiliar with coastal Carolina, the unique aspects of its landscapes may seem exaggerated in these pages; the observant visitor and the native will, it is hoped, recognize that neither the colors nor the shadows are too strong. These poems, however, are not local only, they are stories and pictures of a chapter of American history little known, but dramatic and colorful, and in the relation of an important part to the whole they may carry a decided interest to the country at large.

Local color has a fatal tendency to remain local; but it is also true that the universal often borders on the void. It has been said, perhaps wisely, that the immediate future of American Poetry lies rather in the intimate feeling of

SOURCE: DuBose Heyward and Hervey Allen, *Carolina Chansons: Legends of the Low Country* (New York: Macmillan, 1922), 9–11.

local poets who can interpret their own sections to the rest of the country as Robinson[1] and Frost have done so nobly for New England, rather than in the effort to *yawp* universally. Hence there is no attempt here to say, "O New York, O Pennsylvania," but simply, "O Carolina."[2]

The South, however, has been "interpreted" so often, either with condescending pity or nauseous sentimentality, that it is the aim of this book to speak simply and carefully amid a babel of unauthentic utterance. Nevertheless, the contents of this volume do not pretend to exact historical accuracy; this is poetry rather than history, although the legends and facts upon which it rests have been gathered with much painstaking research and careful verification. It should be kept in mind that these poems are impressionistic attempts to present the fleeting feeling of the moment, landscape moods, and the ephemeral attitudes of the past. Legends are material to be moulded, and not facts to be recorded. Above all here is no pretence of propaganda.

As some of the material touched on is not accessible in standard reference, prose notes have been included giving the historical facts of background of legend upon which a poem has been based. These notes together with a bibliography will be found at the back of the volume.

If the only result of this book is to call attention to the literary and artistic values inherent in the South, and to the essentially unique and yet nationally interesting qualities of the Carolina *Low Country*, its landscapes and legends, the labor bestowed here will have secured its harvest.

And Once Again—the Negro

I HAVE BEEN READING an article in a magazine that takes itself very seriously. It is a well-written article by a most zealous person who has solved the perplexing problem of what is to become of "Our Colored Brother." Education, we are informed comprehensively, especially education in the moral code of the white race, will bring enlightenment, and as an inevitable result, happiness.

I close the book, and look out of my window across a wide court brimful of heavy, languorous sunshine, and droning a slow symphony of humming insects, and drowsy child voices. The old walls show every color through flaking stucco, and, in a pool of cool shadow along the eastern wall, the five happiest curs in the world are dozing away the morning. In the centre of the enclosure, basking in the sweltering heat of the sun, a great black sprawls in the wreck of a chair, and with rhythmic, practised hands, peels stalk after stalk of stout, purple sugar cane. About him the debris accumulates steadily as he chews and discards successive joints of the succulent cane. In this fashion he has spent three days of this week. Last month his stevedoring gang struck for a raise, and got it. Now he can earn in three days sufficient money to support life for a week. We are beginning to realize that, in an ideal civilization, a man should expend but half of his power to secure the necessities of physical existence, and devote the remainder of his time to the realization and enjoyment of life. Students of sociology have many theories by which this desirable end may be attained, but, as yet, the white race is probably centuries away from its practical application. My neighbor, ignoring the conventional attitude towards labor, has decided for himself, quite without the aid of the statistician. He is superlatively happy now. And I am filled with a wistful envy.

SOURCE: *Reviewer* 4 (October 1923), 39–42.

Last month the negro who does my gardening informed me that he was going to quit his wife. To my inquiry as to whether he could afford a divorce, he laughed, and replied that he needed none; and added, "Ain't yer done know, boss, that I married Satira on trial. We done agreed on a one-year trial, and not satisfied with that, I done throw in an extry two years beside. Satira ain't got no complaint. An' what's more, Mr. Rutledge's butler is ready to marry her today."

"But," I protested in an outraged voice, "she cannot marry again without a divorce."

My informant studied me for a long minute, and then, as a concession to my abysmal ignorance, explained slowly, as one might to a child.

"Yer ain't understan', boss. There ain't no papers to a trial marriage. Yer jus' promises for one year; then, if yer can't stand each other, the gentleman most always throws in a little extry before he quits. But, at the end of the year, if you still loves each other, yer ain't takin' no chances, and yer can be safe with goin' ahead with the ceremony."

"But there are two children, Elijah. Who will assume responsibility for them?"

He favored me with a reproachful glance. "Now, boss," he protested. "Yer ain't' think I would take them children from Satira. Who goin' to work for she when she old?"

"But they must be supported," I urged weakly. "Do you deny all responsibility for that?"

He regarded me with an expression akin to pity. "Must be yer don't know the Rutledges, boss. Must be yer think they is poor white trash, that their own butler can't raise his own wife's children offen their table." Then concluding that one so ignorant of social usage was unworthy of further conversation, he gathered his gardening implements and with a blithe hail to a passing friend, departed.

And so, this was the system. This was why many of the married negro couples that I chanced to know could afford to be happy. There was some assurance of compatibility before the final forging of the chain. My gardener had fulfilled every obligation according to the accepted code. The children were assets instead of liabilities; and were magnanimously given over to the wife in lieu of alimony. It was mid-August, and fine alligator weather. The song of the liberated husband trailed back to me on the waves of heat. My eyes wandered back to the magazine that lay before me, and I indulged in a slow—and honesty compels me to add—superior smile.

In a recent poll taken to ascertain, if possible, the feeling of a cross-section of the public, as to the solution of the many new problems between the sexes, a surprising number favored a more flexible marriage bond. Some of the more daring hinted at contracts that might, if possible, allow the contracting parties to carry on their own lives and careers, and then, if living together should become unbearable, part without the clumsy and scandalous machinery of the divorce court. In Europe the movement is fairly well advanced. In America, a century hence perhaps, the march of civilization may bring about a saner, and fairer condition of affairs between the sexes, and especially as regards the marital relationship. In the meantime, my gardener and his wife, who have solved the problem to their mutual satisfaction and happiness, live their lives, blissfully oblivious of the impending advancement that is being prepared for them by their solemn and consecrated white neighbor.

During the past summer, I met, in an advanced art circle, a young couple. The wife insisted upon retaining the "Miss" and her maiden name. They were really quite devil-may-care, and advanced about it, and submitted to the embarrassment of explaining themselves to hotel clerks, and others who made bold to enquire, for the good of the cause.

My washerwoman announced the other day that she had married. To my inquiry as to her present name, she replied: "My Lord, do listen to the gentleman! Yer sure don't think I goin' ter be responsible for any nigger's name. No sir! And he ain't goin' ter get my name neither. I is a good washerwoman, an' I got my reputation to live up to. He can go along with his shoe-carpentering if he wants to, but it is me as brings home the chicken on Saturday night. Me take his name. No suh! Not me!"

And so I listen to their stories, and let them go, but for them I experience a profound sadness. Are they an aeon behind, or an aeon ahead of us? Who knows? But one thing is certain: the reformer will have them in the fullness of time. They will surely be cleaned, married, conventionalized. They will be taken from the fields, and given to machines. Their instinctive feeling for the way that leads to happiness, saved as it is from selfishness, by humour and genuine kindness of heart, will be supplanted by a stifling moral straightjacket. They will languish, but they will submit, because they will be trained into a habit of thought that makes blind submission a virtue.

And my stevedore, there out of the window. I look at him again. I cannot see him as a joke. Most certainly I cannot contort him into a menace. I can only be profoundly sorry for him, for there he sits in the sunshine unconsciously awaiting his supreme tragedy. He is about to be saved.

Year Book of the Poetry Society of South Carolina

(1923)

Prosperously proceeding on the way mapped for it from its outset, the Poetry Society of South Carolina salutes its contemporaries at home and abroad. Its modest Year Book, which, upon its first appearance, was hailed as the "Voice of one crying in the wilderness," is now but a single note in a chorus of voices so numerous, and, honesty compels us to admit, so vociferous, that further assertion on our part that the South has brought forth a literary revival would be to stress the obvious. In point of fact, the Southern Poetry Movement bears a striking resemblance to the legendary matron who inhabited a discarded boot, and was confused by the multiplicity of her progeny. For, in all parts of the South, her robust youngsters, in the guise of poetry societies and magazines, are speaking for their schools and groups; and are producing staggering masses of verse, much of which shows promise, and some of which is poetry.

In the Southeast the movement thus far has organized itself into poetry societies, following the general plan of the Poetry Society of South Carolina, and, with slight changes to meet local conditions, adopting the constitution of the older society. Unquestionably this method has proved itself to be the best adapted to breaking ground in a new field. Through the medium of lectures and readings by well-known poets, open criticism and discussion of original verse, and the publication of yearbooks, an ever-increasing number of the public is developing into a discriminating audience; while generous

SOURCE: *Year Book of the Poetry Society of South Carolina* (Charleston: n.p., 1923), 9–13.

prizes, and actual study groups, conducted by creative poets themselves, are discovering and developing latent talent.

When our last year-book went to press, the Poetry Society of Texas, under the leadership of Therese Lindsey, Karle Wilson Baker, and Hilton R. Greer, was just getting under way. Today its activities extend over the whole of the Lone-Star State, and it has published its first year-book—a most creditable volume.[1]

Early in the autumn of 1922, The Poetry Society of Maryland, under the guiding hand of Sally Bruce Kinsolving,[2] who had visited Charleston to study our methods, was successfully launched, and has closed its first season firmly established as one of the most significant influences in its locality.

The Poetry Society of Georgia, which came into being in the Winter of 1922–1923, under the capable guidance of Elfrida DeRenne Barrow and Marie Conway Oemler,[3] is working in close touch with the Poetry Society of South Carolina, having adopted its general plan. The proximity of Savannah to Charleston makes possible a happy intervisiting of the two memberships when either society is at home to a visiting poet.

Under the auspices of Charles N. Feidelson, a group at William and Mary College, (with which we are cooperating), a number of writers of Richmond, and the Poets' Club of Norfolk, successful organization was made in May for the Poetry Society of Virginia; a call issued to all Virginians interested in poetic art met a wide and cordial response.[4] Though too early to report concrete achievement from this movement, Virginia's prospects are as bright as any of even the older societies.

The combined memberships of these societies, which already total considerably over one thousand, distributed widely over the South, enthusiastically working in concert for the development of an art, represent a cultural influence that can scarcely be estimated.

Tennessee, though having no poetry society, speaks eloquently its interest in the Southern Movement through its magazine of verse, *The Fugitive*, published by a virile group at Nashville. Evidence of the genuine talent which speaks through this medium is found in the fact that the Southern Prize, of one hundred dollars, offered through the Poetry Society of South Carolina, was this year taken by one of their group, John Crowe Ransom;[5] while another member of "The Fugitive Group," Donald Davidson, was one of two poets who in that contest received honorable mention.[6]

Alabama is another Southern State vocal through the medium of a magazine. *The Nomad,* published at Birmingham, backed by a group of which Albert A. Rosenthal and Scottie McKenzie Frasier are leaders, has published some extremely readable verse.[7]

Mention must be made of *The Lyric,* of Norfolk, the South's oldest poetry magazine. That little but clear-voiced publication is now in its third year, and has given its readers much poetry of an unusually high level for so modest an effort. The Poets' Club of Norfolk is to be congratulated upon the authentic success of their organ, and the editor, John R. Moreland, upon the fruit of this, his particular labor.

North Carolina, though not yet represented by a poetry society, has taken her place in the field of literary criticism. The articles of Dr. Archibald Henderson,[8] which have appeared in the *New York Herald,* and other papers and magazines, have done much to remove false and erroneous impressions regarding the literature of the South. In the drama, especially the folk play, North Carolina has come to fore. The theatre at the University of North Carolina, under the direction of Frederick H. Koch,[9] backed by the complete and intelligent cooperation of the University, has bent its energies to the development of a genuine folk drama, written and acted by the people themselves about their own lives and traditions. The success of the experiment has been almost startling, and the first published volume of their plays has received favorable nationwide comment.

The South Carolina Poetry Society, in Charleston, has carried forward its original plan, of lectures, readings, prize contests, and group meetings. Each year an increasing number of names of members, many of whom were discovered and introduced by the Poetry Society of South Carolina, are appearing in well-known literary publications in the United States and England, and there is not a contemporary anthology of any importance which does not contain work of our poets. Braithwaite's *Anthology of Magazine Verse* for 1922 numbered eight of our writers among its contributors; and Gorman's *Peterborough Anthology* contains thirteen poems written by members of the South Carolina society.

Working in close cooperation with the other arts, the Society has extended its field to include poetic drama. Under the capable direction of Daniel Reed[10] of the Town Theatre of Columbia, S.C., assisted by Mrs. Olivia Connor Fuller, Synge's *Deirdre of the Sorrows* was presented in Charleston by a cast from the society, and later taken on tour to Columbia for several performances.[11]

The Folk-lore Committee of the Society, Mrs. Clelia P. McGowan,[12] chairman, has devoted itself to the preservation of the unique Negro spirituals of the Carolina Low Country; and, through its assistance, the second annual concert by Negroes of their own racial music, which took place in January, was an unqualified success. Negro schools in twenty-five counties have been urged to substitute spirituals for cheap popular music. The response has been immediate, a number of institutions already having introduced the old racial chants and hymns. As "The Society for the Preservation of Spirituals," a rather unnecessarily solemn name, a white chorus of forty voices have banded together. Most of this group are "plantation people" from coast counties. By teaching each other their own neighborhood spirituals and dialect, and by excursions to outlying plantations where the Negroes can be studied first hand, a collection of about twenty-five spirituals has already been made, only two or three of which are in print. Mrs. William Heyward Grimball, a member of the Folk-lore Committee, and Mrs. Herbert R. Sass, who are leaders of the "spiritual group," are not planning to publish these songs, but to hold the chorus together so that, as tradition, they may be passed to the next generation by word of mouth, and thus retain their original weird tonal qualities and peculiar harmony.[13]

The appearance of *The Black Border* from the pen of Ambrose E. Gonzales, during the past year, has given the folklore of South Carolina its most important volume.[14] This remarkable book contains, besides its inimitable group of short and humorous studies of the "Gullah" Negro, a glossary of nearly two thousand words and phrases, from that unique, grotesque, fast-disappearing dialect of the Carolina Coast.

Events so closely allied to the activities of the Poetry Society as hardly here to be separately considered were: first, the Author's Reading, given in March 1923, under the auspices of the Society, by a group of eight writers of the city for the benefit of the MacDowell Colony, of Peterborough, N.H. The affair was an unqualified success, and resulted in the substantial contribution toward the support of America's most important art colony. Second, in May an event of peculiar interest to all real poetry lovers; the installation and unveiling at the Charleston Museum of the "Poe Group," or miniature landscape statuette, by Dwight Franklin,[15] to mark and to hold fresh in memory the connection of Edgar Allan Poe with sea-coast South Carolina, during his service in the United States Army in the garrison at Ft. Moultrie on Sullivan's Island. This was the Museum's realization of a dream; the Society did its part, the unveiling exercises being in the hands of Hervey Allen,[16] DuBose Heyward and John Bennett,[17] of the Poetry Society.

It is in this spirit the Society lives, and will live, cordially cooperating with every power that lends a hand to the revival of Southern letters and to the encouragement of art.

It has been our custom in previous years to note the activities of the related arts in the community about us. This pleasure we are now compelled regretfully to forgo, our own increased activity engaging our entire space and attention.

Yet we cannot close this foreword without complimenting in highest terms the Carolina Art Association upon the notable and increasing success of its school, directed by Alfred Hutty;[18] the musical organization ably managed by Misses Maud W. Gibbon, Ella I. Hyams, and Addie Howell;[19] the remarkable constructive cooperation that science, historical culture, and practical art are receiving from the entire staff of the Charleston Museum through the brilliant directorship of Miss Laura M. Bragg;[20] and the never-failing and untiring service given literature and all arts by the small but devoted corps of the Charleston Library Society, under the librarianship of Miss Ellen M. FitzSimons.[21] Not one of these but through the years has played its part with courage: their names thus stand recorded along the road to better things that shall and must befall us all.

This Year Book is, for good or bad, the record of our own course.

The New Note in
Southern Literature

IT HAS BEEN SAID that good taste is an outstanding characteristic of southern letters, and that this in itself constitutes no mean contribution to contemporary American art. That such is the case is undeniable. The southern writer has applied himself with energy and ability to his task, and he has produced a literature that has reflected certain aspects of his environment with fidelity and feeling. Most important of all, he accepted the trust imposed in him by his audience, respected its taboos, and so produced literature that was characterized by "good taste."

In many ways he was fortunate. The audience was already cultivated; it was rooted deep in Anglo-Saxon tradition. It knew and demanded good English in what it read. It was conservative, and was uninterested in sensational filth. But now came the fatal flaw. *This audience also demanded strict adherence to its code of good taste, and the code which it prescribed was that of the Victorian drawing room—not art.* There were, therefore, certain aspects of the life of the region that the writer must see only in part. Occasionally a daring spirit would ignore the signs. The case of George Cable has been pointed out to more than one aspiring southern writer as a horrible example of the retribution of an outraged society. He had broken the "code of manners," and he was hanged in chains that others might see and profit.[1]

To illustrate how this false standard could inhibit, one has only to look upon the Negro in literature during the period following the Civil War. In the well-bred southern drawing room of a decade ago, the "Negro problem" was never mentioned. A discussion of the economic and spiritual strivings of the race would have implied that such a problem existed; that in turn would

SOURCE: *Bookman* 61 (April 1925), 153–56.

have been disturbing and accordingly "bad taste." This attitude was trans-
mitted, simply by the weight of public opinion, to the writer. He knew that
the raw stuff of human drama was there to his hand. But then—there was
George Cable. And so the authors who undertook to interpret Negro life
divided themselves into two general classes: those who dealt altogether de-
lightfully with the Negro of the past; and those who took the Negro's sense
of humor as a keynote, caricatured it beyond recognition, and produced a co-
median so detached from life that he could be laughed at heartily without the
least disloyalty to the taboo.

Now the task that confronts the South today is simply this: to readjust its
standards of good taste. Good taste in manners, if you will. But for art, its
own code of good taste, based upon a fearless and veracious molding of the
raw human material that lies beneath its hand.

That an increasing number from the audience are realizing this, there can
be no doubt. And in this fact lies the encouragement and hope for southern letters of the future. No longer isolated by geographical detachment, the
southern audience is eager for light and, possessing a congenial feeling for literature, it needs only to be made familiar with the new symbols to recognize
the authentic in modern art.

Poetry societies which are enjoying flourishing existences in five southern
states bring to their members each year a number of America's leading poets
and critics in lectures and readings. Newspaper subscribers to the circulation
of 300,000 scattered from Texas to Virginia read each week the excellent syndicated column edited by Addison Hibbard under the name of Telfair, Jr.,
with its trenchant and interesting comments.[2] Book pages are today part of
almost every paper of importance, and are read with eagerness and intelligence. Then there are *The Reviewer, The Southwest Review, The Sewanee Review*, several other quarterlies, and *The Double Dealer*, all seeking eagerly for the young
writer with something to say. The fact that these publications are entirely un-
commercial in intention or appeal renders their editorial policy unfettered.

Subjected to these and other similar influences, the prejudices of the audience are dissolving. It is beginning to concede that, after all, an artist may be
permitted to see the whole of his subject and still not be a public menace.

Already, encouraged by this change in attitude, there has come a new note
in southern literature. There need be no fear of open license. Good taste still
holds good. But there is a new method of approach, and a new and daring
handling of old material that promises much vitality for the new school.

Within a surprisingly short time several writers have appeared who have for-
sworn the shackles of their immediate predecessors, and are observing and
recording with honesty and fearlessness.

It is not the purpose of this article to cover the general field of southern
literature; that has been done most admirably by Professor Richard Burton
in his recent survey in this magazine.[3] It is merely my intention to indicate
this new quality, not yet discernible from the lecture platform, and to offer a
few examples which will make clear its actual existence. Some of the names I
shall mention may thus far have escaped the notice of all but a discriminating few, but they are destined to be heard from in the immediate future, for
they have evidenced qualities that have already laid the foundation for a new
phase of southern letters.

Let us take first the drama, in which there occur more manifestations of
the quality to which I refer than in either poetry or fiction. Consider the plays
of the Carolina mountains that have enjoyed such a vogue in New York. In
Sun-up and *The Shame Woman* Lula Vollmer, of North Carolina, has given us a
cross section of the lives of these dwellers in the southern Appalachians as il-
luminatingly and poignantly true as life itself.[4] And Hatcher Hughes, a native of South Carolina, in *Hell-Bent Fer Heaven* has taken the effect of religious
fanaticism on the same repressed and isolated people, and shown it as a
deadly instrument of evil and destruction.[5] At least two of these plays would
have trod upon the toes of certain conventions of a decade ago, and yet—
there they are. Now turn to *Roseanne*, by Nan Bagby Stephens of Atlanta,
which, although praised by critics, did not receive the popular attention that
it deserved.[6] Confronted by insurmountable mechanical difficulties, this
playwright nevertheless presented in her drama, for the first time on the
American stage, a psychologically true serious picture of contemporary
southern Negro life. In this demonstration she was gallantly backed by Mary
Kirkpatrick of Alabama, who allowed the play to close only after experience
had proved that it is as impossible for the southern black to be portrayed by
the Harlem Negro as by a northern white, plus grease paint.

Then, of course, there is Laurence Stallings, of Georgia, not dealing with
southern material it is true, but displaying, in *What Price Glory?*, an artistic ideal
rather than a Victorian good taste of manners which would have been imposed upon him, I do not doubt, by his forebears, and which would have for-
bidden the employment of his agonizing realism, thus destroying the masterpiece created by Maxwell Anderson and himself.[7]

In the South, which is hampered by the lack of a professional producing theatre, the little theatre has spoken clearly and fearlessly. At the University of North Carolina, Frederick H. Koch, with his own student playwrights, the most distinguished of whom is Paul Green, has presented and published folk plays of a high quality, and these have not hesitated to touch upon the evils of tenant farming and religious fanaticism.[8]

Those who attended the little theatre tournament in New York last spring will not soon forget the dynamic play, *Judge Lynch,* carried on by Oliver Hinsdell, director of the Dallas Theatre, to capture the national trophy for the year. Written by J. W. Rogers, Jr., of Dallas, and produced in the heart of the South, this one act play struck with the full power of its emotional and artistic force at the root of the lynching evil.[9] Out of an overlong and rather appalling silence, it spoke clearly for a vast and enlightened number throughout the south. And has Mr. Rogers been hanged in chains at Galveston Bar? On the contrary, he has since been made an associate editor of the reorganized *Southwest Review.* This would not have happened even five years ago. It did not happen to the pioneer, George Cable.

Two books by South Carolinians cannot be passed without comment, each being in its way an innovation in its approach to the Negro in the south. In *The Black Border,* Ambrose E. Gonzales has combined the talents of a philologist, psychologist, and narrator in an authentic and priceless record of the fast disappearing Gullah Negro of the Carolina Low Country. While it is true that his sketches accent the humorous aspect of his subject, they differ from the comic Negro fiction in that they do not exaggerate the racial characteristics. His people are essentially human beings.

Green Thursday, the second of the books that I have in mind, is by Julia Peterkin, and presents a number of portraits done with an intense, but sympathetic, analysis.[10] Her Negro is still the primitive, living close to the soil. She has watched him at his tasks, and about his home, and what she has seen she has recorded, with neither a conscious nor unconscious superiority but with a strict economy of means, and an effect of stark veracity.

It may be said that both of these books give only the rural Negro, and that the authentic word has yet to be spoken for the Negro of education who is striving to adjust himself to the civilization about him. Unfortunately, this is so. *The Fire in the Flint,* by Walter White, a book by a Negro,[11] doubtless the advance guard of a long procession of novels of protest by members of the race, fails to convince, just as the comic fiction Negro type failed to convince, and from much the same cause. Here we have an author who sees the grave and not the gay, and with good reason; but the material has been subjected to such excessive exaggeration that the illusion of truth cannot survive. The book appeals only by reason of its sensational content. It is the cry of the propagandist rather than the voice of art. This is a pity. It is high time that the Negro produced his own literature showing lights and shadows in their true value.

Turning from fiction to poetry, I will cite but a single case. Not because it stands alone as an example of excellence, but because in *Chills and Fever*, by John Crowe Ransom, published last autumn, I find this new note most evident. In fact, I know of nothing quite like it in American poetry. It is highly intellectual, and possessed of an almost diabolically humorous quality. Unlike the drama, and fiction, it does not turn inward upon its environment for inspiration, but is inclined to be metaphysical. Christopher Morley has liked it for what he described as its "pretty and intricate savagery."[12]

Among critics, and writers of special articles for the magazines, the names of Gerald W. Johnson, Frances Newman, and Howard W. Odum stand out for their courageous, and not invariably popular, utterances upon matters vital to the South.

And so, I believe that we are due for a new phase of southern letters. The skies may not be as blue, nor the women as universally beautiful, as when yesterday was at its high noon. Its good taste may be questioned when the standard of the Victorian drawing room is applied, but it will at least have the virtues of honesty and simplicity, and it will attempt to leave an authentic record of the period that produced it.

The American Negro in Art

MY PREOCCUPATION WITH the primitive Southern Negro as a subject for art derives from the often unworthy, but certainly powerfully motivating quality of curiosity. What, I wondered, was the unique characteristic in the life of the people who formed the sub-stratum of the society in which I had been born that endowed them with the power to stir me suddenly and inexplicably to tears or laughter; when the chaste beauty of the old city created by my own people awakened a distinctly different and more intellectual sort of delight? What was the mysterious force that for generations had resisted the pressure of our civilization and underlaid the apparently haphazard existence of the Negro with a fundamental unity? Why were certain colour combinations wrong in a formal garden, and yet capable of provoking a mysterious excitement when delivered against the vision from the polychromatic pageantry of a Negro lodge parade? What was it about a file of stevedores across a pier-head that made something inside of me follow them to the hold of a ship and wait, counting the moments, for their return? What was the quality in a spiritual sung in the secrecy of some back room that brought the chance listener up short against the outer wall with a contraction of the solar plexus, and lachrymal glands that he was powerless to control?

Slowly, as I watched and listened, there grew within me the conviction that this life which was going on within our own, yet was apart from it, possessed a certain definite, but indefinable quality that remained with my own people only in a more or less vestigial state, and at times seemed to have departed altogether like our gills and tails. From admiration of the manifestations of this secret law my feeling grew to one of envy; and so, from the beginning, my approach to the subject was never one of pity for, or philanthropic urge

SOURCE: Introduction to *Porgy: A Play in Four Acts,* by Dorothy and DuBose Heyward (Garden City, N.Y.: Doubleday, Doran, 1928), ix–xxi. Title supplied by the editor.

to succour, an unfortunate race. I saw the primitive Negro as the inheritor of a source of delight that I would have given much to possess. Why, then, should I weep over him?

Strangely enough, it was not until later that I identified this secret law as rhythm. In fact, not until it had, in my imagination, emerged as what I can only describe as a sort of race personality that dominated and swayed the mass, making of it a sum vastly greater than the total of its individual entities. It was at first this basic law with which I was preoccupied. The behavior of individuals was a secondary consideration, because I felt that it derived from the actuating principle. Then one day a paragraph from the court proceedings of the *Charleston News and Courier* caught my attention, and immediately personalized the vast abstraction with which I was struggling. It was, I feel, significant enough to justify quotation:

> Samuel Smalls, who is a cripple and is familiar to King Street with his goat and cart, was held for the June term of court of sessions on an aggravated assault charge. It is alleged that on Saturday night he attempted to shoot Maggie Barnes at number four Romney Street. His shots went wide of the mark. Smalls was up on a similar charge some months ago and was given a suspended sentence.

Here was something amazing. I had been familiar with the tragic figure of the beggar making his rounds of the Charleston streets. Thinking in terms of my own environment, I had concluded that such a life could never lift above the dead level of the commonplace. And yet this crushed, serio-comic figure, over on the other side of the colour wall, had known not only one, but two, tremendous moments. Into the brief paragraph one could read passion, hate, despair.

Inquiry on my part added only one fact to the brief newspaper note. Smalls had attempted to escape in his wagon, and had been run down and captured by the police patrol.

I am particularly anxious to have these details written into this record. Already the romantically inclined have forgotten that there was a beggar named Smalls, and speak of him only as Porgy, and the story to which I have given that name has assumed the significance of a biographical sketch. The obscure beggar with his malodorous goat bids fair to become a local legend.

As one with a profound respect for the authentic in folklore, I desire to record the exact point at which fact ends and the unfettered hand of the story writer takes up a tale.

To Smalls I make acknowledgment of my obligation. From contemplation of his real, and deeply moving, tragedy sprang Porgy, a creature of my imagination, who synthesized for me a number of divergent impressions and emotions, and upon whom, being my own creation, I could impose my own white man's conception of a summer of aspiration, devotion, and heartbreak across the colour wall.

In fact from the inception of the story I had been sensible of my audacity in attempting an interpretation of the inner life of an alien people. For this reason the presentation of the play with a Negro cast, two years after publication of the novel, represents a much closer approximation of an artistic ideal.

When dramatization was first suggested to me by Dorothy Heyward I was skeptical, believing that the difficulties would only be multiplied by the uncompromising objectivity of the stage. It was not until she submitted her first rough draft of the manuscript that I agreed to the experiment and offered my services as collaborator. It was obvious to both of us that, in spite of the many difficulties, the play would permit of the interpretation of the story by the race with which it was concerned. Our first resolution was that we would stand or fall with a Negro cast. That if no such cast was yet available we would hold the play indefinitely rather than resort to the use of disguised white actors.

Dramatization of a novel, always a difficult and hazardous undertaking, was further complicated in the case of *Porgy* by our determination to give the flow of life—which I have striven and, I fear, with only partial success, to define—its proper place in the canvas. That it was bigger than the individual who moved upon it was evident, for it had driven its dark stream on under our civilization, while generations came, were swept forward by it, and vanished. As with singing, where the Negro seldom excels as a soloist and yet with three or four friends picked up almost at random creates a successful chorus, so in their work and play it is the mass rhythms, the concerted movements, the crowd laughter, the communal interrelationships of the Negro quarter that differentiate it most sharply from its white slum neighbour. We felt that the play in order to possess any degree of verisimilitude must show its people moving in response to the deep undertow of this tide; that the background itself must be an active, significant factor, a powerfully flowing stream of movement, colour, and sound, upon which the story could depend for its motivation as though it were a dominating human force. That this was a highly dangerous experiment we well knew. We were also aware that it was diametrically opposed to the Broadway formula; and that it was one in which we could hope to awaken the curiosity of Broadway we doubted. We even questioned in our own minds whether, with the best intentions, it would be physically possible to capture this elusive quality and make it come to life upon a stage. That we attained a measure of success has been due to an extraordinarily fortunate sequence of circumstances. Had the Theatre Guild not made its small beginning ten years ago, and had not a sympathetic public assisted it in building up the financially strong and artistically enlightened organization that it is to-day, there would have been no adequate producer for the play. Its many difficulties and highly experimental nature would have militated fatally against it with a purely commercial stage, and the necessarily heavy expense of production would have been a serious obstacle in the way of a smaller art group.

Having decided to produce *Porgy*, the Guild commissioned Cleon Throck-morton,[1] a native Southerner, to design the sets, and, as an earnest of their desire for complete authenticity, despatched him to Charleston to study the environment. As a result, the great tenement with its court and many windows, in which most of the action takes place, is an actual stage adaptation of the building that I had in mind when I first wrote Catfish Row into the novel.

The delicate task of direction was then placed in the hands of Rouben Mamoulian, a young Armenian, born in the Caucasus, and trained in the Moscow Art Theatre.[2] I think that at the time even the Guild had very little idea of the extent of their good fortune in making this choice. That he had already done brilliant work we were aware, but of his power to observe and assimilate new material, and his genius for rhythm, we had yet to learn. Like Throckmorton he visited Charleston and absorbed and recorded impressions and, incidentally, under the spell of the lovely and unique old city, he developed an enormous enthusiasm for his task.

Of the many unknown quantities that were encountered in the highly experimental production of *Porgy*, to me the most interesting, the most unknown, and, in the final analysis, the most satisfactorily solved was that presented by the cast.

On the first day of reading and attempting to assign parts we found ourselves in the library of the theatre with a group of Negroes who had been located during months of searching by the casting director and been asked to attend and try out for parts. In the white theatre casting is a comparatively simple matter. The producer in all probability has his principals in mind before he contracts for the play, having seen each in a certain type of role. He, therefore, casts with a degree of certainty which is based upon known experience. But unfortunately, America has not yet had an opportunity of developing a Negro theatre with its proven performers. Our only procedure was to use a drag-net, and bring in every available actor of the least promise. And there we sat facing each other, on the brink of a new and mutual adventure and wondering what would come of it.[3]

With a cast of more than thirty-five people, and with very few from whom to choose, casting resolved itself into taking those that were there and assigning parts, much as is done in a stock company. It was out of the question to search further for a preconceived type for a particular character. We found this painful at first. The Bess of my novel had been a gaunt, tragic figure such as I had often seen on the Charleston waterfront. The part was given to Evelyn Ellis, young, slender, and immediately noticeable for a certain radiant charm.[4] Frank Wilson, whose work in *In Abraham's Bosom* had thrilled us by its emotional power, was equally far from our idea of what Porgy should look like in the flesh.[5] It was not until rehearsals had proved their ability to interpret the parts emotionally that I felt them to be really Porgy and Bess. But, on the other hand, Georgette Harvey was a reincarnation of Black Maria.[6] Rose McClendon was perfect as the Catfish Row aristocrat, Serena;[7] R. J. Huey was born for Mingo, and Dorothy Paul for Lily.[8]

Then the long and nerve-racking ordeal of rehearsal commenced. Many of our people had been trained for the vaudeville stage, and what they had learned had to be laboriously broken down before they could start out correctly. It was then that we realized the tremendous asset that we had in our director. Rouben Mamoulian was not merely a director: he was a creative instructor as well. In the Negro cast he had wonderfully plastic material. They liked him. It was amazing to watch a cast of New York people, most of whom had never seen the South Atlantic Seaboard, slowly bring to life upon a New York stage a living representation of a Charleston Negro tenement, with its laughter and its tragedy.

Then we began to realize the interesting fact that the labour that was being put into atmosphere was contributing directly to the acting of the cast, helping them to forget that they were playing parts, and aiding in the development of the naturalistic performance which they eventually attained. The use of rhythm in the play as it occurs without conscious effort in the life of the primitive Negro was a telling means toward this end. We used the spirituals as they actually occur to express emotional stress when the limited spoken vocabulary becomes inadequate. We employed the rhythmic, and spontaneous prayer with which the primitive Negro makes his supplications; the unfaltering rhythm of time, compressed in the ebb and flow of day and night, and the chiming of St. Michael's bells;[9] and the crowd movements, with their shifting pattern of colour and sound.

As the play took shape and the cast began to merge their own identities into those of the characters that they represented, we became aware that the thing for which we had hoped was actually materializing, and that the performance was developing into collaboration upon a broad scale.

One day, Leigh Whipper, who plays the undertaker, came to us and introduced himself as a fellow Charlestonian.[10] His boyhood had been spent in the old city. We got him to help us check the atmosphere of the play. Then he asked if I remembered the old crab vendor who had been a figure about the streets years ago. I did remember him only vaguely. Our undertaker then illustrated him for us. "Go ahead and put him in Catfish Row," we told him. The result is the "bit" in the second act of the production upon the Guild stage, of which he is not only the actor, but playwright as well.

Another "bit" which appeared on the Guild stage but is not to be found in the printed play, is the quarrel between Annie and Jake at the Sea Island picnic. The authors have no claim to it. It is a spontaneous collaboration between Annie (Ella Madison) and Jake (Wesley Hill).[11] In fact this instinctive, creative gift is the most outstanding characteristic of the Negro as an actor, and one can never be quite sure when and where it will strike, or at what moment an irresistible improvisation will leap into the dialogue.

I have been asked for my impressions of the Northern Negro as compared with those of whom I write in *Porgy*. In temperament, so far as I have noticed, there is no difference. There is the same resilience of spirits, the same sense of humour—especially for the ridiculous—and the same immediate emotional responsiveness which fits them so admirably for the stage. But I feel that there is one decided and very interesting difference—one which may be merely climatic, or which may spring from the broader opportunity for the Negro in the North, with its resultant incentive to effort. It is characteristic of the Southern Negro that he will work magnificently under excitement, or for a reasonably short shift, but that on a long, routine job of sustained effort he loses interest. I have been deeply impressed with the tenacity and determination which the *Porgy* cast have put into their work.

But it has not been only in the mass, but as individuals also, that I have found my co-workers on the play interesting. In the usual play the habitual theatregoer finds an actor of whom he is more than apt to know. His history (thanks to the industry of his press agent) is public knowledge. In some cases there is even a family tradition going back through several generations of actor ancestors. Confronted by a group of Negro artists who are not generally known to the public, one wonders about their background, and eventually one inquires. Rose McClendon is remembered for her distinguished stairway descent in *Deep River* and, with Evelyn Ellis, in *Roseanne*, and again with Frank Wilson and R. J. Huey in *In Abraham's Bosom*. With most of the other players *Porgy* means a Broadway debut.

It is a far cry from the music and dancing of *Shuffle Along*, *Runnin' Wild*, and the coloured Night Club Revue,[12] to the spirituals, with their depth and sincerity, and the rhythmic swaying that accompanies them, and yet from these shows came many of the voices that are heard in the mourning scene over the body of the murdered Robbins.

That the Negro has already made his place in the American drama there can be no doubt. The period following his physical emancipation developed in the race a protective facility for dramatic imitation. He was too preoccupied with his impersonation of the farceur, that he was supposed to be, to be himself. The minstrel show and vaudeville stage marked the limit of his opportunity. Now at the dawn of an artistic emancipation he may reach back across the years, forgetting for the time the well-worn mask of laughter, and speak seriously of his own themes, his hopes and aspirations. That, almost without preparation, he is able to acquit himself with honour in serious drama is not a matter for wonder. He has always possessed a natural talent, and he is at last permitted to be merely himself.

The Negro in the Low-Country

IN ATTEMPTING A PORTRAIT of the Negro who created the spirituals of the Carolina Low-Country one is faced at the outset with an almost insurmountable difficulty. Standing upon the high ground of the twentieth century and looking back along the years, he is at once confused by the varied and contradictory aspects that his subject presents. His gaze must traverse the vale of humiliation that marks the reconstruction period, when his former slave sat in his legislative halls. He must lift the pall of the Civil War that hangs over his middle distance, and project his vision into the dazzling and already legendary period that lay between America's two great wars and brought the State's most glamorous epoch to flower. And there, in the golden haze of the past, the figure that he has been following has vanished. The Negro has ceased to be a human entity and has become a symbol. On one hand, out of the pamphlets of the Abolitionists, he looms chained, heroic, uncomplaining under the lash of a brutal owner. On the other, he stands, the creation of a defensive South, reared in love, utterly content, faithful even in the moment of death to an incredibly benevolent master. Somewhere between these two diametrically opposed conceptions the real Negro slave must stand, but his outlines are blurred in the glare that beats about him from the symbolic presences that tower on either side. He split a nation asunder, and he endowed both with the attributes of crusaders. It is not to be wondered at, therefore, that, as a simple mortal blindly yet courageously working out his humble destiny, he has very nearly ceased to exist as a figure in the past.

It is obvious therefore that if the artist aspires to the creation of a convincing and realistic portrait he must immediately forget all of his precon-

SOURCE: *The Carolina Low-Country*, ed. Augustine T. Smythe et al. (New York: Macmillan, 1932), 171–87.

ceptions, and submit his emotions to the stern and unbiased discipline of his
art. He must go back into the dawn of our own beginnings on the American
continent and consider the Negro, not as a human chattel to be bought and
sold, but as an immigrant arriving out of an old world to take his place in a
new and strange one. Then, taking this as his starting point, he must follow
the Negro up along the years assuming his development in the light of certain known racial characteristics which were his heritage from the past, and
certain physical and spiritual influences to which he was exposed in his new
and amazing environment.

At its peak the slave trade transported to the new world as many voyagers
as sailed from the white lands lying to the north of the hot dark continent. In
the popular mind of today the African slave of the early days of the trade
stands simply and conclusively as a Negro, and he is endowed with certain
universally accepted Negroid characteristics, most of which in turn are derived
from the literary representations—or misrepresentations—of a favorite author. Nothing could be further from an accurate conception. The various
strains that composed this momentous migration differed as widely in many
cases as did the highland Scot from the Italian of the Roman Campagna. At
a given time one vessel lying off the northern limits of the slave coast, would
be packing her holds with hill men marched on the chain from a thousand
miles inland; two thousand miles to the southeast at Calabar, a second ship
would be stowing a cargo fresh from the malarial swamps of the Equator;
and a third lying to the southward of Calabar at a distance as great as that
which separates New York from Florida would be shipping her capacity in
the natives of Angola, the most highly prized strain in the Carolina markets.[1]

But although the tribal differences seem of little moment to us now after
the lapse of more than a century, it is not to be supposed that either the
traders or planters were unaware of the respective advantages and disadvan-
tages of the different tribes. Had the Negroes come voluntarily as merely individual adventurers to the new world it is likely that small account would
have been taken of their tribal characteristics, but, as articles of commerce,
certain excellences become intrinsically valuable. It was natural that, as the
plantations developed a gentry that prided themselves on the strains in their
racing stables, they would be at least equally mindful of the racial traits that
distinguished the accretions in the Negro yards. And so out of the long past
come echoes of the various tribes that supplied the colonies, their virtues,

their failings, and their net worth as revealed under the acid test of the auctioneer's hammer.

There is little doubt that the factors of Charleston found most ready sale for cargoes from Angola, and posters announcing their arrival were probably a common sight upon the wharves where the plantation barges landed their masters on their visits to town. Indeed it is logical to suppose that the title "Gullah Negro," which time has rendered applicable to all Negroes of the Carolina Low-Country, was a corruption of the word "Angola." But in this connection it is worthy of note that John Bennett, whose exhaustive studies on the subject have made him an authority, maintains that the word is derived from Gola, a tribe that inhabited Western Liberia and which also contributed largely to the trade.

Of the Angola Negro it was said that he was of a gentle and affectionate nature and faithful to a trust. But, of rather low mentality, he was gullible and easily swayed by others. This possibly accounted for his proclivity for running away—which counted somewhat against him in the markets.

Advertisements for the sale, in Charleston, of Gold Coast Negroes, which appeared in 1785, suggest the probability that the Corramantees, who came from that section of Africa, may have contributed largely to the Negro race during its period of development under slavery.[2] In fact it is likely that this strain entered the colony with its very beginning, for it was at that time the most highly prized on the plantations of Barbadoes and Jamaica. And when, with the opening of Charles Town, a number of gentlemen planters arrived from the British Islands to the South it is logical to assume that they introduced Corramantees into the Colony. As to this tribe, Christopher Codrington, one time Governor of the Leeward Islands,[3] expressed himself in a letter addressed to the English Board of Trade:

> The Corramantees are not only the best and most faithful of our slaves, but are really all born heroes. There is a difference between them and all other negroes beyond which 'tis possible for your Lordships to conceive. There never was a raskal or coward of that nation. Intrepid to the last degree, not a man of them but will stand to be cut to pieces without a sigh or groan, grateful and obedient to a kind master, but implacably revengeful when ill-treated. My father, who had studied the genius and temper of all kinds of negroes forty-five years with a very nice observation, would say no man deserved a Corramantee that would not treat him like a friend rather than a slave.[4]

Gambia Negroes were not an uncommon importation and apparently found a ready market. They were reputed to be industrious, and "seasoned" readily in our latitude, with but small mortality in the process.[5]

But these strains were only a beginning. By 1750, with the citizens of our own Rhode Island vying—and by no means unsuccessfully—with the vast fleets out of Liverpool and Bristol, the life of Africa poured in a steady stream into the Antilles and British West Indies, then it lifted like a tidal wave and washed along the whole Southern seaboard.

It was difficult to say where the cargoes would land as the slave-ships often traded from port to port in search of a market. And so into the broad dark stream of life that was beginning to settle into a channel of its own making in the Carolina Low-Country trickled accretions of Senegalese, with their decided Arabic strain, their sensitive intelligent faces; Mandangoes reputed gentle in demeanor but prone to theft; Whydahs, Nagoes, and Pow Pows, all industrious and sturdy of body; Congoes, Gaboons, and finally Eboes, malarial yellow of complexion, despondent, and so apt to commit suicide on the middle passage that they were considered unprofitable by the traders. In fact, there was probably no tribe on the West Coast that did not contribute to the tide that during these decades was always at the flood.[6]

By the middle of the eighteenth century, the melting pot was seething. And it is likely that nowhere else on the Continent was there so ideal a condition for accomplishing the complete homogeneity of various immigrant strains as on the Southern plantation. While white immigration to the northward was settling its Ghettos, its Little Italys, even its self-contained rural districts, which clung to imported languages and traditions, probably an equal number of Negro races were arbitrarily disintegrated and thrown immediately upon the resources of a new language, a new religion, a new conception of morality.

If we accept as American a people who have most entirely abandoned a number of alien cultures for one which had its origin with their arrival upon our shores, and who have developed from that beginning into a race that has no counterpart elsewhere on the globe, we must concede the Negroes' possession of at least as pure an Americanism as any presented in the spectacle of our national life.

It is evident from the writings and legislation of the early eighteenth century that the Southern conscience was none too easy upon the moral aspect of the institution of slavery. Colonization schemes for the return of the African to his native land, the Randolph movement looking toward emancipation in Virginia, the general practice of manumission, as a reward for faithful service, or by the will of a deceased master, all met with some popular following.[7]

It is notable that in all of these movements the responsibility of the owner for the well-being of the slave after freedom was the prime concern. The idea of loosing an enormous, ignorant, pauper population upon a community to fend for itself was one that could never have had its inception in the Southern mind which from the beginning, had been conscious of the obligation to, as well as the benefits to be derived from, its slave labor.

In Charleston the law governing manumission provided that the owner appear with his slave before a committee and demonstrate the future freeman's ability to earn a living for himself by the practice of some adequate trade. Only then was freedom granted, and, thereafter, the former master continued as a patron of the Negro in a sort of informal guardianship.

That under this benign form of emancipation the free population grew with considerable rapidity in Charleston was evidenced by the fact that when the Vesey insurrection took place in 1822, and precipitated the series of laws that stopped the practice, there was a free population numbering several thousand.

While it is my desire to encumber this article with as little of the dry material of history as may be possible, the attitude of mind in the ruling class toward slavery can be seen in retrospect to have changed from time to time in definite response to certain significant events. If we follow these dates with an imaginary line that rises and falls with the sentiment toward slavery, we will see the process of solidification of opinion and the trend in the South not towards emancipation but away from it, culminating with the secession of South Carolina as a Slave State in 1860, with the Negro fetching a higher price in the market than at any period in his history with but one exception.

The introduction of rice in 1694 marked the termination of the frontier period when the pioneers hewed out their clearings, farmed in a small way, and lumbered for export. But rice called for heavy labor and Africa furnished it.

The introduction of indigo in 1741 sends our imaginary line up another notch, for the process of indigo planting and preparation could be dovetailed with that of rice and the same gangs could be utilized for both crops. Then followed the evolution of the rice field from patches planted on high land to swamp areas flooded by reserves, and finally on to the perfection in 1783 of the tideflow system which marked the birth of the rice plantation as we know it, with its huge labor demand for maintaining dikes and producing crops. This lifted the line to a peak at which it remained until sent to a higher level by the introduction of cotton in 1790.

It is true that during the period of depression following the Revolution, South Carolina passed laws prohibiting the importation of slaves. But history will not allow us to attribute this cessation to a humanitarian impulse. Slave property had become the greatest investment of the Carolina ruling class. This investment was seriously jeopardized by a market flooded with raw importations from Africa. The overlords simply eliminated this competition, and, in the face of our first great national depression, held up the value of their "Negro Yards" in what was probably America's first successful combination in restraint of trade.

But cotton opened up a new demand for labor. There was no longer any fear of over-stocking. In 1804 the traffic was resumed and between that year and national prohibition of the trade which became a law in 1808 the slavers poured thirty-nine thousand and seventy-five raw Africans through the port of Charleston, and on in a dark wave across the rice and cotton lands of the Low-Country. The statistics of these four years of intensive immigration, which come to us from an authoritative source, are so illuminating that they should have a place in this record, even though it essays neither a justification of, nor an apology for, the South for the institution of Slavery.

During these four years, when the harbor was never free from the evil stench of the slave ships, of the total of 39,075 Negroes, 21,027 were transported in British and French vessels; by the citizens of Rhode Island 8,238; by the citizens of other nonslave holding States 6,367; and by the citizens of slave-holding States only 3,443.[8]

And now the forces that directed the trend of the race away from freedom came from outside the state and had nothing to do with economics. The Abolitionists of the North had grown strong enough to make themselves heard. Inflammatory pamphlets were finding their way into the hands of the Negroes. Finally in 1822 the vague uneasiness occasioned by the Abolitionist propaganda was crystallized into the constant fear of rebellion which, until the Civil War, hung like a menacing shadow over the smiling prospect of Southern life, and prompted the elaborate series of restrictive measures that were piled upon the statute books affecting the status of the slave.[9] The event which crystallized this fear was the Vesey insurrection in 1822. This uprising, although frustrated almost in the moment of its accomplishment, was so daring in its conception, so far-reaching in its consequences, and so illuminating in all of its aspects, that it leaps from the faded pages of the official reports and captures the imagination by the sheer power of its drama.

Of Denmark Vesey we know little. He must have been possessed of a sublime belief in his own destiny. And at the beginning he must have been convinced that his Gods were with him, for, through the incredibly long odds of a lottery ticket, they presented him with fifteen hundred dollars with which to purchase his freedom. He was evidently possessed of those rare qualities among Negroes, a genius for organization, leadership, and infinite patience and sustained determination in the face of difficulties, for he spent four years perfecting his plan. Having taught himself to read, he studied the Bible and took as the symbol for his revolution the liberation of the Children of Israel from Egypt.

Confronted by the barrier of tribal prejudice which was still evidently strong among the Africans, he appointed lieutenants from the various dominant strains, who organized the Angolas, the Eboes, the Corramantees, and others into tribal units. His most valued assistant was called Gullah Jack. He was evidently a Witch-doctor, and worked among the less intelligent slaves. By his charms, he promised immunity from danger to all who joined the insurrection, and threatened the recalcitrant with the wrath of the Gods.

Vesey's organization acted as a distributing agency for Abolitionist propaganda, and the successful looting of San Domingo by the Negroes was held as an example before the credulous Charleston blacks.[10] His plan even included a contact with the Negroes of San Domingo who were invited to reinforce the Charleston Negroes when the insurrection became an accomplished fact. The revolt was set for midnight on Sunday, June the sixteenth, 1822. At that hour all of the drivers in the city were to seize the horses of their masters to form a sort of irregular cavalry. Certain stores that had arms for sale were scheduled for immediate looting, and the two city arsenals were then to be the objectives of the slaves. Immediately upon the capture of the town, slaves on the outlying plantations were to rise, assassinate their masters, destroy the plantations, and march to town. The plan contemplated the complete extermination of the white population.

Over this seething volcano Charleston lay between her twin rivers happy in her fancied security. Behind deep windows, shuttered against the noon glare, and around tea tables in walled gardens in the cool of the evenings, the social life, yielding to the languor of summer, pursued its happy and leisurely way.

Then, two weeks before the date set for the uprising, a slave who comes down the years to us by the single name of George whispered a terrified word of warning to his master. A Negro named William, belonging to Mr. Paul, had invited him to join the rebellion. William was seized and after a week of solitary confinement told the plans and the date set for their execution. But so incredible to the authorities did the elaborate scheme appear that after a few days of caution they were about to dismiss it as a sheer fiction, when another master came to them with an identical story brought to him by one of his slaves.

Accordingly, on the night of June 16th, the militia was called and the city waited tensely for the outbreak. But the appearance of the soldiers gave pause to the followers of Vesey and the night passed quietly. Immediately a special court was called consisting of two magistrates and five outstanding citizens. These in turn appointed a vigilance committee and arrests of Vesey and his lieutenants followed. Confessions revealed the magnitude of the plot and 130 Negroes were arrested, of whom 9 were free men. Four white men, of whom only one is described as Charlestonian, were also arrested for complicity.

The account of the trial contained in an official pamphlet[11] is extremely significant because of the unquestioned evidence which it presents of the treatment which a slave received in a court of law, and the value which was placed upon his life. The skeptic will say, and with a large measure of truth, that this consideration had more to do with a Negro's property value than with humanitarianism. But whether as valuable property of a powerful master, or a human being asking justice in a court of law, the evidence points to the conclusion that during the slave regime the Negro received in the courts infinitely more consideration than he has found at the hands of an average jury since he has attained to freedom.

In the Vesey trials the committee appointed to serve with the magistrates was composed of William Drayton, Robert J. Turnbull, James Legare, James R. Pringle, and Nathaniel Heyward. All, of course, slave holders.[12] These gentlemen at once laid down the rule that no Negro was to be tried unless either his master or attorney was present; and, furthermore, realizing the possibility of the occasion for paying off old scores among the Negroes, that none should be convicted upon the testimony of a single witness.

Of the 130 arrested, 52 were promptly discharged. Nine were acquitted with recommendations that their masters have them transported, which doubtless meant that they were privileged to sell them beyond the borders of the state.

Of those who remained, 34 were deported by the state, and 35 were hanged, among the latter being Denmark Vesey and Gullah Jack. Somehow, of these two, the one who seizes upon the imagination is not Vesey with his tremendous schemes for revenge and liberation, but Gullah Jack, who looms above the ruins of the evil-starred insurrection a tragic symbol of the failure of the old African Gods. It is not difficult to imagine him going to his death clutching to the last the charmed crab-claw which was supposed to render him invulnerable to the hostile magic of the white man.

That free Negroes were held largely responsible for this trouble was evidenced by the immediate action of the white population in requesting the legislature to pass a law expelling them all from the state. This failed, but as a compromise further manumission was prohibited.[13] New and heavy penalties were imposed upon white people who might be implicated in future uprisings, and the control over blacks was stiffened, with the augmented patrol empowered to administer punishments when deemed necessary. It also became illegal to teach a Negro to read and write. What was probably the most dire result of the uprising was that the former Southern advocate of a benign and intelligent form of freedom was silenced by overwhelming public opinion, and was promptly damned as an Abolitionist with all the opprobrium that the title then implied.

We have seen how the ascendency of the plantation system on the one hand, and the militant hostility of the Abolitionists, with its resultant fear of insurrection, on the other, solidified public opinion in the South. But, paradoxically, this definite closing of the Southern mind to the idea of emancipation undoubtedly created a condition that made for the well being of the slave as an individual. With the anti-slavery movement gaining momentum in all parts of the civilized world, the Southern planter could not escape the realization that here, in his own fields, the institution was on trial for its life. As the ascendency of "King Cotton" continued, and the South entered upon the period that saw the full flowering of its ante-bellum civilization, it is likely that here in the Carolina Low-Country, with which specifically, we are now concerned, the rural Negro experienced a higher state of physical and moral well being than at any other period in his history. Labor was abundant, the plantations were for the most part self-sustaining units and produced an abundance of food and even clothing, and these necessities were not subject to those seasonal famines which are inevitable with a primitive and improvident people. Records of the time show that in cotton, and even to a certain extent in rice, the task system was favored by the owners. With these tasks, which were not excessive, accomplished, the time of the slaves was their own for the tending of their private vegetable gardens and chicken yards. Churches were built and preachers provided, and medical attendance, usually by a white contract physician.

The ridiculous accusation that stocks were bred up by the forced mating of particularly fine specimens finds not the slightest corroboration in fact.[14] On the contrary vestiges of the Negro yards with their separate cabins which still stand, and which alone in so many cases escaped the torch of an invading army, prove conclusively that the development of the family was the invariable law. And if further evidence is needed it is provided by the slave rosters of the period. Before me as I write lies a large book bound in faded buckram—the slave register of Harbin Plantation, St. Johns Berkeley.[15] On page one we find the names:

Plenty	age 41
Diana	age 38

and under these the children:

Edward	22
August	15
Solomon	13
Finette	5
Rubelle	1

then follow other family groups with the children listed in order of their arrival.

Slaves were punished. The lash was employed. But we must not forget that during the period of slavery the cat-o-nine-tails was used in the United States Navy, and in the City of Charleston, as well as in New England, the public whipping post was commonly employed as a disciplinary measure for white petty offenders.

That the system of slavery by its very nature protected the sadist in the practice of cruelty cannot be denied, nor can it be doubted that there were individual instances of injustice. But we must remember that the Negro probably to a greater extent than any other living race is possessed of a genius for forming happy human relationships, for inspiring affection, for instinctively divining the mood of one with whom he comes in contact, and of accommodating his own mood to that of the other. He was temperamentally ideally suited to make his own way in a state of slavery, and, where he came in personal touch with his master, to weld a bond of friendship and sympathetic understanding between them so close and so interdependent that the idea of excessive cruelty on the part of the master would have been preposterous. It is true that this relationship has been sentimentalized and utilized *ad nauseam* in writing of the slave period. But all of the bathos cannot obliterate the fact that there was something beautiful and tender and enriching to both black and white in the ante-bellum relationship that existed between master and servant.

No, hatred cannot breed affection, and cruelty cannot beget loyalty, and when, in 1863, with their masters at the front and the women and children at their mercy, the slaves were liberated, there was no repetition of the San Domingo horror. On the contrary, undoubtedly to the amazement of the radical Abolitionist faction in the North, they remained where they were as the protectors of the homes of their absent masters. And yet the Negroes were of the identical parent stocks with those who had risen in the West Indian Island, slaughtered their masters and plunged the country into a state of utter barbarism. Evolution is a slow process. Human nature does not come a full circle in a century. Perhaps after all something can be said for a master who can inspire the higher rather than the baser emotions.

It is not to be wondered at that out of a past of such inextricably interwoven destinies the black and white races of the Carolina Low-Country have emerged with a relationship that baffles the stranger.

In America where we hold before every native-born man-child the prospect of becoming the president of the United States, and where we promulgate the fallacious theory that we are living in a true democracy, we have forgotten that there can be such a thing as pride of caste among the lowly, that there could exist in a man who had been born a servant and expected to die a servant a self-respect equally as great, and as jealously guarded as that enjoyed by the master, and yet, paradoxically, this very cleavage between the ruling and servant classes in the South which has imposed an obligation to respect the dignity of each other has constituted the bond which has held the two classes together in affection and mutual understanding through the vicissitudes of two and a half centuries. It has made possible an intercourse so lacking in racial self-consciousness, so utterly free from inhibiting modern attitudes, that, in the hands of the white people of the Low-Country, the task of salvaging the spirituals of the Negroes from a mutual past becomes not an unwarranted audacity, not a gesture of patronizing superiority, but a natural and harmonious collaboration wrought in affection and with a deep sense of reverence.

But to those who have undertaken this task it has become more than merely a matter of recording a folk expression of the locality. As the work has progressed under our hands it has assumed a deeper significance. The plantation Master and the plantation Negro stand today definitely at the parting of the ways. This then becomes our valedictory—our requiem for a lost yesterday.

The fire-lit rooms, the broad acres that for generations have dreamed through the short winter and in the spring have burgeoned into productive life are gone. Space, the tonguing of the pack on a frosty morning, the rhythm of a running horse between gripped knees, the laughter of plow hands and the chime of trace-chains in the still evenings, the swarming life of the quarters,—these are memories now. It was our destiny that sooner or later the city would have us, for when all else fails the city offers nourishment to the body.

And the plantation Negro, too, will pass. The rhythm of our National life, so alien to him at first, will eventually possess him. Upon the vast, sterile tracts of the hunting preserves that have superseded the plantations he will survive in small numbers. He is authentic Southern atmosphere, and, as such, has something to sell in a limited, but rich and highly specialized market. He will enliven the sportsman's day with his native wit, and in the evening he will don his Sunday clothes and appear punctually at the Big House to render spirituals for the delectation of the guests.

But for the Negro in the mass the call of the city has already been heeded. The migration has commenced. The old, uncomplicated pattern of life is broken. The forces of advancement are at work and will prove irresistible. They will be taken from our fields, fired with ambition, and fed to the machines of our glittering new civilization.

But here in the semi-tropical belt of the Carolina Low-Country, where isolation and time have retarded the process, we can still hear the Negro singing the songs of his own creation. We can see him hale, vigorous, and glad under the sun by day, and at night surrounded by wide, still fields and moon-drenched marshes. We watch him with his family, his unquestioning belief in a personal God, his spontaneous abandonment to emotion, his faith in his simple destiny. And, seeing these things, out of our own fuller and sadder knowledge, we wonder whether he will be much happier when the last of the bonds are severed and finally and triumphantly he has conformed to the stereotyped pattern of American success.

Porgy and Bess Return on Wings of Song

NOTHING could be more ill-advised than the writing of this article. It exhibits all too clearly the decay of a human will, and it is strewn with the debris of broken resolutions. Out of a limited but illuminating Broadway experience, I have grasped the simple fact that a play does not exist until the critics and the public have looked upon it and found it good. Could there then be a more perfect example of artless, parental exhibitionism than the spectacle of a playwright prattling about his expected brain-child a full month before the hazardous accouchement?

How did it happen? I will tell you. I can at least expose the system of which I am a victim.

You leave the first rehearsal, hypnotized by the music of your own words. You are beguiled into the sanctum of an editor. Your fingers close of their own volition about a cocktail glass. You are told things about your work which, in your state of initial intoxication, you are fatuous enough to believe. You conclude that the editor is also a discriminating critic and altogether an excellent fellow. And then, since, in any event it is against nature for an author to say "no" to an editor, you find yourself committed. It is not until later that you realize your deadline for a monthly periodical is a month in advance of publication, and that your story may burst from the presses, not as a bright paean for the living, but a sad and ironical epitaph for the dead.

But the story of *Porgy* has a definite past, as well as a projected reincarnation, and the production of the opera is the materialization of an idea suggested by George Gershwin in a letter written to me nine years ago.[1] The drama had not yet been produced, but was being written by my wife, Dorothy Heyward,

SOURCE: *Stage* 13 (October 1935), 25–28.

and myself for the Theatre Guild,[2] when George read the novel and suggested a meeting.

My first impression of my collaborator remains with me and is singularly vivid. A young man of enormous physical and emotional vitality, who possessed the faculty of seeing himself quite impersonally and realistically, and who knew exactly what he wanted and where he was going. This characteristic put him beyond both modesty and conceit. About himself he would merely mention certain facts, aspirations, failings. They were usually right.

We discussed *Porgy.* He said that it would not matter about the dramatic production, as it would be a number of years before he would be prepared to compose an opera.[3] At the time he had numerous Broadway successes to his credit, and his *Rhapsody in Blue,* published three years before, had placed him in the front rank of American composers.[4] It was extraordinary, I thought, that, in view of a success that might well have dazzled any man, he could appraise his talent with such complete detachment. And so we decided then that some day when we were both prepared we would do an operatic version of my simple Negro beggar of the Charleston streets.

In the meantime, the play went into rehearsal at the Theatre Guild. Rouben Mamoulian, in his first appearance on Broadway, was entrusted with its direction. A cast was assembled from Negro night clubs and Harlem theatres. Then for six weeks, what we all believed to be Broadway's most highly speculative venture dragged its personnel through the extremes of hope and despair toward the opening night.

I suppose it is sheer physical exhaustion, plus the emotional bludgeoning an author undergoes during rehearsals, that reduces him to pessimistic witlessness on the night of the premiere. Out of that night, I remember only vaguely a few moments of startling beauty: Mamoulian's fantastic shadows, the heartbreaking quality of the funeral spiritual, Porgy's pathetic leave taking. But never to be forgotten was that awful moment when Crown shouted to the silent heavens, "Gawd laugh and Crown laugh back."[5] Then, after an aching interval, came the belated clap of thunder that was supposed to be the laugh of God. The scene shifts seemed interminable. And lastly, and most crushing, as we cowered at the back of the house under the protective wing of Philip Moeller, came the exit of Woolcott before the last scene of the play.[6]

I have never seen him since, but I could point him out immediately in any crowd, so vivid is my impression of him. He stands about forty feet in his stockings, is about thirty feet broad; and when he rises to his full height from the second row in the orchestra, he can blot out an entire proscenium arch. His mouth is that of a medieval executioner, and when he strides down a theatre aisle and past a terror-stricken playwright, his footsteps shake the building with the tread of doom. Somebody might have warned us that he had an early deadline, and had to get his copy in, but nobody did. To us it was a walk-out. He gave us a fine review. He proved that dramatic critics really are omniscient by knowing how the show ended. But the mischief had been done. Thirty months later, when the play closed after a run in America and a successful journey across the Atlantic, the authors are still more or less nervous wrecks.[7]

Time passed and Porgy and the goat lay comfortably dossed down in Cain's warehouse. But every year, between novels with me, and Broadway productions with George, I would journey North and we would meet and discuss our opera. I remember George saying once—it was, I think, when he was planning to stage *An American in Paris*—that he would stay abroad and put in some intensive study in counterpoint.[8] As always, he knew just where he was going. The success of his symphonic poem in Paris was flattering, but the main idea was to build toward the opera.

Later he worked with Joseph Schillinger, the musicologist, who carried him from Bach to Schoenberg, concentrating his attention on polytonality— modern harmony, and counterpoint.[9]

It is the fashion in America to lament the prostitution of art by the big magazine, the radio, the moving pictures. With this I have little patience. Properly utilized, the radio and the pictures may be to the present-day writer what his prince was to Villon, the king of Bavaria was to Wagner.[10]

At no other time has it been possible for a writer to earn by hiring himself out as a skilled technician for, say, two months, sufficient income to sustain him for a year. And yet the moving pictures have made it possible. I decided that the silver screen should be my Maecenas,[11] and George elected to serve the radio.

During my first year I wrote the screen version of *The Emperor Jones*. For this I may have lost the friendship of Eugene O'Neill. I haven't dared to look him up since. And to finance my second year I made a pilgrimage to Hollywood to tinker at Pearl Buck's *Good Earth*. My selection for this assignment presented a perfect example of motion picture logic. When I arrived on the lot and asked why I had been offered the job, it was made perfectly plain to me.

Negroes were not a Caucasian people. Neither were Chinamen. I wrote understandingly of Negroes. It was obvious then that I would understand the Chinese. I suspect that before my engagement closed their faith in their reasoning power was shaken. But I gave them my best, and when I left for the East I was free to complete my work on the opera.

Statistics record the fact that there are 25,000,000 radios in America. Their contribution to the opera was indirect but important. Out of them for half an hour each week poured the glad tidings that Feenamint could be wheedled away from virtually any drug clerk in America for one dime—the tenth part of a dollar. And with the authentic medicine-man flair, the manufacturer distributed this information in an irresistible wrapper of Gershwin hits, with the composer at the piano.

At the outset we were faced with a difficult problem. I was firm in my refusal to leave the South and live in New York. Gershwin was bound for the duration of his contract to the microphone at Radio City. The matter of effecting a happy union between words and music across a thousand miles of Atlantic seaboard baffled us for a moment. The solution came quite naturally when we associated Ira Gershwin with us. Presently we evolved a system by which, between my visits North, or George's dash to Charleston, I could send scenes and lyrics. Then the brothers Gershwin, after their extraordinary fashion, would get at the piano, pound, wrangle, swear, burst into weird snatches of song, and eventually emerge with a polished lyric. Then too, Ira's gift for the more sophisticated lyric was exactly suited to the task of writing the songs for Sporting Life, the Harlem gambler who had drifted into Catfish Row.[12]

I imagine that in after years when George looks back upon this time, he will feel that the summer of 1934 furnished him with one of the most satisfying as well as exciting experiences of his career. Under the baking suns of July and August we established ourselves on Folly Island, a small barrier island ten miles from Charleston.[13] James Island with its large population of primitive Gullah Negroes lay adjacent, and furnished us with a laboratory in which to test our theories, as well as an inexhaustible source of folk material. But the most interesting discovery to me, as we sat listening to their spirituals, was that to George it was more like a homecoming than an exploration. The quality in him which had produced the *Rhapsody in Blue* in the most sophisticated city in America, found its counterpart in the impulse behind the music and bodily rhythms of the simple Negro peasant of the South.

The Gullah Negro prides himself on what he calls "shouting." This is a complicated rhythmic pattern beaten out by feet and hands as an accompaniment to the spirituals, and is indubitably an African survival. I shall never forget the night when, at a Negro meeting on a remote sea-island, George started "shouting" with them, and eventually to their huge delight stole the show from their champion "shouter." I think that he is probably the only white man in America who could have done it.

Another night as we were about to enter a dilapidated cabin that had been taken as a meeting house by a group of Negro Holy Rollers, George caught my arm and held me. The sound that had arrested him was one to which, through long familiarity, I attached no special importance. But now, listening to it with him, and noticing his excitement, I began to catch its extraordinary quality. It consisted of perhaps a dozen voices raised in loud rhythmic prayer. The odd thing about it was that while each had started at a different time, upon a different theme, they formed a clearly defined rhythmic pattern, and that this, with the actual words lost, and the inevitable pounding of the rhythm, produced an effect almost terrifying in its primitive intensity. Inspired by the extraordinary effect, George wrote six simultaneous prayers producing a terrifying primitive invocation to God in the face of the hurricane.[14]

We had hoped, and it was logical, that the Theatre Guild would produce the opera. An excursion into that field of the theatre was a new idea to the directors. But then they had gambled once on *Porgy* and won. There was a sort of indulgent affection for the cripple and his goat on Fifty-second Street. Most certainly they did not want anybody else to do it, and so contracts were signed.[15]

Having committed themselves, the Guild proceeded to deprive us of all alibis in the event of failure by giving us a free hand in the casting and a star producing staff.

Mamoulian returned from Hollywood to assume the direction. (Alexander Smallens, who had conducted the Philharmonic Stadium Concerts, and the Philadelphia Symphony, and who, in spite of having conducted the orchestra of *Four Saints in Three Acts,* still made his wants known in comprehensible English, was made conductor.)[16]

Alexander Steinert, pianist and composer, with a Prix de Rome to his credit, was entrusted with the coaching of the principals.[17]

For a year George had been cast-hunting. It had been an exciting, if at times a strenuous sport. But last April, when I journeyed North to hear the aspirants and advise on the final decisions, I was amazed at the amount of promising talent exhibited. The cast was assembled. Steinert took them in hand, and at the first rehearsal he had them ready to read the difficult score from beginning to end.

We were in rather a dither about the name. The composer and author both felt that the opera should be called simply *Porgy*. But there was a feeling in the publicity department that this would lead to a confusion in that amorphous region known as the public mind, and that *Porgy* in lights might be construed as a revival of the original play, rather than as the Gershwin opus.

There had of course been *Pelleas and Melisande, Samson and Delilah, Tristan and Isolde*.[18]

"And so," said Heyward, with the humility characteristic of those who draw their sustenance from the theatre, "why not *Porgy and Bess?*"

To which Gershwin replied with the detachment to which I have referred and which could not possibly be mistaken for conceit, "Of course, it's right in the operatic tradition."

Two years! It doesn't seem that long. There has been so much to do. The published version of the piano and vocal score, fresh from the press, runs to five hundred and sixty pages. And when that was finished, George tackled the orchestration single handed. The resulting manuscript is impressive. It contains seven hundred pages of closely written music, and it is the fruit of nine months of unremitting labor.

For my own part, I had a play which needed to be cut forty per cent for the libretto, yet nothing of dramatic value could be sacrificed. The dialogue had to follow that of the drama, but it had to be arranged to form a new pattern, to escape monotony and adapt itself to the music. And then there were the spirituals, and the lyrics upon which Ira and I worked.

In the theatre every production is a gamble. In some, naturally, the odds are greater than in others. *Porgy and Bess* has, I believe a fair chance of scoring. But whether it does or not, we who have written and composed the opera cannot lose. We have spent two years doing exactly what we wanted to. It has been a very especial sort of adventure. That, at any rate, is in the bag.

Dock Street Theatre

EARLY IN THE NINETEEN-TWENTIES, when a liberated spirit began to express itself in the arts, it became evident that the South was prepared to take its place in the national revival. The silence which had followed the tragic 'sixties was at last being broken.

Poets appeared simultaneously in most of the states south of the line, and their work was accorded flattering attention beyond regional borders. Traveling exhibitions by southern painters pushed northward across the Potomac and won substantial recognition for their artists. Music felt the surge of new vitality, and spring festivals, concert seasons and local symphony orchestras flowered in the most unexpected places.

With all of this activity abroad in the land it was inevitable that Charleston should resume her ante-bellum position as one of the cultural centers of the region. Behind her garden walls and shuttered drawing-room windows there was an awareness of the arts which, if it had been inarticulate, had remained very much alive. The Poetry Society of South Carolina sprang into being. The Society for the Preservation of Spirituals entered upon its work of perpetuating and presenting negro folk music. The musical interests formed a symphony orchestra and arranged a concert series. A group of writers emerged, and, contrary to custom, instead of flocking to New York preferred to remain and interpret their own locale. The Carolina Art Association opened a winter school with classes in the various plastic media. The Footlight Players, an able dramatic organization, took its place in the community to fill a vacancy left in the cultural life by the passing of the road show in the remoter provinces, and furthermore to foster a creative spirit in the theatre.

With all of this activity scattered about the city, and in most cases inadequately housed, the time was obviously ripe when a significant meeting was

SOURCE: *Magazine of Art* 31 (January 1938), 10–15.

held in Charleston early in 1935 between Mr. Harry L. Hopkins and the local authorities to decide upon the disposition of a certain appropriation by the Emergency Relief Administration.[1]

It was the sense of this meeting that the funds could best be utilized by combining with a practical objective the restoration of some characteristic old building and the perpetuation of a valued tradition. This idea found expression in the plan to remodel a group of dilapidated buildings on the corner of Church and Queen Streets into a center which would serve all of the cultural groups of the community.

Research had revealed the fact that upon this site on February 12, 1736, was opened the Dock Street Theatre, the first building designed for theatrical use in America.[2] This building, destroyed by fire, had been succeeded by another playhouse, and that in turn by a group of residences erected during the late eighteenth and early nineteenth centuries.[3] These buildings were of the usual Charleston type, brick and stucco, and presented severely plain façades to both streets.

At some date prior to 1835 these buildings had been brought together and converted into the Planter's Hotel,[4] which remained a famous haunt of the aristocracy until the Civil War. It was during its adaptation to the purposes of a hotel that the group, now become a unit, acquired the entrance lobby with its much admired sandstone columns, massive brackets of Barbadian mahogany, and overhanging cast iron balcony; and it is to the bold thrusting of this Classic Revival ornamentation into the almost austere façade of the earlier period that the architecture owes much of its charm.

In February of 1935, the site and the general nature of the project having been approved, Douglas D. Ellington, Architectural Research Consultant for the Government,[5] was assigned to the task of conducting the preliminary studies, and of remaining in touch with the project until completion, in the capacity of active consultant for the ERA. The working drawings and supervision of construction were entrusted to the architectural firm of Simons and Lapham of Charleston.[6] The Dock Street Theatre, as it stands completed, attests not only to the extraordinary success of this collaboration but to the enlightened cooperation of the community as well.

The problem faced was one requiring an unfailing sense of values past and present, and a daring originality in approach and execution. For here was no slavish reproduction of a single period, but a bringing together under a single roof of an early eighteenth-century theatre, a group of simple early Charleston dwelling houses, an unmistakable example of the Classic Revival, and the harmonious incorporation therein of interior decoration removed bodily from a Georgian mansion. The harmonizing of these various factors, the ingenuity and taste with which they were merged one into another, and the delightful element of the unexpected which one now encounters in passing from room to room, give this building a character unique in American restorations.

Much of the success of the undertaking was due to the action of the City of Charleston and the Charleston Museum in making available the interior decoration from the old Mitchell King mansion.[7] It is not a digression to touch here upon the history of this dwelling, for it will now be a part of the Dock Street Theatre, and it brings to the newer structure not only its beauty of plaster and woodwork but its wealth of tradition extending far back into Charleston's past.

The dwelling, built prior to 1806, was an outstanding example of late Georgian architecture. For many years it was the home of the late Mitchell King. General Robert E. Lee was entertained there, and Thackeray, and many other notables of his day. It was there that, during the brief literary flowering before the Civil War, Timrod, Hayne and Gilmore Simms would meet frequently to sip the Judge's Madeira and discuss the coming of that new literature of the South which was destined to die so tragically in the first thundering of Sumter's guns.[8] And so into the mosaic of this unique building fit these memories as well as those of the nation's earliest drama.

One of the project's signal successes is the completeness with which the modern structural work has been concealed, and it is difficult to realize that between the shell of old English brick of the original walls and the transplanted Adam plaster of the interior, there exists a modern structure of reinforced concrete that should withstand the assaults of centuries.

In entering the building from Church Street, one passes beneath the balcony, with its gracefully patterned ironwork, into the spacious lobby—formerly of the Planter's Hotel—now of the Dock Street Theatre. To the left, as one stands with the street behind him, is a door opening into the dining room. This room, large and octagonal in form, with its Adam decoration, might have been brought hither bodily from one of Charleston's Georgian mansions. From its western end it opens on a patio around three sides of which a dining cloister extends, affording space for tables during the long summers, or for pleasant loitering on sunny winter days.

To the right of the lobby at the end of a short passage lies the Green

Room. This charming apartment is designed to take care of the social life of the center. It can accommodate an audience of two hundred for intimate recitals or lectures, and could serve well as a ballroom or reception room for functions following a performance in the auditorium. The small stage which occupies its western end opens through a large door directly into the wings of the theatre, permitting its use for the assembling of large crowds or processions when a performance should require them. In this room, not only the plaster decoration, but door and window frames from the King mansion have been utilized effectively.

Returning to the lobby, broad stairs rise from right and left to meet in a landing which opens into the auditorium, then turn and continue to the spacious foyer. Here again we find ourselves in Colonial Charleston, with glimpses of the iron-work balcony through high French windows.

Adjoining the foyer is the bar, included in the plans in a spirit of optimism, looking toward some remote future when liquors may again be sold over the counter in South Carolina, and first nighters may be permitted to sip a liqueur between the acts. In the meantime it is to be hoped that the soft drinks which are allowed by law will draw a touch of glamour from the high old-fashioned bar, and the copies of Hogarth prints in panels about the room, which were admirably executed for the building by William Halsey.[9]

The third floor of the building contains eight small apartments and these eventually may be made available for occupancy by visiting artists.

The theatre proper occupies the western end of the building and combines to an extraordinary degree the atmosphere of the past with the elaborate equipment of the modern theatre. The stage covers the site of the old play-house, and is approximately 56 by 36 feet in size. The auditorium, modelled after the London theatre of the early eighteenth century, is treated in plain plaster and well rubbed cypress, the effect being simple, vigorous and robust.

The auditorium opens not only into the lobby, but through wide doors across its rear wall into the court, and there, during mild weather, one may spend the entr'acte surrounded by old brick walls and roofed by stars.

The modern lighting equipment and projection booth are cunningly concealed, and the comfortable auditorium seats are ranged in high-backed benches to carry out the general effect. Backstage the equipment is equal to that of any small theatre in America.

Here then is a center which may well serve as an artistic and intellectual inspiration to a community. It will bring to the city singers, lecturers, orchestras and ballets, and can offer inducements for the return of an occasional road show where the character of the performance is of a high order. Here plays may be written and given tryouts, and proven successes presented by the Footlight Players. And here all of the cultural groups in the community will find the facilities which they have long needed.

Although the theatre belongs to the city, its management has been completely divorced from politics, Mayor Burnet R. Maybank[10] having with rare judgment placed it, during an experimental period of two years, under the control of the Carolina Art Association, of which Robert N. S. Whitelaw[11] is the enthusiastic and capable director.

On November 25 the Dock Street Theatre was formally opened to the public.[12] Brief speeches by Mr. Hopkins and the Mayor preceded music furnished by Charleston's Symphony Orchestra and the Society for the Preservation of Spirituals. The Footlight Players then presented *The Recruiting Officer*, a comedy by Farquhar,[13] thus bridging the gap between the present and the past. For this same comedy had been presented on this site as the opening piece of the old Dock Street Theatre just a little over two centuries ago.

Charleston

WHERE MELLOW PAST AND PRESENT MEET

IN 1670 A STURDY BAND of Englishmen under the command of William Sayle planted, on the west bank of the Ashley River at a distance of about two miles from the present city of Charleston, the first permanent colony in South Carolina.[1]

A hundred years earlier, an expedition of French Huguenots had attempted a settlement near what is now the town of Beaufort, but their venture had come to an early and tragic end.[2]

Still earlier, in the 1520s, only thirty-odd years after Columbus first set foot in the Western Hemisphere, Spain had made unsuccessful attempts to plant colonies in South Carolina, especially in the neighborhoods of Georgetown; and again in 1540 Don Hernando de Soto, the great Conquistador, had pursued his dream of gold northward from Florida across what is now the Savannah River, and had planted the banner of Spain on Carolina soil. But his avarice would not let him rest and he pushed on to the westward until he met death in the American wilderness.

The dwellers on the coastal islands will tell you now that their wild and mettlesome salt marsh ponies are descendants of his Spanish stallions. That tradition is all that is left in South Carolina of the fame and splendor of Spain.

Then Came the English—with the Plows and Sickles

BUT WHERE OTHERS had failed, the English succeeded, and perhaps the reason lies in the fact that they came armed not with pikes and arquebuses,[3]

SOURCE: *National Geographic* 75 (March 1939), 273–312.

but with plows and sickles; not to loot, but to found an agricultural empire overseas; and the new land with its mild winters, its fertile soil and vast virgin forests, after subjecting them to a rigorous probation, opened to receive them and made them rich.

In their first cargo the English fetched with them from Barbados little tubs containing olive sets and cuttings of cane and many seeds and roots, and established what was probably one of the first agricultural stations in the South. When Governor Sir John Yeamans arrived to assume authority under the Lords Proprietors, he imported a number of negro slaves from his Barbadian estates.[4]

Doubtless the pick of his plantations, these blacks, seasoned to labor under tropical suns, were the vanguard of the vast importations which were destined to build up a civilization in the sweat of their brow, to color the lives and influence the destinies of their masters.

In 1680 the town was moved to its present strategic site upon a peninsula commanding the entrances to its two rivers. These streams, called the Ashley and the Cooper after one of the Lords Proprietors, Lord Ashley Cooper,[5] were the arteries which, as the decades passed, pumped life in a steadily mounting tide into the city and gave it the sobriquet, "The Capital of the Plantations."

Today you can take a launch and in three hours you can reach the headwaters of either river, and you will have passed through a country that has seen one civilization rise and fall, and another utterly different rise to take its place.

The Era of Indigo

THE GREAT PLANTATION TRACTS are still there. From bluffs overlooking the rivers old mansions peer from under deep porticoes like spectacled ancients, bewildered by change but tranquil and acquiescent.[6]

These vast baronies have seen the rise and fall of indigo.

For more than a century they made Carolina rice a standard in the markets of the world. Then rice passed, a victim of competition from the West with its modern irrigation. There followed an economic twilight; but now a new day has dawned along the rivers. Scarcely any of the plantations remain in the hands of the original families.

The vast abandoned rice fields attract wild ducks by the thousands, and northern sportsmen have followed them south, to hunt, to enjoy the winter—balmy, yet bracing—and to establish a new gentry in the ancient bailiwicks.

Wealth again flows into "The Capital of the Plantations" from its two rivers, but its source lies closer to Wall Street and the great economic structures of the North than it does to the land.

King Cotton Supplants Rice

BUT IF THE RICE COUNTRY is out of production, such is not the case in Charleston's hinterland, where, in spite of the boll weevil, Cotton is still King. The gins start clattering in the outlying counties by mid-September, and all fall the staple moves down upon the city to be compressed for shipment and hurried over long cotton docks to the holds of waiting tramp steamers.[7]

Here, too, garden truck[8] is raised on a large scale, and one has only to cross the modern concrete bridge which spans the Ashley River to find himself almost immediately surrounded by far-flung fields whose rich black loam is green nearly every month of the year from its rotating crops.

Probably more than any other city on our continent, Charleston has experienced extremes of good and evil fortune. Founded shortly before the most distinguished period of English residential architecture, and with the tide of its prosperity rising as that period came to full flower, it still contains within the confines of its narrow peninsula more fine examples of Georgian architecture than any other similar area in the United States.

The explanation of this is simple. Carolina was conceived in the aristocratic tradition, and, within its provincial limitations, was brought to birth in the grand manner. Its Lords Proprietors were gallant Cavaliers who had remained loyal to the Crown while Cromwell was at his rabble-rousing, and in token of his appreciation Charles II had handed them an American subdivision lying between Virginia and Florida and extending westward to the South Seas (the term then applied to the Pacific Ocean).

The distinguished philosopher, John Locke, was called to their assistance, and the result was the "Fundamental Constitutions," which, while liberal in many respects, provided for a "nobility" in order "to avoid erecting a numerous democracy."[9]

This nobility consisted of baron, with an estate of 12,000 acres; cassique, with 24,000 acres; and landgrave, whose domain of 48,000 acres might have been the size of a small county today.[10] But in spite of this undemocratic setup, the constitution was so liberal regarding the personal liberty of the individual that the tides of immigration set southward, and, while the city was still in the making, the English nucleus absorbed accretions of French Huguenots, Irish, Scotch, Germans, Dutch, Quakers, Swiss, and Jews.

There were even several shiploads of refugees from New England who had fled the rigors of climate and religion for the broader moral latitude favored by the Cavaliers, and the balmy Carolina winters. And so, even before 1700, the melting pot was seething, and from the four corners of the world began to come the ingredients that went into the making of what we are pleased to designate today as the one hundred percent American.

A Succession of Disasters

IN A STEADILY mounting wave, prosperity flowed in from the back country until, a century after its founding, Charleston was numbered among the four major ports of the Atlantic seaboard. But her entries were not all upon the credit side of the ledger. In the 268 years of her life, Charleston has possessed the stamina to take an appalling succession of disasters and survive, to wit: several major conflagrations, more than fifteen hurricanes, and two earthquakes. Two wars have trampled her: the British occupation during the Revolution, and the great siege of the Confederate War, which lasted for 567 days.

Toward the close of this war she escaped complete annihilation by a hairsbreadth. General Sherman, then on his historic March to the Sea, received from Major General H. W. Halleck,[11] Chief of Staff, instructions that "Should you capture Charleston, I hope that by some accident the place may be destroyed, and if a little salt should be sown upon its site it might prevent the growth of future crops of nullification and secession."

Fortunately, however, after the burning of Columbia, Sherman changed his course to intercept one of the last armies of the South under General Joseph E. Johnston,[12] and the old city was spared.

An Unchanging City

So, MUCH OF HISTORY one must know if he would grasp the significance of what he sees today. Noble mansions here and there show scars of hurricane or bombardment. The great iron bolts passing through the houses from wall to wall, and revealed by large washers on the façades, tell of the night in August, 1886, when the great earthquake left gaping fissures in pre-Revolutionary masonry.

Charleston to this day, with the colonial life one hundred and fifty years behind it, seems in many respects more British than American. There is a definite resistance to sudden change, and a stubborn clinging to modes of life and thought that have been tried and proved.

But it is British with certain differences; and it is these variations that give the city its unique character. The early builders took the foursquare Georgian dwelling house, elongated it so that the prevailing breezes could blow through all of the rooms, and set it with its narrow gable end to the street.[13] Then along its entire side they hung galleries (they call them piazzas in Charleston) which shaded the walls during the long summers and looked down into walled gardens.

This type of dwelling, unique to Charleston, is a perfect adaptation to the subtropical climate.

The exigencies of the climate undoubtedly shaped customs, as it had houses, and these customs, like the solid buildings, resist change. True there is a season now when the azaleas, wisteria, and camellias convert the city into a fairyland of color and perfume, and when, during several weeks in the spring, visitors to the estimated number of two thousand a day pour through the streets. But when they are gone the city heaves a sigh of relief, forgets its hospitable efforts to be other than itself, and settles down into its accustomed routine.

Now the visitor may breakfast when he will, but he will not be fed again until 2:30, or even 3 o'clock; then it will not be luncheon, but dinner, and "Southern" in all the culinary implications of the word.

Before sitting to table he will have been constrained to join his host in a toddy; and when he arises replete from the board, it is not difficult to show him the logic of a siesta, which, especially during hot weather, is the custom of the country.

In the cool of the afternoon the city rubs its eyes, takes its cold plunge, and enters into the social life of the day. The evening meal, called "tea," is usually a casual buffet affair.

To the unthinking this arrangement may seem an evidence of Southern indolence. It is, as a matter of fact, a perfect climatic adaptation. Your Charleston business man will have put in five or six hours of uninterrupted labor during the cool of the morning.

But how, one might wonder, with other old cities changing with the times, did Charleston preserve its unique character? There are several explanations.

The period following the War between the States, with its jig-saw woodwork, grotesque residential spires and cupolas, found Charleston prostrate, economically. Poverty may well have been the ally of good taste which kept the people for the most part living in the houses which had sheltered them for over a century, and limited the erection of the newer type of dwelling largely to the upper and western sections.

But, that good taste and sound esthetic appreciation were present is evidenced by the fact that in 1930 they passed a zoning law which will preserve the architectural landmarks of the city intact for future generations. Encouraged by this legislation, the lower half of the peninsula, extending from Broad Street to the beautiful White Point Gardens (usually referred to as the Battery), is reassuming the character of an early American town, with every householder intent upon achieving as scrupulously exact a restoration as possible.

As Charleston has brought down through the generations tangible survivals of an early civilization, so also has she preserved through the assaults of a mechanized civilization a mode and manner of life which are an antidote for the jangled nerves of today. She has drawn her sustenance from the plantations on the one hand and the sea on the other, and her life has been lived in harmony with the great deliberate forces of Nature. She has listened to the march of modernity, but she has not yet been stampeded into the procession.

Today, within five minutes of her borders by motor, or immediately, from one of her wharves or boat clubs, one can reestablish the life-giving contact with woods or sea.

Perhaps it is due to this realization, that life at its fullest comes through these contacts rather than through the amassing of wealth, that Charleston incomes are small. There are no large fortunes. Salaries even in times of relative prosperity remain at what would be described in the North as a depression level.

But, strangely enough, your Charlestonian is not particularly concerned.

He is a provincial, and he is proud of it. He knows upon a salary which in New York would give him three rooms and a bath, and a subway strap to and from the office, he can in his own province keep a small car, enjoy golf on one of two good courses, or sail, if he has a mind to, in his own yacht. Of an evening he may see a current play interpreted by his Little Theater company, view an exhibition at the Gibbes Art Gallery, or listen to a concert by the local symphony orchestra.

In summer a twenty-minute drive in either direction will bring him to one of the palm-crowned barrier islands with its mile on mile of incomparable beach, and its unflagging sea breeze.

In winter the white community, which during the long summer has golfed, boated, and commuted to and from its islands together, tends to retire behind the barriers of its separate associations for its more formal entertainment.

There are the St. Andrews Society, now more than two centuries old, the Hibernian Society, and the German Friendly Society, both of which have over a century of life behind them, and the St. Cecilia Society.[14] This last, through the changes of 177 years of its existence, has preserved the aristocratic tradition which the Lords Proprietors had planted in the New World through their provincial nobility for the discouragement of a "numerous democracy."

It has resolutely clung to its customs in the face of social change, and it prides itself upon adherence to a code of manners and morals of an earlier day. Its two balls which are given each season are the social events of the year, and are examples of social decorum and formal elegance. Chaperones are present, not as exhibition pieces, as one might guess in this modern age, but as gracious mentors and hostesses to their charges; and it is not uncommon to see upon the dance floor at the same time representatives of three generations of the same family.

The ancient custom prohibiting the attendance of any actress or divorced person still obtains, and the admission of a new family to the society is so rare that membership may well be considered hereditary.

A City of Gardens

USUALLY BY THE FIRST of March the short winter is over, and spring pre-empts the city. This is a dramatic invasion. Starting with the waxy perfection of the camellia bloom, and a spray or two of yellow jessamine while the nights are still frosty, it seems to hang poised, then descends, sweeping the parks and gardens with a tidal wave of color and perfume. Climbing roses foam over old garden walls. Wisteria hangs like purple clouds in ancient pine and oak; and everywhere the azalea seems determined to spend itself utterly in a short, breath-taking burst of color.

Later will come the red of the pomegranate, the gay profusion of the oleander, and the great waxy magnolia with its almost narcotic perfume.

But in Charleston the azalea is the acknowledged queen of the spring. During the month of its flowering, which usually lasts from the middle of March to the middle of April, the town is in holiday mood. Music of an outlandish but gaily negroid character will assault the ear of the visitor, and upon turning a corner he will find himself face to face with a brass band from the Jenkins Negro Orphanage.[15]

Almost hidden by enormous battered horns, a dozen negro boys will be performing to the antics of a maestro, scarcely yet in his teens, and all will be enjoying it hugely. Other black urchins will solicit a nickel to dance and sing. Then perhaps the guest within Charleston's gates will remember that his first waking impression was the chanting of the hucksters as they strode through the early morning streets, balancing large baskets, West Indian fashion, on their heads.

He will recall also the beauty of spirituals heard from the open windows of a negro church during a nocturnal ramble, and the music, color, and humor of "Heaven Bound," the negro pageant recently presented in a big church. And he will realize that the city owes much of its atmosphere and light-hearted charm to the black half of its population, these people who had brought with them to America, besides the gift of labor, the gifts of laughter and song.

During the garden season, Charleston is "at home" to the Nation, and last year more than 270,000 of her neighbors from every State in the Union availed themselves of the invitation to share her beauty.

Within a short motor drive of the city, upon the banks of the Ashley, lie the most renowned of the plantation gardens. (See "Ashley River and Its Gardens," by E. T. H. Shaffer, *National Geographic Magazine*, May, 1926.) Sherman's army passed this way in 1865 and burned all the of the great houses save one, but the gardens, which had been in the making while generations came and went, held their indestructible beauty locked in the soil, to flower again in the spring.

Magnolia, which John Galsworthy called "the world's most beautiful garden," is over a century old, and, in addition to its flowering shrubs, contains many unique botanical exhibits. One of the largest redwoods east of the Rockies is there, a Chinese yew, the sweet olive, the incense cedar, and many others.[16]

Middleton Gardens, situated three miles beyond Magnolia on a historic plantation estate of which some 7,000 acres still remain in the family, is the oldest landscape garden in America. In a way it stands as a monument to the slave regime in the South, for into its creation, which dates from 1740, went the labor of a hundred slaves for a period of ten years. Its hedges and walks, terraces, and ornamental waters bear eloquent witness to the long, patient labor of the slave as well as the taste and vision of the master.[17]

Differing greatly in character, Magnolia and Middleton supplement each other admirably. Painted from the same magnificent palette, the burning glory of the azalea is flung into contrast with the somber beauty of giant, moss-draped live oak and dark, cypress-haunted water in a range of values that amazes while it delights. But in Middleton the dominant note is formal. In Magnolia it is the unexpected.

Continuing along the Ashley River, a twenty-minute drive will bring the visitor to Summerville, "The Flower Town in the Pines," and for blocks his way will lead him beneath festoons of wisteria that sway from tree to tree, and between widely spaced cottages bowered in color and drowned in perfume. A visit to Cypress Gardens, of Dean Hall Plantation, on the Cooper River, will complete this circuit.

Seeing a Garden by Boat

PERHAPS the most unusual of all of Charleston's gardens is Cypress. Upon arriving, one is conducted to a landing and seated in the bow of a small bateau. A negro paddler takes his place in the stern, and his passenger is off on a voyage of discovery. For Cypress is a water garden, planted in the "reserve" of an ancient rice plantation. With only the dip of the paddle and an occasional birdcall for an accompaniment, the voyager has ample time to note the extraordinary, almost weird beauty of the scene.[18]

Beneath him lies the water, brilliantly clear and colored like old sherry, and over his head towering cypress trees brush the spring sky with their first faintly yellow leaves. Along the banks are low, brilliant lines of flowering bulbs, and on small islands azaleas and other shrubs form avenues and masses of glowing color. These cast reflections which shatter soundlessly beneath the advancing bows.

There have been seasons when the full moon came at the zenith of the flowers' beauty, and Cypress has been opened to the visitor at night. The effect at these times is almost supernatural. Great cypresses rise out of the water, casting shadows that seem as substantial as the trees themselves, so that the boat in which you sit seems to hover in a space of moonlight and shadow, with treetops and stars far above and far below you.

Only half an hour of easy motoring lies between Cypress Gardens and the city, and the whole circuit can be accomplished in the course of a morning. Recently three other plantation gardens have been opened to the public: Brookgreen and Belle Isle in the old Santee region, and Runnymede on the Ashley, and each of these as it matured through successive generations has developed its unique differences within the general pattern and tradition.[19]

The Azalea Festival

AS A CULMINATION to the season of flowers, Charleston celebrates usually about mid-April its annual Azalea Festival. During these six gala days of pageantry, beauty, sport, and entertainment, the city is more especially at home to its State, and from various sections of South Carolina come representative beauty queens to participate in the festivities. Opening with the parade of gorgeous floats and visiting queens, the program embraces a water carnival and boat races in full view of the Battery, a pageant re-enacting the trial and conviction of Stede Bonnet and his pirates (presumably as the event occurred on the same spot over two centuries ago),[20] street criers' contests, balls, and the final coronation of the State Queen.

Streets are roped off at night for dancing and gay carnivals, and there are concerts and excursions. And when the last azalea wilts on its stem, it must be admitted that the population feels and looks a little like its bedraggled floral confederate; but Charleston thinks that it is well worth it, for it prides itself upon the fact that in this fevered age it is one city that has not altogether forgotten how to play.

A Morning Constitutional

IT IS NOT a long walk from New York's Central Park southward to Times Square, a mile let us say, and a modest constitutional for a brisk morning. Now, transfer our mile-long walk to Charleston, and let us see what of drama and history is packed into its brief span.

We will start from the point of the Battery where Charleston's two rivers meet and flow eastward, as a native son will tell you, to form the Atlantic Ocean. Out of the east, as likely as not, will come a soft drumming, and a fleet of seaplanes will appear over the low, dark line of Fort Sumter and drive a wedge northward to where the Navy Yard is waiting to receive them a few miles above the city.

Again that dramatic juxtaposition between today and yesterday, between news and history. For Fort Sumter and the commodious landlocked harbor which lies before us have been the stage upon which momentous drama has been enacted. From these surrounding islands, on the morning of April 12, 1861, Confederate cannon opened fire on Major Anderson, who with his Union artillerymen was holding the fortress under orders from President Lincoln. On the 13th, with his flag shot away and the fort on fire about him, Anderson surrendered, and the Nation entered upon its four years of devastating civil war.

And here in 1863, with the Confederate forces in possession of the fortress, came the first large fleet of ironclads, to try their strength against man's immemorial stronghold of brick and stone and to sustain one of the worst naval defeats in the history of the Nation—but to demonstrate anew the superiority of iron ships and thus to revolutionize the navies of the world.

Here again, during the Confederate War, while the blockading fleet drew its iron circle tighter and tighter about the harbor mouth, came the first submarine to sink an enemy ship in time of war, February 17, 1864.

On the Battery stands a granite shaft which commemorates the event and lists the names of the known dead. That is all—yet this is the untold story: The "Fish Boat" of the Confederate Navy, designed by Horace L. Hunley, was 20 feet long, 3½ feet wide, and 5 feet deep. Her motive power consisted of eight men who sat in a row with their knees drawn up to their chins and turned a crankshaft by hand.[21]

When this metal shell was closed for diving, it contained sufficient air to support life for only half an hour. Since the torpedo was attached to the boat itself, there was little hope of escape. The crew, sealed in their metal coffin, hoped only to reach and destroy a Federal battleship before they were suffocated or drowned. Five successive volunteer crews died without accomplishing the destruction of an enemy ship. After each attempt the craft was salvaged and new volunteers stepped forward.

The sixth crew succeeded in exploding the torpedo against the blockading ship *Housatonic*, the "Fish Boat" being caught and sucked down with the foundering vessel. These crews went to what was virtually certain death in such secrecy that it was often months before the names of the dead were made known, and when, after the lapse of half a century, the commemorating tablet was being cast, it was possible to identify only sixteen of the forty-odd who gave their lives.

This is the stark outline of a story of such exalted heroism that now, in a reunited nation, not only Charleston but America may well be proud of it.

Let us continue a few hundred feet along the sea-wall parade of East Battery and we come to Water Street. It is well named, for it was once a narrow stream and upon its banks were hanged the great pirate, Stede Bonnet, and his cutthroat crew, when an expedition from Charles Town (the original name of the city) captured them and put an end to piracy off the Carolina coast for the time being.

Ahead of us looms a fine square building of the early colonial type. It is known as the Old Exchange, and was once the property of John Bull; but when Boston was having its historic "Tea Party," the Carolinians, less spectacularly perhaps but equally effectively, having seized all the tea in port, locked it up in the dungeonlike cellars to rot, rather than pay duty.

Turning into Queen Street and stopping at Church, we find ourselves again reminded of the meeting of the past with the present. A lovely old façade with an iron balcony is the newly restored Dock Street Theater and that here stood one of the first buildings in the Colonies fully equipped as a theater and dedicated exclusively to the presentation of dramatic performances.[22]

The architects incorporated in the restoration plan the site of the old playhouse and the walls of an early American hotel. The project was carried out with historical and architectural accuracy, and with extraordinary taste, with the result that Charleston now possesses as finely equipped a small theater as any in the country.

Leaving the theater, the gaze of the visitor is immediately caught by the soaring spire of St. Philip's, and a few steps will bring him to one of the most beautiful churches in America. Known as the "Westminster of the South," St. Philip's is the oldest Protestant Episcopal parish south of Virginia.[23] Presidents Washington and Monroe have worshipped with its congregation, and under the great oaks of its graveyard names that have made history are etched upon aging marble.

It is characteristic of human nature that our possessions increase in value when coveted by others. Next in our walk we come to the Heyward-Washington House on lower Church Street, the former residence of Thomas Heyward, Jr., a signer of the Declaration of Independence from South Carolina.[24]

Here in 1791 President George Washington was domiciled by the city when on his famous swing by coach and four through the southern States of his new republic. A decade or so ago, Charleston learned to its horror that the building, then the property of a local baker, was about to be purchased and that the paneling and woodwork were to be shipped away.

The resulting indignation occasioned the founding of the Society for the Preservation of Old Dwellings.[25] A fund was raised and the early Georgian mansion, with its spacious rooms, unusually fine woodwork and historical significance, was saved as a local shrine. Gradually the building has been restored to its original condition, and through the co-operation of the Charleston Museum the small formal garden has been planted in the shrubs and flowers that are recorded as being coeval with the mansion.

The First Fireproof Building

NEAR THE Heyward-Washington House we meet another of Charleston's "firsts," America's first fireproof building. Built in 1822 to house the country records,[26] the structure, Greek Doric in type, massive yet gracefully proportioned, is a monument to its architect, that same Robert Mills,[27] born in Charleston, who gave to the National Capital the Washington Monument.

But now with our walk already half finished, and as we turn into Meeting Street and face again toward the Battery, we realize the impossibility of examining in detail all of the characteristic and interesting buildings that we shall see.

Before us, as the wide thoroughfare narrows in perspective towards the

Battery, they take their places quietly in converging rows and it is the street itself which challenges our attention, with its atmosphere of Old Charleston. Here we see at its best that infinite variety within a general pattern which never fails to delight.

High overhead from the steeple of St. Michael's, resembling that of St. Martin's-in-the-Field's, in London, mellow chimes announce the hour. Since 1764 that clock, a primitive system of wooden cogs, rope and weights, has been the arbiter of the city's time.[28] Today, feeling its age, it is subject to occasional lapses; but no modern timepiece would dare argue with it. In Charleston you are not late to an appointment unless you are late by St. Michael's.

Proceeding toward the Battery, we stroll beneath porticoes of the old church and the hall of the South Carolina Society, which lies just beyond. Across the way the sidewalk passed beneath the broad piazzas of the Horry House, all built in the days when the street was less sacred, and a man might span the sidewalk with his piazza if he had a mind to, and listen to the talk of his neighbors and the hucksters' songs beneath his feet.

As we near the Battery and glance down an approach of a short city block, we are brought up standing by one of the most nearly perfect Georgian residences in America, the Miles Brewton House at 27 King Street. Mention the name to any architect and he will probably tell you that he cut his professional teeth on drawings of it in college; then, becoming technical, he will launch into explanations of the unusually light and intricate plaster decoration.

Here, during the Revolution, Sir Henry Clinton,[29] attracted no doubt by its flawless English atmosphere, established headquarters for the British army. Here again during the War for Southern Independence, when the city was evacuated by the Confederates, the general commanding the Federal forces ensconced himself and his staff.

Considered by many the loveliest of the residential gardens is that which hides behind the high brick walls of the William Gibbes House at 64 South Battery. The dwelling, dating prior to 1776, is an outstanding example of the wooden colonial Georgian, and, with its modern garden, preserves the atmosphere of the city in the days when it was the capital of its plantation principality.

The Charleston of 1938

BUT CHARLESTON is not a museum piece, nor do the 105,000 residents of city and suburbs (divided almost equally between white and black) sit in retrospective and unproductive contemplation of its glamorous past. It is true that this heritage forms a background to its life, endowing it with a special color and flavor; but its illuminating statistics tell a different story.

Besides possessing the finest deep-water harbor south of Hampton Roads, Charleston has 86 major manufacturing plants and 125 wholesale establishments; its municipal college, established in 1770, was the first municipal college in America; its South Carolina Military Academy, now called "The Citadel," picturesquely situated on the banks of the Ashley, is one of the crack military schools of the country and is known as the "West Point of the South"; and the Charleston Museum, another of the city's "firsts," antedates all other public museums in the United States.

Springing from the rural mainland on the east, a modern steel bridge over two miles in length hurls its two mighty spans across Cooper River and Town Creek and plunges downward to the city's streets. Resembling a giant roller coaster, its more than five million dollars' worth of concrete and structural steel, attaining a height of 150 feet above high water, looms over the low line of the city and offers a magnificent bird's-eye view of the region. To the northward on the neck of the peninsula industrial Charleston reveals itself, segregated among its noises and stenches from the lower city.

Massed stacks rise from factories that have made the city one of the leading fertilizer ports of the Atlantic seaboard. Great oil tanks squat among the belching funnels of refineries, and far up the Cooper, beyond the gibbetlike cranes of the Navy Yard, lies the new plant of the West Virginia Pulp and Paper Company, which, when running at capacity, adds half a million dollars a year to the city's payrolls.

Looking directly downward, the visitor will be struck by the cleanliness of the streets which spread their geometric pattern below him. For quietly, in its own way, the city has been working at its slum problem, and has just thrown open to occupancy two trim little villages, one for whites and one for negroes, which have been constructed with Government grants.

With its subtropical climate, and ranking high in hours of sunshine, Charleston's tourist traffic has been building steadily until it has become an economic "back log" against evil days. Housing accommodations and transportation facilities have been pushing forward to keep abreast of the seasonal increase in population.

Beyond the city to the north lies one of the finest municipal airports in the South. The great planes of two main lines shuttle north and south, pausing on their way between New York and Florida, or, heading westward, hurtle away racing the sun toward the Pacific. A transatlantic seaplane base is nearing completion upon the bank of the Ashley, Charleston having been selected as the terminal for Clipper service via the Azores and Bermuda.

Adjacent to the seaplane base lies the Municipal Yacht Basin, to furnish accommodations for pleasure craft which, like great migratory birds, follow the seasons north and south or linger on the Carolina coast for the fishing and duck shooting.

But what of the future for Charleston? Can she hold the characteristics that make her so individual a note in the American scene, and at the same time bid for success in a mechanized field in competition with the great manufacturing centers? If present plans carry through, the next decade will have to find an answer to that question.

Funds have been allocated for the Santee-Cooper hydroelectric development, now under way. When completed, it will release an enormous power output at rates comparable with any in the Nation. Where quiet marshes now spread along the river banks, great factories may rise.

The Charleston business man of another generation may forego the leisurely dinner and traditional siesta for a luncheon bolted while a deal is being closed. With his income doubled or tripled, he may find himself the beneficiary of an infinitely more abundant life. But will he be happier, and will his home be as quiet, his town as serenely lovely, as it is today?

That is Charleston's enigma of tomorrow.

Poetry

Carolina Chansons

Silences

You who have known my city for a day
And heard the music of her steepled bells,
Then laughed, and passed along your vagrant way,
Carrying only what the city tells
To those who listen solely with their ears;
You know St. Matthew's swinging harmonies,
And old St. Michael's tale of golden years
Far less like bells than chanted memories.

Yet there is something wanting in the song
Of lyric youth with voice unschooled by pain.
And there are breathing stillnesses that throng
Dim corners, and that only stir again
When bells are dumb. Not even bronze that beats
Our heart-throbs back can tell of old defeats.

But you who take the city for your own,
Come with me when the night flows deep and kind
Along these narrow ways of troubled stone,
And floods the wide savannas of the mind
With tides that cool the fever of the day:

SOURCE: DuBose Heyward and Hervey Allen, *Carolina Chansons: Legends of the Low Country* (New York: Macmillan, 1922), 20–22, 25–33, 54–64, 72, 76–80, 117–18.

One with the dark, companioned by the stars,
We'll seek St. Philip's, nebulous and gray,
Holding its throbbing beacon to the bars,
A prisoned spirit vibrant in the stone
That knew its empire of forgotten things.
Then will the city know you for her own,
And feel you meet to share her sufferings;
While down a swirl of poignant memories,
Herself shall find you in her silences.

Once coaches waited row on shining row
Before this door; and where the thirsty street
Drank the deep shadow of the portico
The Sunday hush was stirred by happy feet,
Low greetings, and the rustle of brocade,
The organ throb, and warmth of sunny eyes
That flashed and smiled beneath a bonnet shade;
Life with the lure of all its swift disguise.

Then from the soaring lyric of the spire,
Like the composite voice of all the town,
The bells burst swiftly into singing fire
That wrapped the building, and which showered down
Bright cadences to flash along the ways
Loud with the splendid gladness of the days.

War took the city, and the laughter died
From lips that pain had kissed. One after one
All lovely things went down the sanguine tide,
While death made moaning answer to the gun.
Then, as a golden voice dies in the throat
Of one who lives, but whose glad heart is dead,
The bells were taken; and a sterner note
Rang from their bronze where Lee and Jackson led.

The rhythmic seasons chill and burn and chill,
Cooling old angers, warming hearts again.

The ancient building quickens to the thrill
Of lilting feet; but only singing rain
Flutters old echoes in the portico;
Those who can still remember love it so.

NOTE ON THE CHIMES TO ACCOMPANY "SILENCES"
The bells of Charleston, like the bells of London town, have a peculiar interest. St. Michael's
bells and clock were brought from England in 1764. When the British evacuated Charleston
in 1782 they took the bells with them. A Mr. Ryhineu bought them in England and returned
them. They were rehung in November 1783. During the Civil War, St. Michael's steeple was
the target for Federal artillery and fleet guns. In 1861 the bells were taken to Columbia, S.C.,
where two of them were stolen, and the rest injured by fire when the city was burned. Those
left were again sent to England, and recast in the original moulds. In March 1867 they once
again rang out from the spire.

St. Philip's Church stands in the old part of the town. During the Civil War its bells were
cast into cannon. For a long time its steeple was used as a lighthouse. It is the center of forgotten things.

The bells of St. Matthew's are modern and speak of a new order, but all the bells are the
voice of the town. They speak for her silences, which are eloquent. [Heyward's note]

The Pirates

I stood once where these rows of deep piazzas
Frown on the harbor from their columned pride,
And saw the gallant youngest of the cities
Lift from the jealous many-fingered tide.
Flanked by the multi-colored sweeping marshes,
Among the little hummocks choked with thorn,
I saw the first, small, dauntless row of buildings
Give back the rose and orange of the dawn.
Above them swayed the shining green palmettoes
Vocal and plaintive at the winds' caress;
While, at the edge of sight, the fluent silver
Of sea and bay framed the wide loneliness.

Out of the East came gaunt razees[1] of commerce
Troubling the dappled azure of the seas;

While sleeping marsh awoke, and vanquished under
The thrusting open fingers of the quays.

Ever, and more, came ships, while others followed.
Feeling their way among unsounded bars,
Heaping their freights upon the groaning wharf-heads,
Filling their holds with turpentines and tars,
Until the little twisting streets all vanished
Into a blur of interwoven spars.

II

One with the rest, I saw the commerce dwindle,
High bosomed, sturdy vessels take the main
And leave us, with the morning in their faces,
Never to come to any port again.
Slowly an ominous and pregnant silence
Grew deep upon the wharves where ships had lain.

Laughter rang hollow in those days of waiting,
And nameless fears came drifting down the night.
The tides swung in from sea, hung, and retreated,
Bearing their secrets back beyond our sight;
Till, like the sudden rending of a curtain,
The East reeled with the lightnings of a fight.

Never was a night so long with waiting.
Never was the dark more prone to stay.
And, in the whispering gloom, taut, listening faces
Hung in a pallid line along the bay.
Slowly at last the mists dissolved, revealing
A fearful silhouette against the day.

Blue on a saffron dawn, a frigate lifted
Out of the fog that veiled her fold on fold,
Taking the early sunlight on her cannon
In running spurts and rings of molten gold;

No flag of any nation at her masthead.
Small wonder that our pulses fluttered cold.

Never a shot she fired on the city,
But, when the night came blowing in from sea,
And our ruddy windows warmed the darkness,
Through the surrounding gloom we heard the free
Strong sweep and clank of rowing in the harbor,
And on the wharves raw jest and revelry.

She was the first, but many others followed;
Insolent, keen, and swift to come-about,
I have seen them go smashing down the harbor,
Loud with the boom of canvas and the shout
Of lusty voices at the crowded bulwarks,
Where tattooed hands were swinging long-boats out.

Up through the streets the roisterers would swagger,
Filling the narrow ways from wall to wall,
Scattering gold like ringing summer showers,
Ready with song and jest and cheery call
For those who passed; buying the little taverns
At any cost; opening wine for all.

There were rare evenings when we used to gather
Down in a coffee-house beside the square.
Morgan knew well our little favored corner;
Black Beard the sinister was often there;
And we have watched the night blur into morning
While Bonnet, quiet-voiced and debonnaire,

Would throw the glamor of the seas about us
In archipelagoes of mad romances;
Pointing a story with a line from Shakespeare,
Quoting a Latin proverb; while his glance,
Flashing across the eager, listening circle,
Fettered—blinded—held us in a trance.

Their bags of Spanish gold bribed our juries,
Bought dignified officials of the Crown;
Money and wine were ours for the asking;
The Orient flamed out in shawl and gown,
Until a sudden and unholy splendor
Irradiated all the quiet town.

Those were the days when there was open gaming,
And roaring song in tongue of every race.
Evil, as colorful as poison weeds,
Bloomed in the market place.
And those who should have known, shared in the revels,
And passed their neighbors with averted face.

Until one day a frigate entered harbor,
And passed the city, with a Spanish prize,
Then insolently came-about, despoiled her,
And fired her before our very eyes,
While the vagrant breezes left the streaming vapor
Like red rust on the clean steel of the skies.

III

All in the sullied hours,
While the pirates stood away
Out of the murk and horror
In a sheer white burst of spray,

Leaving the wreck to settle
Under its winding sheet,
I felt the city shudder
And stir beneath my feet.

Thrilling against the morning,
As audible as song,
I heard the city waken
Out of her night of wrong.

That was a day to cherish
When Rhett and a gallant few
Summoned the bets among us;
Called for a daring crew.

New and raw at the business,
To the smithy's roar and clang,
We drove our aching muscles
And as we worked we sang,

Until one blowing morning
With summer on the sea,
The *Henry* to the windward,
The *Sea Nymph* down alee,

Flecking the wide Atlantic
With a flaring, lacy track,
We went, as glad as the winds are glad,
To buy our honor back.

IV

Over the wooded shore-line,
Where the hidden rivers stray
Down to the sea like timid girls,
I saw in the first faint gray

A burst of cloudy topsails
Go blowing swiftly by,
With the stars aswirl behind them
Like bright dust down the sky.

Gone were the days of waiting,
And the long, blind search was gone;
With a cheer we swung to meet them
On the forefoot of the dawn.

Out of the screening woodland
Into the open sound
The frigate crashed, then staggered
Careening, fast aground.

White water tugged behind us,
We felt the *Henry* reel
And spin as the hard impartial sand
Closed on her vibrant keel.

All through the high white morning,
While the lagging tide crawled out,
Fate held us bound and waiting,
While, turn and turn about,

We manned the fuming cannon
And bartered hell for hell,
While the scuppers sang with coursing life
Where the dead and dying fell.

Till, like the break of fever
When life thrills up through pain,
We felt the current stirring
Under the keel again.

Then it was hand to cutlass,
And pistols in the sash.
"All hands stand by for boarding,—
Now, close abeam and lash!"

But the ensign that had mocked us
With its symbol of the dead
Fluttered and dropped to the bloody deck,
And a white square spoke instead.

Home from the kill we thundered
On the tail of the quinox.

To the thrum of straining canvas,
And the whine and groan of blocks.

Leaping clear of the shallows,
Chancing the creaming bars,
We heard the first faint cheering
As the late sun limned our spars.

Safe in the lee of the city
We moored in the afterglow,
The *Sea Nymph* and the *Henry*
With the buccaneers in tow.

Glad we had been in the going,
But God! It was good to come
Out of the sky-wide loneliness
To the walls and lights of home.

V

Under these shouldering rows of stone
That notch the quiet sky;
Under the asphalt's transient seal
The same old mud-flats lie;
And I have felt them surge and lift
At night as I passed by.

Yes, I have seen them sprawling nude
While an Autumn moon hung chill,
And the tide came shuddering in from sea,
Lift by lift, until
It held them under a silver mesh,
Responsive to its will.

Then slowly out from the crowding walls
I have seen the gibbets grow,

And stand against the empty sky
In a desolate, windblown row,
While their dancers swayed, and turned, and spun,
Tripping it heel and toe;
With a flash of gold where the peering moon
Saw an earring as it swung,
And a silver line that leapt and died
Where the salt-white sea-boots hung,
And the pitiful, nodding, silent heads,
With half of their songs unsung.

NOTE ON "THE PIRATES"

The many inlets and sheltering coves of the Carolina coasts very early made the "low country" seaboard a rendezvous for pirates and a shelter to refit, and to bury their treasure.

As early as 1565 the French from Ribault's settlement[2] succumbed to the temptation to plunder their rich Spanish neighbors; and in the century before the coming of the English, the lonely bays and estuaries saw strange ships from time to time. There was a pirate settlement by 1664 at Cape Fear River, where Governor Sayle[3] did not arrive until 1670 to take formal possession for the Lords Proprietors of the colony.

The Peace of Utrecht turned many privateers into pirates, ships which had been habitually preying upon Spanish commerce since Blake's victory at Santa Cruz in 1657, and these gentlemen of fortune were at first welcome in the Carolinas. Nearly all the coin in circulation then was at first brought by such doubtful adventurers, and they were regarded as the natural protectors of the Carolinas against their powerful enemy, the Spaniard, to the south.

Gradually, however, this cordial attitude changed. It was a small step from attacking Spanish to plundering English commerce, and, with the cultivations and export of rice and indigo, the demand for a safe sea passage grew overwhelming, while the coasts continued to be ravaged. The royal government was slow to act. In 1684 we learn that "the governor will not in all probability always reside in Charles Town, which is so near the sea as to be in danger of sudden attack by pirates"; nor was this an idle thought, for the town was blockaded by pirate ships at the harbor's mouth, and medicines and supplies demanded while citizens were held as hostages.

In 1718 Governor Spotswood of Virginia sent an expedition to North Carolina, which succeeded in surprising, capturing, and beheading the notorious "Black Beard," who, in company with one Stede Bonnet, had long ravaged the coast with impunity.[4]

In August of the same year word was brought to Charles Town that Bonnet with his ship the *Royal James* was refitting in the Cape Fear River. Colonel William Rhett volunteered to attack him.[5] With two sloops of eight guns each, the *Henry* and the *Nymph*, and about 130 men in all, he set sail, and found Bonnet at anchor in the Cape Fear River. In making the attack, and during the encounter, all three ships ran aground. The fight raged desperately all day between the *Henry* and the *Royal James*, the *Nymph* being unable to get off the shoal and come to the help of her companion ship. Bonnet finally surrendered and was taken prisoner to Charles Town. It is this adventure which the poem celebrates.

Bonnet escaped, but was afterwards recaptured by Colonel Rhett on Sullivan's Island. He and about thirty of his crew were hanged about the corner of Meeting and Water Streets. Bonnet, himself, was hanged later than his crew, after a masterpiece of invective by the judge, who painted hell vividly. This pirate leader was dragged fainting to the gallows, and there was much sympathy for him, as it was said, "His humor of going a-pirating proceeded from a disorder of the mind . . . occasioned by some discomforts he found in the married state." [Heyward's note]

The Last Crew

I

Spring found us early that eventful year,
Seeming to know in her clairvoyant way
The bitterness of hunger and despair
That lay upon the town.
Out of the sheer
Thin altitudes of day
She drifted down
Over the grim blockade
At the harbor mouth,
Trailing her beauty over the decay
That war had made,
Gilding old ruins with her jasmine spray,
Distilling warm moist perfume
From chill winter shade.

Out of the south
She brought the whisperings
Of questing wings.
Then, flame on flame,
The cardinals came,
Blowing like driven brands
Up from the sultry lands
Where Summer's happy fires always burn.

Old silences, that pain
Had held too close and long,
Stirred to the mocker's song,
And hope looked out again
From tired eyes.

Down where the White Point Gardens drank the sun,
And rippled to the lift of springing grass,
The women came;
And after them the aged, and the lame
That war had hurled back at them like a taunt.
And always, as they talked of little things,
How violets were purpling the shade
More early than in all remembered Springs,
And how the tides seemed higher than last year,
Their gaze went drifting out across the bay
To where,
Thrusting out of the mists,
Like hostile fists,
Waited the close blockade—
Then, dim to left and right,
The curving islands with their shattered mounds
That had been forts;
Mounds, which in spite
Of four long years of rending agony
Still held against the light;
Faint wraiths of color
For the breeze to lift
And flatten into faded red and white.

These sunny islands were not meant for wars;
See, how they curve away
Before the bay,
Bidding the voyager pause.
Warm with the hoarded suns of centuries,
Young with the garnered youth of many Springs,

They laugh like happy bathers, while the seas
Break in their open arms,
And the slow-moving breeze
Draws languid fingers down their placid brows.
Even the surly ocean knows their charms,
And under the shrill laughter of the surf,
He booms and sings his heavy monotone.

II

There are rare nights among these waterways
When Spring first treads the meadow of the marsh,
Leaving faint footprints of elusive green
To glimmer as she strays,
Breaking the Winter silence with the harsh
Sharp call of waterfowl;
Rubbing dim shifting pastels in the scene
With white of moon
And blur of scudding cloud,
Until the myrtle thickets
And the sand,
The silent streams,
And the substantial land
Go drifting down the tide of night
Aswoon.

On such a night as this
I saw the last crew go
Out of a world too beautiful to leave.
Only a chosen few
Besides the crew
Were gathered on the pier;
And in the ebb and flow
Of dark and moon, we saw them fare
Straight past the row of coffins

Where the fifth crew lay
Waiting their last short voyage
Across the bay.

And, as they went, not one among them swerved,
But eyes went homing swiftly to the West,
Where, faint and very few,
The windows of the town called out to them
Yet held them nerved
And ready for the test.
Young every one, they brought life at its best.
In the taut stillness, not a word
Was uttered but one heard
The deep slow orchestration of the night
Swell and relapse; as swiftly, one by one,
Cutting a silhouette against the gray,
They rose, then dropped out softly like a dream
Into the rocking shadows of the stream.

A sudden grind of metal scarred the hush;
A marsh-hen threshed the water with her wings,
And, for a breath, the marsh life woke and throbbed.
Then, down beneath our feet, we caught the gleam
Of folded water flaring left and right,
While, with a noiseless rush,
A shadow darker than the rest
Drew from its fellows swarming round the quay,
Took an oncoming breaker,
Shook its shoulders free,
And faced the sea.

Then came an interval that seemed to be
Part of eternity.
Years might have passed, or seconds;
No one knew!
Close in the dark we huddled, each to each,

Too stirred for speech.
Our senses, sharpened to an agony,
Drew out across the water till the ache
Was more than we could bear;
Till eyes could almost see,
Ears almost hear.
And waiting there,
I seemed to feel the beach
Slip from my reach,
While all the stars went blank.
The smell of oil and death enveloped me,
And I could feel
The crouching figures straining at a crank,
Knees under chins, and heads drawn sharply down,
The heave and sag of shoulders,
Sting of sweat;
An eighth braced figure stooping to a wheel,
Body to body in the stifling gloom,
The sob and gasp of breath against an air
Empty and damp and fetid as a tomb.
With them I seemed to reel
Beneath the spin and heel
When combers took them fair,
Bruising their bodies,
Lifting black water where
Their feet clutched desperate at the floor.

And as each body spent out of its ebbing store
Of strength and hope,
I felt the forward thrust,
At first so sure,
Fail in its rhythm,
Falter slow,
And slower—
Hang an endless moment—
Till in a rush came fear—

Fear of the sea, that it might win again,
Gathering one crew more,
Making them pay in vain.

Then through the horror of it, like a clear
Sweet wind among the stars,
I felt the lift
And drive of heart and will
Working their miracles until
Spent muscles tensed again to offer all
In one transcendent gift.

III

A sudden flood of moonlight drenched the sea,
Pointing the scene in sharp, strong black and white.
Sumter came shouldering through the night,
Battered and grim
The curve of ships shook off their dim
Vague outlines of a dream;
And stood, patient as death,
So certain in their pride,
So satisfied
To wait
The slow inevitableness of Fate.

Close, where the channel
Narrowed to the bay,
The *Housatonic* lay
Black on the moonlit tide,
Her wide
High sweep of spars
Flaunting their arrogance among the stars.

Darkness again
Swift-winged and absolute,

Gulping the stars,
Folding the ships and sea,
Holding us waiting, mute.
Then, slowly in the void,
There grew a certainty
That silenced fear.
The very air
Was stirring to the march of Destiny.

One blinding second out of endless time
Fell, sundering the night.
I saw the *Housatonic* hurled,
A ship of light,
Out of a molten sea,
Hang an unending pulse-beat,
Glowing stark;
While the hot clouds flung back a sullen roar.
Then all her pride, so confident and sure,
Went reeling down the dark.

Out of the blackened wave on livid wave
Leapt into being—thundered to our feet;
Counting the moments for us, beat by beat,
Until the last and smallest dwindled past,
Trailing its pallor like a winding-sheet
Over the last crew and its chosen grave.

IV

Morning swirled in from the sea,
And down by the low river-wall,
In a long unforgettable row,
Many faces tremulous, old;
Terrible faces of youth,
Broken and seared by the war,
Where swift fire kindled and blazed

From embers hot under the years,
While hands gripped a cane or a crutch;
Patient dumb faces of women,
Mothers, sisters, and wives:
And the vessel hull-down in the sea,
Where the waters just stirring from sleep,
Lifted bright hands to the sun,
Hiding their lusty young dead,
Holding them jealously close
Down to the cold harbor floor.

There would be eight of them.
Here in the gathering light
Were waiting eight women or more
Who were destined forever to pay,
Who never again would laugh back
Into the eyes of life
In the old glad, confident way.
Each huddled dumbly to each;
But eyes could not lift from the sea,
Only hands touched in the dawn.

"He would have gone, my man;
He was like that. In the night
When I awoke with a start,
And brought his voice up from my dream:
That was goodbye and godspeed.
I know he is there with the rest."

Brave, but with quivering lips,
Each alone in the press of the crowd,
Was saying it over and over.

The day flooded all of the sky;
And the ships of the sullen blockade
Weighed anchor and drew down the wind,

Leaving their wreck to the waves.
Hour heaved slowly on hour,
Yet how could the city rejoice
With the women out there by the Wall!
Night grew under the wharves,
And crept through the listening streets,
Until only the red of the tiles
Seemed warm from the breath of the day;
And the faces that waited and watched
Blurred into a wavering line,
Like a foam on the curve of the dark,
Down there by the reticent sea.

What if the darkness should bring
The lean blockade-runners across
With food for the hungry and spent . . .
Who could joy in the sudden release
While the faces, still-smiling, but wan,
Turned slowly to hallow the town?

NOTE TO "THE LAST CREW"

The "Fish-Boat" of the Confederate Navy, which exhaustive research indicates to have been the first submarine vessel to sink an enemy ship in time of war, was designed by Horace L. Hunley in 1863. This boat was twenty feet long, three and one-half feet wide, and five feet deep. Her motive power consisted of eight men whose duty it was to turn the crank of the propeller shaft by hand until the target had been reached. When this primitive craft was closed for diving there was only sufficient air to support life for half an hour. Since the torpedo was attached to the boat itself there was no chance of escape. The only hope was to reach and destroy the enemy vessel before the crew were suffocated or drowned.

Five successive volunteer crews died without reaching their objectives. But the sixth crew was successful in sinking the Federal blockading ship *Housatonic,* their own craft being caught and crushed beneath the foundering vessel. These crews went to certain death in the night time, in such secrecy that it was often months before their own families knew the names of the men. And now, with the lapse of scarcely more than half a century, it has been possible to find the names of only sixteen of those who paid the price.

Because no nation of any time can point to a more inspiring example of self-sacrifice, and because now, in a country reunited and indissoluble, the traditions of both the North and the South are a common, glorious heritage, the poem, which presents the final episode in the drama, is written as a memorial to all who gave their lives in the venture. [Heyward's note]

Modern Philosopher

They fight your battles for you every day,
The zealous ones, who sorrow in your life.
Undaunted by a century of strife,
With urgent fingers still they point the way
To drawing rooms, in decorous array,
And moral Heavens where no casual wife
May share your lot; where dice and ready knife
Are barred; and feet are silent when you pray.

But you have music in your shuffling feet,
And spirituals for a lenient Lord,
Who lets you sing your promises away.
You hold your sunny corner of the street,
And pluck deep beauty from a banjo chord:
Philosopher whose future is today.

Gamesters All

The river boat had loitered down its way;
The ropes were coiled, and business for the day
Was done.
The cruel noon closed down
And cupped the town.
Stray voices called across the blinding heat,
Then drifted off to shadowy retreat
Among the sheds.
The waters of the bay
Sucked away
In tepid swirls, as listless as the day.
Silence closed about me, like a wall,
Final and obstinate as death.
Until I longed to break it with a call,
Or barter life for one deep, windy breath.

A mellow laugh came rippling
Across the stagnant air,
Lifting it into little waves of life.
Then, true and clear,
I caught a snatch of harmony;
Sure lilting tenor, and a drowsing bass,
Elusive chords to weave and interlace,
And poignant little minors, broken short,
Like robins calling June—
And then the tune:
"Oh, nobody knows when de Lord is goin ter call,
Roll dem bones.
It may be in de Winter time, and maybe in de Fall,
Roll dem bones.
But yer got ter leabe yer baby an yer home an all—
So roll dem bones,
Oh my brudder,
Oh my brudder,
Oh my brudder,
Roll dem bones!"

There they squatted, gambling away
Their meagre pay;
Fatalists all.
I heard the muted fall
Of dice, then the assured,
Retrieving sweep of hand on roughened board.

I thought it good to see
Four lives so free
From care, so indolently sure of each tomorrow,
And hearts attuned to sing away a sorrow.

Then, like a shot
Out of the hot
Still air, I heard a call:

"Throw up your hands! I've got you all!
It's thirty days for craps.
Come, Tony, Paul!
Now, Joe, don't be a fool!
I've got you cool."

I saw Joe's eyes, and knew he'd never go.
Not Joe, the swiftest hand in River Bow!
Springing from where he sat, straight, cleanly made,
He soared, a leaping shadow from the shade
With fifty feet to go.
It was the stiffest hand he ever played.
To win the corner meant
Deep, sweet content
Among his laughing kind;
To lose, to suffer blind,
Degrading slavery upon "the gang,"
With killing suns, and fever-ridden nights
Behind relentless bars
Of prison cars.

He hung a breathless second in the sun,
The staring road before him.
Then, like one
Who stakes his all, and has a gamester's heart,
His laughter flashed.
He lunged—I gave a start.
God! What a man!
The massive shoulders hunched, and as he ran
With a head bent low, and splendid length of limb,
I almost felt the beat
Of passionate life that surged in him
And winged his spurning feet.

And then my eyes went dim.
The Marshal's gun was out.
I saw the grim

Short barrel, and his face
Aflame with the excitement of the chase.
He was an honest sportsman, as they go.
He never shot a doe,
Or spotted fawn,
Or partridge on the ground.
And, as for Joe,
He'd wait until he had a yard to go.
Then, if he missed, he'd laugh and call it square.
My gaze leapt to the corner—waited there.
And now an arm would reach it. I saw hope flare
Across the runner's face.

Then, like a pang
In my own heart,
The pistol rang.

The form I watched soared forward, spun the curve.
"By God, you've missed!"
The Marshal shook his head.
No, there he lay, face downward in the road.
"I reckon he was dead
Before he hit the ground,"
The Marshal said.
"Just once, at fifty feet,
A moving target too.
That's just about
As good as any man could do!
A little tough;
But, since he ran,
I call it fair enough."

He mopped his head, and started down the road.
The silence eddied round him, turned and flowed
Slowly back and pressed against the ears.
Until unnumbered flies set it to droning
And, down the heat, I heard a woman moaning.

Dusk

They tell me she is beautiful, my City,
That she is colorful and quaint, alone
Among the cities. But I, I who have known
Her tenderness, her courage, and her pity,
Have felt her forces mould me, mind and bone,
Life after life, up from her first beginning.
How can I think of her in wood and stone!
To others she has given of her beauty,
Her gardens, and her dim, old, faded ways,
Her laughter, and her happy, drifting hours,
Glad, spendthrift April, squandering her flowers,
The sharp, still wonder of her Autumn days;
Her chimes that shimmer from St. Michael's steeple
Across the deep maturity of June,
Like sunlight slanting over open water
Under a high, blue, listless afternoon.
But when the dusk is deep upon the harbor,
She finds *me* where her rivers meet and speak,
And while the constellations ride the silence
High overhead, her cheek is on *my* cheek.
I know her in the thrill behind the dark
When sleep brims all her silent thoroughfares.
She is the glamor in the quiet park
That kindles simple things like grass and trees.
Wistful and wanton as her sea-born airs,
Bringer of dim, rich, age-old memories.
Out on the gloom-deep water, when the nights
Are choked with fog, and perilous, and blind,
She is the faith that tends the calling lights.
Hers is the stifled voice of harbor bells
Muffled and broken by the mist and wind.
Hers are the eyes through which I look on life
And find it brave and splendid. And the stir
Of hidden music shaping all my songs,
And these my songs, my all, belong to her.

Skylines and Horizons

Your Gifts

You could not give me toys in those bleak days;
So when my playmates proudly boasted theirs,
You caught me to the shelter of your arms,
And taught me how to laugh away my tears.
Having no books, you sang a shining word
Into my open palm, and closed it tight.
And some far God of Little Children heard,
And gave you of His best for my delight.
So, when the neighbors' children shouted by,
Their hired nurse-maids herding them like sheep;
Then, that old dauntless look of yours would leap,
And, leading me beneath the western skies,
You woke their mirrored glory in my eyes.

And there were nights; do you remember still?
Forgetting playthings we could never buy,
We journeyed out beyond the farthest bill,
Adventuring along the evening sky,
And you would teach the meaning of the stars.
Not the dull purpose vaguely guessed by sages,
And catalogued in musty study-books.
But wild, fantastic legends of lost ages,

SOURCE: *Skylines and Horizons* (New York: Macmillan, 1924), vii–viii, 17, 18, 21–22, 25, 47, 50, 51, 62, 65–71.

That none but their Creator ever knew,
And that He whispered only once to one
Frail, lonely mother—and that mother—you.

Now autumn years are blowing swiftly by,
And I come empty-handed from my quest;
Save for a captured wraith of sunset sky,
A star or two, and last and loveliest,
The little shining word you gave to me:
Treasures no human hand may ever hold.
But you first knew their wonder and their worth;
You who have made me rich with more than gold.

A Yoke of Steers

A heave of mighty shoulders to the yoke,
Square, patient heads, and flaring sweep of horn;
The darkness swirling down beneath their feet
Where sleeping valleys stir, and feel the dawn;
Uncouth and primal, on and up they sway,
Taking the summit in a drench of day.
The night-winds volley upward bitter-sweet,
And the dew shatters to a rainbow spray
Under the slow-moving, cloven feet.

There is a power here that grips the mind;
A force repressed and inarticulate,
Slow as the swing of centuries, as blind
As destiny, and as deliberate.

They will arrive in their appointed hour
Unhurried by the goad of lesser wills
Bearing vast burdens on.

They are the great
Unconquerable spirit of these hills.

The Mountain Woman

Among the sullen peaks she stood at bay
And paid life's hard account from her small store.
Knowing the code of mountain wives; she bore
The burden of the days without a sigh;
And, sharp against the somber winter sky,
I saw her drive her steers afield each day.

Hers was the hand that sunk the furrows deep
Across the rocky, grudging southern slope.
At first youth left her face, and later, hope;
Yet through each mocking spring and barren fall,
She reared her lusty brood, and gave them all
That gladder wives and mothers love to keep.

And when the sheriff shot her eldest son
Beside his still, so well she knew her part,
She gave no healing tears to ease her heart;
But took the blow upstanding, with her eyes
As drear and bitter as the winter skies.
Seeing her then, I thought that she had won.

But yesterday her man returned too soon
And found her tending, with a reverent touch,
One scarlet bloom; and, having drunk too much,
He snatched its flame and quenched it in the dirt.
Then, like a creature with a mortal hurt,
She fell, and wept away the afternoon.

The Mountain Preacher

In the red church with its checkered window-panes,
That squats among its cluttered graves, and stains
The laurelled clearing with its ugly blot,
He preached his God on Sunday, while the hot

Thin mountain air vibrated to the sound
Of hotter threats, and in from miles around,
Threading still trails through rhododendron gloom,
Came silent groups to fill his house of doom.

Raw-boned and thunder-voiced, with brandished fist,
He shouted of an arrant egotist
Swift to avenge a wrong, carrying hate
Beyond the grave, hurling a dire fate
On all who failed to follow his decree.
Until his God emerged, the Deity
Behind the mountain feud—the iron code
Of eye for eye was His. Slowly there showed,
Behind impassive faces, sullen fear
Of the all-seeing Foe they worshipped there.

Wednesday the freshet came; and Pigeon Creek,
That threads the laurel blossoms on a streak
Of morning sunshine, dropped its slender song,
Drew one deep breath, then lifting with a long
Slow shudder, hurtled like a tawny beast,
Froth-lipped and baying, oceanward and east.
Where the trail leads from church to Garvin's house,
Tom Garvin's boy was driving up the cows.
A vaulting seethe of water, trees, and foam
Lunged for the bank, then curved and tumbled home.
On yellow chaos, and the sky's hard slate,
For one swift heart-beat, beauty, slim and straight,
Swung sharply upward, crumpled, hung and fell:
There may have been a cry—no one could tell.

That night, ten miles away, the preacher heard.
The first stream took his horse and rig; the third
Hurled him a mile down stream and gashed his head.
A sallow morning light lay on the bed
At Garvin's when he staggered through the door
And closed it very softly on the road

Of hungry water. Slowly silence grew
And spread—and suddenly the watchers knew
There was a God, and He was very kind.
While the grim, silent man, with eyes gone blind,
Gathered the broken form that never stirred
Into his bleeding arms—and said no word.

Black Christmas

*"It is cruel for a woman with her man gone,
An' the younguns allus hungry, an' winter comin' on."*

I thought the feud was ended last Christmas Day,
When Darrell sent the preacher to the Galloways to say
That they could come and get him, if they had a mind:
He was done with rifle-totin' for his fellow-kind.
An' a year gone by, with everythin' *thet still;*
An' never once a Galloway on our side the hill.
Oh I was glad this mornin' when Dal hollered up to me
To sen' the younguns runnin' to help him fetch a tree.
"There's a fine young balsam by the wood-house shed,
An' we'll have it in for Christmas, like we used to do!" he said.
I watched him drop the saplin' with a single stroke;
An' the snow all whirlin' round him like a shinin' smoke;
While the younguns tumbled, and laughed, and sang:
Then someone shouted sudden—an' a rifle rang.
Now the folks are gatherin' to bring him from the shed;
An' I got to stop denyin' that my man is dead.

New England Landscape

On a sepia ground
Shot with orange light,
The pines,
In blue-black lines,

And birches, slender,
Diagonal, and white,
Stencil compact designs.
The inevitable wall,
As it leaves the woods,
Breaks to a sprawl
Of separate stones
Echoing the tones
Of sepia and orange
With high lights
Of chrome and red,
Until they find a bed
In the splotched lilac
Of the meadow,
Or chill to blue in shadow.
In the valley's cupped palm
Lies a handful of ripening grain.
And, riding the high blue calm
Over Monadnock,[1]
A decorous cloud
Is slowly unwinding its skein.

Suffrage

The mother in her was the last to die
In the strong chains of "What will neighbors say!"
She could have painted; and she'd make you cry,
Singing familiar songs her different way.
But vaguely art connoted blasphemy
And idleness. She could have married Will,
And reared his young above the grocery.
But something in her sang that he would kill.

At thirty-five *he* came; and then the day
He drew her close; but told her of old ties—

Yet there was France—and love. She turned away,
For Heaven fastened her with watchful eyes.

The women at the polls all swear her daft.
Today she tore her vote to bits—*and laughed.*

Weariness

I do not dread the coming of Old Age:
I am so tired today—so wholly spent.
Kind hands are suddenly belligerent.
"If you lack strength to earn your daily wage,
Give us your soul," they cry, "your heritage
Of pride." Revengeful winds that I have bent
Before my body's strength, finding me impotent,
Lash me to cover with their blinding rage.

Now, if the form that I have always feared
Should take my nerveless hand, and, like a friend,
Say "Come and rest a while, Forget the mad
And futile fight—the thinking that you cared—
The shout—the kiss. Come, dream until the end
Here with me in the sun," I could be glad.

Buzzard Island

A frieze of naked limbs, gaunt, sinister,
Against the sanguine anguish of the west.
No sound except the steady cluck and purr
Of thirsty streams that tap the sky's bared breast,
And crawl through blind canals until they flood
The barren levels of the empty fields,
The fallen dikes, the rotting trunks with blood.

Now, as the fading horror swoons tonight,
Like cinders scattered from a funeral pyre,
Coursing and veering in the upper light,
With bellies ruddy from the ebbing fire,
The vultures circle down until their breath
Poisons the stagnant air, until the stark
Awaiting trees blossom and leaf with death.

Beyond these rice-fields and their crawling streams,
Young voices ring; white cities lift and spread.
This is the rookery of still-born dreams;
Here old faiths gather after they are dead,
Outlived despairs slant by on evil wing,
And bitter memories that time has starved
Home down the closing dusk for comforting.

NOTE: Buzzard Island is a buzzard rookery among abandoned rice-fields on the coast of
South Carolina. [Heyward's note]

Chant for an Old Town

Builders of high white towers in the sun;
Masters, yet driven by the force you spend;
Can you not feel beneath the soil you rend
A surer rhythm than you have yet begun:
The drum of steady pulses that have done
With stone and iron, colors, and the bend
Of certain beauty; workers, friend and friend,
Whose hands wrought slowly until grace was won.

Trading new lamps for old, you storm the street.
Then, heedless of the magic in the old,
You leave them strewn in fragments at our gate.
Oh, Pause before the ruin is complete.
For that which stands have pity, and withhold.
Leave for your sons these walls inviolate.

I.

It has been told above the fading embers
That once beneath a cloud-wracked, frightened moon,
When the Governor's ships drove down upon the pirates,
And days were numbered for the picaroon,
A long-boat swept from the sea toward the city,
Slender, and dark, and eager as a sword,
Cleaving the swirling play of light and shadow
That made the bay a crazy checker-board.

And once the light drenched down and limned a picture
That caused the blood to stagger, hang, and freeze;
For the boat leapt clear, and in the stern sat Blackbeard
Nursing a bloody cutlass on his knees.

And the watchers paled and shifted in the darkness,
Hugging the shadows when the moon flared through;
For the ships were out, and gaunt below the city
Stood gibbets that had swung a pirate crew;
While a Judas wind went whispering among them,
And bent palmettoes muttered all they knew.

But the drone of parted water never slackened.
The slash of oars and tumble of the wake
Dwindled and ebbed along the windy river,
And died at the city's edge where forests break.
And silence fluttered back from the hidden marshes,
Throbbed, and bore upon them like an ache.

But the negroes tell of a silent landing-party
That hacked a path through tangled scrub and vine,
And a long-boat beached where greying live-oaks crowded
About a creek to dabble their beards in brine.

Of a sullen torch that splashed vermillion patches
On a face from hell, and sweat upon the backs

Of diggers working heavily in silence;
And a cheat borne down by two great straining blacks
Into a yawning hole. Then color of fire
Poured from a sudden blade to the stooping men
Terribly cleaving souls from splendid bodies;
And a voice: "Guard well until I come again."

Darkness then, and the heavy rhythmic thudding
Of sods on wood and the flesh of those on guard;
A hush that built about them slowly, stilling
Even a distant pulse where tholepins jarred.

2.

A gust of years went by, and then the blowing
Of steady decades kind to a new land.
Like a spent storm, the head of Blackbeard glowered
Through rainbows at a frigate's prow, while sand
And the terrible strong teeth of deep-sea hunters
Fretted the tarnished cutlass from his hand.

Streets spread, and quiet forest paths receded.
Men built with hands that loved the feel of stone,
And hearts that knew elusive ways of Beauty,
Who mates a loving touch—or lives alone.
Where forests fell the grateful soil reflowered
In slender portico and stuccoed wall.
Old stones from France lay in the narrow driveways,
And through their crevices the many small
Sweet fingers of the Spring would lift unhindered.
Summer would mount there like a tropic wave
Spilling pomegranate coral through the gardens.

There figs, sea-purple, ripened, and the brave
Old tattered banners of bananas fluttered

About their heavy fruit. White mornings sprawled
On wharves that loved the bay, where chanties rang;
And August courtyards, flagged and lichen-walled,
Where negroes bought and sold, and laughed and sang.
Above deep streets hung weathered copper spires
And domes to take the sun, and, like a crowd
Of patient watchers over fading splendors,
High toppling dormers, staring shaggy-browed.
Cowled doorways bore the chisel's mark upon them,
And iron-work in many a harp and scroll,
Beaten by hands that shaped red yielding metal,
Still bore the fleeting imprint of a soul.

But there are things that human clay may handle,
And warm its coldness on, and speed its breath
For one brief day. Then, like a flaring candle,
They go. Beauty is such. The seed of death
Is born in lovely things to ripen slowly
And kill them before we are satisfied.
Only the dead are free to give up wholly,
And follow mortal beauty that has died.

3.

The engines come.
Through the short night
They breathe their iron breathing,
Waiting the dawn.
Then *snarl,* and

SHATTER, SHATTER, SHATTER!

"Frail city of hands,
What have you to offer?
Can you prove by mathematics
Why you should survive?
Pierced by plunging caisson,

Walled by towering concrete;
What have you to compare
With the superb accurance
Of a blue-print,
Or a relentless convergence
Of a studied perspective?
Can you give us a sea-wall
Like that of Buenos Aires,
Or a hotel the mate to twenty others
In great American cities?
A hundred Western towns say you are wrong;
And in answer
You smile your faded, wistful smile,
And show us a crooked, moss-hung tree
A century old;
And the way a street
Bends a protecting arm
About an impossible curve.

SHATTER, SHATTER, SHATTER!

See how a house can climb
Sheer to the zenith,
Floor hurled upon floor,
While the girders swing dizzily upward.
We show you a street like
Pennsylvania Avenue,
Canal Street,
Riverside Drive,
All asphalt and uniform concrete.
And you dodder of ancient flagged pavements
That lay like faint pastel mosaics
Between careless gardens
That were like nothing else upon Earth.

SHATTER, SHATTER, SHATTER!

Ah, you are silent at last."

4.

Under the feet of a tall machine,
In the false and tricky dark
That grew where the sky-flung derricks lean
Over the littered park,

A gang of negroes burrowing
With bar, and pick, and spade,
Tugged and bent to an iron ring
In a hole their tools had made.

A sudden give, and the earth fell clear,
A gasp, and seven blacks
Bunched and cringed, and muttered a prayer
To the thing behind their backs.

For a moon grown suddenly old and blue
Laid withered hands upon
A mouldy chest, and a bone or two
From a rotting skeleton;

A shooting-star whined overhead,
The arc-lights winced and failed,
And a lonely wind from the longtime dead
Crept to their ears and wailed.

Then Terror loosed them, and let them go
In a storm of flailing feet,
To tell their tale by the lantern glow
Of the shops in Sailor Street.

But when the engines summoned day
Up from oblivion,
And the gang crept back to loot the clay,
The chest and bones were gone.

5.

Simon, the drunkard, swears he saw them going,
In a shaking world of neither-here-nor-there,
Tottering out of the shades, and slowly blowing
Across the park, lighter than harbor air,
With a wedge of the milky-way serenely showing
Through cloven skulls under the matted hair.
Yes, he will tell you that he watched them travel
Out to the city's edge with a mouldy chest.
How they would bulk in the dark, and then unravel
Under the lights. And when they paused to rest,
Dusted their burden free of city gravel.
And waited tense, lest any should molest.

Heaving their treasure to their backs, they waded
The last salt stream, and where the forests keep
The old lost darks and silences, they faded.

Back in the early grey, steel-throated, deep,
The engines ripped the silence, and the jaded,
Driven city stumbled from its sleep.

Jasbo Brown and Selected Poems

Jasbo Brown

Loose heady laughter shook the humid night,
Bells jangled shrilly, and a whistle flung
A note as lonely as a soul in flight
To fail and die along a mile of river.
Then silence, while a presence moved among
The floating stars and made them swirl and quiver.

Clang-clang! A sudden world swam into view,
Dim windows banked in tiers against the dark,
And paddles threshing phosphorescent blue
Out of abysmal night; tall funnels wreathing
The scene in deeper gloom from their dark breathing.

Twin eyes of red and green sought out the shore,
Found it, and centered on the sagging pier.
A sleepy negro woke and raised a cheer.
A painter slapped the planks, and someone swore.
Out of the gloom the shore-line seemed to stir
And swim to greet the phantom visitor.
"Ahoy! Stand by!" Lithe, fluid shadows massed
Upon the wharf. The gang-plank rattled down.
Faint lights came running from the river town.

SOURCE: *Jasbo Brown and Selected Poems* (New York: Farrar and Rinehart, 1931), 9–17, 95.

A door banged open on the boat and cast
An orange glare across the crowded deck,
Gashing the screen of night, secretive, vast,

And showing life, gregarious and teeming,
Bronze torsos under tatters, ridged and gleaming,
Bandanaed heads, a banjo's round blank face.
A woman's voice shrilled "Honey, I's come home."
And from the wharf: "T'ank Gawd! I's glad yo' come."
  I got a song, yo' got a song,
    All Gawd' chillen got a song.
Up the plank they trooped a hundred strong,
Throats belling in the warm, moist river air.
Hot laughter on the wharf, the flow and fusion
Of reds and greens and purples, then a flare
Of ecstasy that unified confusion.
"Eberybody talk about Heaben ain't goin' dere,
Heaben, Heaben, goin' sing all ober Gawd' Heaben."
From the high pilot house a voice drawled down:
"Got all your niggers off?"
              And from below:
"Ay, ay, sir, let her go."
The gang-plank rattled up against its spars.
The tide with ponderous deliberation
Swung out the boat and drew it down the night
To lose it like a fading constellation
Destined for the graveyard of the stars.

Jasbo reeled slightly as he turned to face
The clustered lights that marked the river town.
"Gawd, I's tired," he said, and then far down
Among the shacks: "Heaben, Heaben,"

He raised his head; so, he was not alone.
The chorus throbbed in his deep baritone:
"Goin' sing all ober Gawd' Heaben,"
But no one answered. Yes, that was their way.

He ought to know by now they'd make him play
Out on the river clean from New Orleans,
But in the town they'd drop him mighty quick.
Churches were no place for muddy jeans.
He was not good enough for city ways,
And songs about their Jesus and his grace.

No, he was not. He knew it. When they whined
Their mournful hymns a trigger in his mind
Would click, and he would yearn to shout
Queer broken measures that his soul flung out
Of some recess where joy and agony
Whirled in a rhythm that he could feel and see.

The river clucked and sobbed among its piles.
A screech-owl launched a wavering ghost of sound
That ranged and circled on the watery miles
And lived to shudder in the heavy air,
Causing the lonely man upon the pier
To turn and look behind him, while his eyes
Widened and whitened. "Gawd it's lonely here."

He drew a sleeve across his sweating brow.
"All Gawd's chillen got a song," I wonder now—
That girl in New Orleans who sent him packing
Because he had to stroke the ivories
To ease the smart
That always kept devouring his heart,
Instead of heaving cotton on the boat
And earning money for her like the rest.
The sudden thought of her caught at his throat.
Old fires seared him, set his temples throbbing.
"Oh Gawd, I got de blues," he said, half sobbing.

Then, suddenly, he heard it down the shore.
A square of light leaped out, and through the door
A tinny clamor smote the heavy night.

Someone sang drunkenly, and then a fight
Flamed up and died. The door went BANG.
Something inside of Jasbo broke and sang.

They saw him reel against a shrunken moon
That hung behind him in the open door.
Scarcely at all he seemed a human being,
Lips hanging loosely and his eyes not seeing.
"My Gawd!" a woman cried, "It's Jasbo Brown,
Git off dat stool yo' empty-headed fool
An' let him play what kin."

          Somebody poured a gin,
Another, and another.
He gulped the liquid fire scarcely knowing,
Lunged heavily and slumped above the keys.
Out of the night a little wind came blowing,
A little wind, and searing memories.
"Oh Gawd, I's lonely," he moaned once, "but what's de use!"
Then crashed an aching chord and sang "I got de blues."

   Oh the hypocritical
   Children of the Lord,
   How he jeered and mocked them
   In a snarling chord.

   Women who had known him,
   Who had passed him by,
   Once again he loved them,
   Spurned them, let them die.

   Bosses who had cursed him
   Over Christendom
   Whimpered as he flung them
   Into Kingdom Come.

Out of clinkered torment
Like a rising steam,
Something spun and glittered,
Waked him, let him dream.

Showed the world, a madness
Cured by ridicule,
Praised him for a prophet,
Damned him for a fool.

Fingers conjured music
From the ivories
Into swaying bodies,
Into flexing knees.

Black face, brown face,
In the smoky light,
Gin and river women,
And the reeling night

Whirled along a rhythm
Crashing through his blood,
Jasbo, ginned and dreaming,
Stained with river mud.

Dawn, and the music tinkled out and died.
"Jus' one more Jas, here take another gin."
Two dancers dropped and sprawled,
A third stood watching with an empty grin.
The door blew open and the day smiled in.
White-footed down the river it came striding,
Beauty upon it, ancient and abiding,
Breathing of April and of jessamine.
The player rose and staggered to the street.
Oh for a place to go, a hole for hiding.

She came and stood beside him in the dew.
They watched the copper sun swing up together.
"Honey," she said at last, "I'd die for you
Most anytime yo' say when yo' are playin'."
"Yo likes my songs?" he asked, "Dat what yo're sayin'?"
The wonder in her eyes left little doubt.
"Come home with me an' rest. Yo're clean wore out."

Down the littered street the player stumbled
With the girl beside him. Once she glanced
Up into his face and found it tranced.
His eyes had lost her, and his loose lips mumbled.
Presently, half aloud, she heard him sing
A low-keyed, minor thing:
 "Yo' got to know
 I ain't de kin' for stayin'
 Always I is movin',
 Always playin'.

 "Life is jus' hello
 An' so-long
 For Gawd's lonely Chillen
 What got a song.

 "Take me home an' res' me
 In de white folks' town.
 "But I got to leabe yo'
 When de boat comes down.

 "De boat, an' de niggers
 What love my song.
 Life is jus' hello
 An' so-long."

Prodigal

Some day when the stern speaker in my brain
Has ceased to drive me stumbling through the dark
Dropping dead cinders for each faint new spark,
Only to see the new one wax and wane.
When all my dreams are numbered with the slain,
And Wisdom, that egregious Patriarch,
Has told his last half truth, and left me stark,
I shall go home. I shall go home again.

Friendship will greet me in the panelled hall,
And Laughter will enfold me on the stairs
Sweet as old rose leaves wrinkled in a jar.
Battles and loves will move me not at all.
There will be juleps, billiards, family prayers,
And a calm crossing to another star.

Porgy and Bess

Summertime

Summertime an' the livin' is easy,
Fish are jumpin', an the cotton is high.
Oh, yo' daddy's rich, and yo' ma is good lookin',
So hush, little baby, don' you cry.

One of these mornin's you goin' to rise up singin',
Then you'll spread yo' wings an' you'll take to the sky.
But till that mornin', there's a-nothin' can harm you
With Daddy an' Mammy standin' by.

My Man's Gone Now

Gone, gone gone.

My man's gone now, ain' no use a-listenin'
for his tired footsteps climbin' up de stairs.
Ah—ah—
Ole Man Sorrow's come to keep me company,
whisperin' beside me when I say my prayers,
Ah—ah—
Ain' dat I min' workin', work an' me is travelers

SOURCE: *Porgy and Bess* (New York: Gershwin Publishing Corp., 1935).

journeyin' togedder to de Promis' Lan'.
But Ole Man Sorrow's marchin' all de way wid me
tellin' me I'm ole now since I lose my man.

Since she lose her man.

Since I lose my man.

Ah—

Ole Man Sorrow's sittin' by de fireplace,
lyin' all night long by me in de bed.
Tellin' me de same thing mornin', noon an' eb'nin',
that I'm all alone now since my man is dead.
Ah—since my man is dead.

A Woman Is a Sometime Thing

Lissen to yo' daddy warn you,
'fore you start a-traveling,
woman may born you, love you an' mourn you,
but a woman is a sometime thing,
yes, a woman is a sometime thing.

Oh, a woman is a sometime thing.

Yo' mammy is the first to name you,
an' she'll tie you to her apron string.
Then she'll shame you and she'll blame you,
till yo' woman comes to claim you,
'cause a woman is a sometime thing.
Yes, a woman is a sometime thing.

Oh, a woman is a sometime thing.

Don't you never let a woman grieve you
jus' 'cause she got yo' weddin' ring.
She'll love you and deceive you,
then she'll take yo' clo'es an' leave you,
'cause a woman is a sometime thing.

Yes, a woman is a sometime thing.

Fiction

The Brute

THE LATE SUN was behind Hal Patton as he crossed Galoway's lot; and that was perhaps the reason why the woman failed to raise her eyes as he approached. Or it may have been that she was altogether engrossed with her task; for, with futile, feminine strokes of an axe she was attacking a heavy log of oak.

Be that as it may, it was not until his shadow slanted, blue, across the mellow radiance at her feet that she lifted her gaze. Then stood with parted lips, while her hand fled with a quick, characteristic gesture to her heart, a little hopelessly, and yet with a gleam of exultation, her eyes met his and held them.

He should not have come to her so out of the glamour of the sunset, and haled forth the youth in her that she was striving to quench and forget. It was not quite fair;—and yet—well, it was all of a piece with life. Behind him the sun sank rapidly, the harsh outline of Greybeard Mountain first distorting, then quenching its glory. She shivered instinctively. Night was even now welling up from the valley; and with it would come her husband, as sinister and unrelenting as the mountain, where he spent his days, endlessly engrossed in some dark and mysterious affair of his own.

With the setting of the sun, Patton, no longer silhouetted against the brilliance, became real—and his companion, searching his features in the dusk, was struck by the intense virility and the intangible suggestion of possession that lit his face as he looked steadily into her eyes. Suddenly she sensed danger. He would speak . . . the night was too intimate; it would lead him to say things that would make her have to send him away. He *must* not. He *must* not.

Almost a minute passed. Then—with fine sensitiveness—he knew, and his face softened. Lapsing into the dialect of the mountain, he held out his hand.

SOURCE: *Pagan* 3 (November 1918), 19–26.

"Let me have that axe, Sary," he said, while she thanked him with her eyes; "'tain't no woman's work nohow. You go and set down." And he took the axe from her not unwilling fingers.

In a moment the clear ring of metal on oak filled the air, and the girl, sagging wearily against the "worm" fence, watched the demolition of the fifteen-inch log.

As her eyes dwelt upon the stalwart figure before her, a faint color brightened her sallow cheeks; and with eyes that held a certain blue wonder, she noted the play of the superb back and arm-muscles as they writhed and stiffened beneath the cotton undershirt, which, with a pair of blue overalls, completed the man's visible apparel.

Unnoticed by the two, Brutus Galoway rounded the corner of the cabin and paused; a slow, dark, malignity gathering in his face; while behind him, immense, sinister, Greybeard Mountain towered twenty-five hundred feet into the purple evening.

To the primitive dwellers of the little neighborhood that wrested a meager living from the rocky and grudging soil, there seemed to exist a sort of grim kinship between the man Galoway and the mountain. Nature had fashioned them, each perfect of his kind, and then had unleashed her forces against them and blasted them in their prime.

Vast landslides had streaked the verdure of the mountainside with great raw scars, through which showed ridges of rock, like gaunt ribs from which the flesh has been torn.

And with the man it had been a cat in a tight place, one black night when the boys had been panther hunting out on Greybeard. They had shot the beast dead on his chest, and had dragged him out alive; but the nearest doctor was fifty miles—and a hundred dollars—away, so Nature had to make her repairs unassisted by modern science, and her work was not artistic. When Galoway stepped from his cabin two months later his coat showed a flapping sleeve from its right elbow where the arm had gone, and a raking claw had left its hideous life-mark upon his face. Among other things that was now a right cheek, the salvage of which was quite inadequate to the task of concealing the strong, fang-like teeth that gleamed nakedly where the sparse beard came to an abrupt end.

There was another change, too, and a deeper one. In a community as primitive as the little scattered settlement that nestled at the mountain's foot, one must find sustenance, as well as recreation, in the exercise of physical faculties. Now Galoway with his empty sleeve was a bankrupt in the one admitted asset; a cipher in the community life: and the acid of it bit deep into him.

From childhood his friends had called him Brute, associating the cognomen only with the name from which it was a contradiction. Now as by common consent the few that remained were heard to address him as "Galoway," realizing in their dull way the cruel appropriateness of the old nickname and wishing to be kind.

Suddenly Galoway strode forward and addressed the woman.

"Since you got a friend to cut your wood for you, Sary, you can go in and start supper."

The girl flinched but rose and obeyed submissively. Galoway faced the younger man, repressed anger in his voice.

"Ain't you got nothing else to do except woman's work?" he rasped.

"This ain't woman's work, where I've been, since I left here," came the defiant reply.

"Well it's woman's work here; and so's plowing, and anything else their men tells 'em to do." Galoway flung the words at him conscious of his right, for he was voicing the time-honored code of the mountaineer; then he added belligerently: "And I don't want you coming around putting notions into the head of my woman."

With an evident effort at repression the youth made no reply but gathered the wood in a great armful, and entered the cabin. Galoway followed in time to intercept a grateful look from Sarah.

When his guest had departed, Galoway lifted a jug from the mantel and poured out a half tumbler of colorless moonshine whiskey, drained the glass, then crossed the room and stood over the girl.

"You'll not see Hal Patton again, do you understand?"

"But Brute," she quavered, "he's my oldest friend."

"Sweetheart, you mean; don't be afeared to say it. And when you thought he had gone to Asheville and gotten shed of you, then you married old Brute Galoway and his safe little farm. Come, answer me. That's right, ain't it?"

Silence in the cabin, and beneath its spur the man's temper bolted. Bending over, he hurried on, the rank breath of the crude whiskey beating into her face.

"And then the cat got your husband, and now you want your fine, handsome young man back again."

Still silence, save for a shuffling of her feet, as she adjusted them to a firm stand upon the sandy floor.

"Answer me, ain't I right?"

For a moment the mask of utter impassivity that is the face of a mountain woman, gave way, and a look of supreme loathing flamed up, and burned whitely as she eyed him face to face.

Then Galoway struck her. The blow, a short, vicious clubbing stroke of his one arm that held the strength of two, extinguished the light in her face as one might snuff a candle, and felled her in a huddle at his feet.

It is to the little commonplaces of life, the little exacting cogs in the machinery of our daily lives, that we owe our sanity in times of terrific stress. It is the clock that must be wound in the house of death, or the hungry dog that lays his muzzle beseechingly in an empty hand, that often sways the balance back into the land of today. And so it was with Sarah. Presently she rose dizzily to her feet and crossed by instinct to the stove, where the bacon was burning.

Still unappeased, Galoway flung at her— "And you'll do your own woman's work from now on do you understand."

At the door there appeared a lean hound, his muzzle high, an attentive forepaw extended across the threshold. Presently he sensed the unrest in the atmosphere, and raised a long, dismal whine. Galoway strode across the room and kicked the animal, straight and swift as a cannon-ball, far into the night.

During the three days that followed, Galoway appeared morose and preoccupied. Leaving early for the mountain, as was his wont, but returning by midday, to spend the afternoon pottering abstractedly about the place. He acquired the habit of coming upon her suddenly and silently, and he seemed to draw amusement from the fear that these appearances surprised into her face. And then on the fourth morning he leaned across the rough table, while they were breakfasting, and addressed her abruptly.

"I got to work the road on yon side of Greybeard today, more slides come down since the rains." Then with a cunning look, he added— "You'll fix me up a can of lunch, then put the steer to the cart and go over to Beartown to visit Ada. I won't have you here alone when I am away."

She looked up in sudden apprehension. "Not the mountain today, Brute," she faltered.

"Why not?" he demanded, his eyes narrowing with quick suspicion.

"You—you—said you were going down the valley pasture after the cow this week, and it's Saturday."

Deigning no reply, the man passed out of the cabin; and in a moment the woman followed timidly.

A great white-lipped storm-head was lifting its leaden bulk over Grey-beard, and now, through a stillness that was not of peace but of taut waiting, came the muffled boom of thunder. The woman shivered and looked down; then she approached Galoway and laid a timid hand upon his arm.

"Oh, not today, Brute—not today," she pleaded. "Hear that thunder. It's a-talkin' to you and to me—can't you just *feel* everythin' a-listenen'? Can't you tell what it's a-sayin'? 'Not today, not today!'"

Among the mountaineers there are many who seem to have a sixth sense; a certain prescience that warns of impending danger. It is nature's gift to her primitive creatures. It is the same faculty that has made a horse go wild with terror a full five minutes before a rattler has sounded his shrill warning; and has driven a flock of sheep from beneath a sheltering tree, out into the full force of a storm at least a minute before the tree has been shattered by a bolt of lightning. And among the simple folk of the mountain, who have not yet altogether passed from the intuitive to the reasoning phase of evolution, it is accepted, not with ridicule, but solemnly and without question, as is their God.

Now Galoway looked into the face of his wife, and saw there a dread as keen as the fear of death.

"I am afeared, Brute, afeared to my soul," she whispered in a tense voice. Then drawing herself up, her manner changed and she added, with a certain calm dignity, "Three years ago I started to do your work—three years—and now I'm askin' my first favor of you, one little thing. Don't go on Greybeard today."

The coming storm had now folded the mountain in its sable embrace, cutting it out of the range that, save for the one peak, still lay shimmering in the clear white sunshine. The girl shivered and laid her face against the arm of the man, in the world-old, involuntary plea for the protection of her mate, and whispered, with a poignant little gesture to her heart:

"I feel it here. That if you say 'No,' it will be the last time—the last time between you and me, Brute."

For a moment Galoway hesitated, the superstition in his being quickened in response to her mood. And then he divined in the situation an opportunity to stab more deeply than any physical hurt that he might inflict. He turned from her and shook her free.

"I done give my word to the boys," he said doggedly; "and I'm a-goin'."

Galoway started his wife off before him, seeing her well on her way. Then, with the long swinging stride of the mountaineer, he commenced the six mile climb that would take him around the shoulder of the mountain, to where the gang would be busy clearing the road of the boulders and debris from the recent slides.

He found operations in full swing when he joined the men. With a supply of dynamite which had been hauled from the railroad forty miles away, they were dislodging the heavier rocks, and blasting out the stumps of trees where new detours were necessary.

Scarcely exchanging greetings, he took his place, preceding the gang by several hundred yards, with the cartridges and fuses rigged for use. Unable to wield a pick or shovel, he had naturally fallen heir to the position of blaster, while the others followed and tidied up by hand.

The work progressed with speed, and a little before midday Galoway rounded the shoulder of the mountain, and came out upon the warm Southern slope.

Here, however, he was brought to a sudden stop. A tremendous slide had started near the summit, and had peeled the surface to the naked rock for five hundred feet above him. The lower edge of the immense deposit had by some odd chance fallen into the narrow road; and the mass had evidently not gained its momentum, for this insignificant hindrance held it poised, as it were, by a hair.

Then fate reached for Galoway, and he raised his eyes from his work.

The thunder-storm had passed down the valley, leaving the atmosphere unbelievably clear; and in the crystalline air of the altitudes, perspective and distance were set at naught. Before him the mountains, range beyond range, seemed piled one on top of the other until the most distant notched the sky in a vivid saw-like line of blue, while, over a thousand feet below, his little farm stood revealed in each minute detail, as though held beneath a lens.

Suddenly Galoway gave a start: in the small pasture he discerned the steer, grazing indolently; and in the untidy barn yard, the cart, resting its empty shafts upon the ground. An ugly fleeting look shone in his eyes, then fixed and hardened into shrewd suspicion.

Face shaded against the glare with his one great hand, he watched.

Presently he noted a man swinging along toward the house, appearing, then vanishing among the thick rhododendrons. Finally the figure emerged at the edge of the woods, descended into a hollow, and paused beside a spring a short distance from his clearing. Raising his hands to his mouth, the man gave a short hallo that ascended as clear as a bell note to the watcher above. A moment later Galoway saw his wife leave the cabin and hasten down to the spring. In the dappled sunlight of the little hollow she went unswervingly to the man, her hands at her breast, her head low; he made no movement until she was at his side; then with a certain awkward dignity he drew her swiftly into his arms.

Then the flare of sudden intelligence lit Galoway's heavy features. He stopped, thrust his crowbar beneath the edge of the mass that lay before him, withdrew it and inserted three cartridges of dynamite strung together on a fuse; this he tamped closely into place, working with the swift thoroughness that had won for him the reputation of the best blaster in the mountains. When he arose and again looked below, the woman was leaving the cabin for the second time. For a moment she stood hesitant in the doorway, her blue calico making a spot of bright color against the darkness within; and Galoway noticed she carried a bundle wrapped in a shawl, such as is always taken by a mountain woman in a journey. Carefully she closed the door, then sped quickly down the path until she was beside the man in the hollow. A moment later, with his arm around her, she turned toward the house as though to send a last good-bye.

Then it was that Galoway stooped and very deliberately applied a match to the end of fuse that lay at his feet. For a moment he listened intently: then a sibilant response reached him as the black cord became a living thing that sent a troop of tiny sparks dancing toward the inert mass of earth. Quickly he stepped around the shoulder of the rock and waited.

Suddenly the earth surged slightly beneath his feet, as though awaking from slumber; and a muffled boom thudded against the deathlike quiet: the great incubus shuddered from end to end, as if throwing off some distasteful, detaining hand; and lifting itself over the slight hindrance, like a great tidal way of earth, crested high with its loot of trees and rocks, it leaped sheer off the edge and hurtled downward.

Below, the two heard the boom and the crash as the slide took the leap, and together raised their heads: it was only a matter of seconds, and minutes would not have sufficed. Quick as thought the man saw this: he divined that this was the end, and the manhood in him leaped to meet it. He turned with his arm still about the woman. All Heaven was one roaring cataclysm now. Standing close with heads high and breasts toward it, they waited; waited with that magnificent physical courage that is the heritage of all primitive people; waited for a space during which a steady heart might beat to ten— THEN—

Above, the destroyer stood watching his handiwork. At the unleashing of the slide he leaned forward eagerly; and as the certainty of his vengeance became manifest, his maimed visage twisted itself into a hideous snarl. Then, as the slide shot clear across the hollow and settled slowly back into place, filling it from pit to brim, he straightened up.

Had he been a pagan, Galoway, in that tremendous moment of conquest and justification, might have compared himself to Thor, with his destroying lightnings. Or, had he reached a higher sphere of soul development, the immensity of the weapon with which he administered his justice might have awakened in him at least a feeling akin to awe.

But, being Brute Galoway of Greybeard Mountain, in this, his supreme moment, there came to him now the pangs of physical hunger; and, spitting contemptuously out over the new-made grave, he snarled, "So yer would, would yer?"—and turned in search of a well filled can of lunch which certain toil-worn hands had prepared for him a brief five hours before.

FROM

Porgy

Part I

[Catfish Row and the Murder of Robbins]

Porgy lived in the Golden Age. Not the Golden Age of a remote and legendary past; nor yet the chimerical era treasured by every man past middle
life, that never existed except in the heart of youth; but an age when men, not
yet old, were boys in an ancient, beautiful city that time had forgotten before
it destroyed.

In this city there persisted the Golden Age of many things, and not the
least among them was that of beggary. In those days the profession was one
with a tradition. A man begged, presumably, because he was hungry, much as
a man of more energetic temperament became a stevedore from the same
cause. His plea for help produced the simple reactions of a generous impulse,
a movement of the hand, and the gift of a coin, instead of the elaborate and
terrifying processes of organized philanthropy. His antecedents and his
mental age were his own affair, and, in the majority of cases, he was as happily oblivious of one as of the other.

Had it all been otherwise, had Porgy come a generation, or even a score of
years, later, there would have been a reception of the old tragedy of genius
without opportunity. For, as the artist is born with vision of beauty, and the
tradesman with an eye for barter, so was Porgy equipped by a beneficent
providence for career of mendicancy. Instead of sturdy legs that would have
predestined him for the life of a stevedore on one of the great cotton wharves,

SOURCE: *Porgy* (New York: George H. Doran Co., 1925), 11–37, 76–96, 133–60, 174–96.

he had, when he entered the world, totally inadequate nether extremities, quick to catch the eye, and touch the ready sympathy of the passer-by. Either by birth, or through the application of a philosophy of life, he had acquired a personality that could not be ignored, one which at the same time interested and subtly disturbed. There was that about him which differentiated him from the hordes of fellow practitioners who competed with him for the notice of the tender-hearted. Where others bid eagerly for attention, and burst into voluble thanks and blessings, Porgy sat silent, rapt. There was something Eastern and mystic about the intense introspection of his look. He never smiled, and he acknowledged gifts only by a slow lifting of the eyes that had odd shadows in them. He was black with the almost purple blackness of unadulterated Congo blood. His hands were very large and muscular, and, even when flexed idly in his lap, seemed shockingly formidable in contrast to his frail body. Unless one were unusually preoccupied at the moment of dropping a coin in his cup, he carried away in return a very definite, yet somewhat disquieting, impression: a sense of infinite patience, and beneath it the vibration of unrealized, but terrific, energy.

No one knew Porgy's age. No one remembered when he first made his appearance among the ranks of the local beggars. A woman who had married twenty years before remembered him because he had been seated on the church steps, and had given her a turn when she went in.

Once a child saw Porgy, and said suddenly, "What is he waiting for?" That expressed him better than anything else. He was waiting, waiting with the concentrating intensity of a burning-glass.

As consistent in the practice of his profession as any of the business and professional men who were his most valued customers, Porgy was to be found any morning, by the first arrival in the financial district, against the wall of the old apothecary shop that stands at the corner of King Charles Street and The Meeting House Road. Long custom, reinforced by an eye for the beautiful, had endeared that spot to him. He would sit there in the cool of the early hours and look across the narrow thoroughfare into the green freshness of Jasper Square, where the children flew their kites, and played hide-and-seek among the shrubs. Then, when the morning advanced, and the sun poured its semi-tropical heat between the twin rows of brick, to lie impounded there, like a stagnant pool of flame, he would experience a pleasant atavistic calm, and would doze lightly under the terrific heat, as only a full-blooded negro can. Toward afternoon a slender blue shadow would commence to grow about him that would broaden with great rapidity, cool the baking flags, and turn the tide of customers home before his empty cup.

But Porgy best loved the late afternoons, when the street was quiet again, and the sunlight, deep with color, shot level over the low roof of the apothecary shop to paint the cream stucco on the opposite dwelling a ruddy gold and turn the old rain-washed tiles on the roof to burnished copper. Then the slender, white-clad lady who lived in the house would throw open the deep French windows of the second story drawing-room, and sitting at the piano, where Porgy could see her dimly, she would play on through the dusk until old Peter drove by with his wagon to carry him home.

PORGY had but one vice. With his day reduced to dead level of commonplace, he was by night an inveterate gambler. Each evening his collections were carefully divided into a minimum for room and food, and the remainder for the evening's game. Seen in the light of the smoking kerosene lamp, with the circle of excited faces about him, he was no longer the beggar in the dust. His stagnant blood leaped to sudden life. He was the peer of the great, hulking fellows who swung cotton bales and stank intolerably from labor in the fertilizer mills. He even knew that he had won their grudging respect, for he had a way of coaxing and wheedling the little ivory cubes that forced them to respond. The loud "Oh, my Baby," and explosive "Come seben," of his fellow gamesters seldom brought silver when he experienced that light, keen feeling and thought of the new, soft-spoken words to say. In those hours he lost his look of living in the future. While the ivories flew, he existed in an intense and burning present.

One Saturday night in late April, with the first premonitory breath of summer in the air, Porgy sat in the gaming circle that had gathered before his door in Catfish Row, and murmured softly to his gods of chance. All day he had been conscious of a vague unrest. There had been no breeze from the bay, and from his seat outside the apothecary shop the sky showed opaque bluegrey and bore heavily upon the town. Towards evening, a thunder-head had lifted over the western horizon and growled ominously; but it had passed, leaving the air hot, vitiated, and moist. The negroes had come in for the night feeling irritable, and, instead of the usual Saturday night of song and talk, the rooms were for the most part dark and silent, and the court deserted.

The game started late, and there were few players. Opposite Porgy, sitting upon his haunches, and casting his dice in moody silence, was a negro called Crown. He was a stevedore, had the body of a gladiator, and a bad name. His cotton-hook, hanging from his belt by a thong, gleamed in the lamplight, and rang a clear note on the flags when he leant forward to throw. Crown had been drinking with Robbins, who sat next to him, and the air was rank with the effluvium of vile corn whisky. Robbins was voluble, and as usual, when in liquor, talked incessantly of his wife and children, of whom he was inordinately proud. He was a good provider, and, except for his Saturday night drink and game, of steady habits.

"Dat lady ob mine is a born white-folks nigger," he boasted. "She fambly belong tuh Gob'ner Rutledge sheself come tuh visit she when she sick? An' dem chillen ob mine, dem is raise wid *ways.*"

"Yo' bes sabe yo' tak for dem damn dice. Dice ain't gots no patience wid 'oman!" cut in a young negro of the group.

"Da's de trut'," called another. "Dey is all two after de same nigger money. Dat mek um can't git 'long."

"Shet yo' damn mout' an' t'row!" growled Crown.

Robbins, taken aback, rolled the dice hastily. Scarcely had they settled before Crown scooped them fiercely into his great hand, and, swearing foully at them, sent them tumbling out across the faintly illuminated circle, to lose them on the first cast. Then Porgy took them up tenderly, and held them for a moment cupped in his muscular, slim-fingered hand.

"Oh, little stars, roll me some light!" he sang softly; made a pass, and won. "Roll me a sun an' moon!" he urged; and again the cubes did his bidding.

"Porgy witch dem dice," Crown snarled, as he drained his flask and sent it shattering against the pavement.

Under the beetling walls of the tenement the game went swiftly forward. In a remote room several voices were singing drowsily, as though burdened by the oppression of the day. In another part of the building some one was picking a guitar monotonously, chord after chord, until the dark throbbed like an old wound. But the players were oblivious of all except the splash of orange light that fell upon the flags, and the living little cubes that flashed or dawdled upon it, according to the mood of hand that propelled them. Peter, the old wagoner, sat quietly smoking in Porgy's doorway, and looked on with the indulgent smile of tolerant age. Once when Crown lost heavily, and turned snarling upon Robbins with, "T'row dem damn dice fair, nigger," he cautioned mildly, "Frien' an' licker an' dice ain't meant tuh 'sociate. Yo' mens bes' go slow."

Then, in a flash, it happened.

Robbins rolled again, called the dice, and retrieved them before Crown's slow wits got the count, then swept the heap of coins into his pocket.

With a low snarl, straight from his crouching position, Crown hurled his tremendous weight forward, shattering the lamp, and bowling Robbins over against the wall. Then they were up and facing each other. The oil from the broken lamp settled between two flags and blazed up ruddily. Crown was crouched for a second spring, with lips drawn from gleaming teeth. The light fell strong upon thrusting jaw, and threw the sloping brow into shadow. One hand touched the ground lightly, balancing the massive torso. The other arm held the cotton-hook forward, ready, like a prehensile claw. In comparison Robbins was pitifully slender and inadequate. There was a single desperate moment of indecision; then he took his only chance. Like a thrown spear, he hurled his lithe body forward under the terrifying hook, and clinched. Down, down, down the centuries they slid. Clothes could not hold them. Miraculously the tawny, ridged bodies tore through the thin coverings. Bronze ropes and bars slid and wove over great shoulders. Bright, ruddy planes leaped out on backs in the fire flare, then were gulped by sliding shadows. A heady, bestial stench absorbed all other odors. A fringe of shadowy watchers crept from cavernous doorways, sensed it, and commenced to wail eerily. Backward and forward, in a space no larger than a small room, the heaving, inseparable mass rocked and swayed. Breath labored like steam. At times the fused single body would thrust out a rigid arm, or the light would point out, for one hideous second, a tortured, mad face. Again the mass would rise as though propelled a short distance from the earth, topple, and crash down upon the pavement with a jarring impact.

Such terrific expenditure of human energy could not last. The end came quickly, and with startling suddenness. Crown broke his adversary's weakening hold, and held him the length of one mighty arm. The other swung the cotton-hook downward. Then he dropped his victim, and swaggered drunkenly toward the street. Even to the most inexperienced the result would have been obvious. Robbins was dead: horribly dead.

A scream rose to a crescendo of unendurable agony, and a woman broke through the circle of spectators and cast herself upon the body. The fire flickered to a faint, blue flame, unearthly, terrifying.

Porgy shivered violently, whimpered in the gloom; then drew himself across his threshold and closed the door.

CATFISH ROW, in which Porgy lived, was not a row at all, but a great brick structure that lifted it three stories about the three sides of a court. The fourth side was partly closed by a high wall, surmounted by jagged edges of broken glass set firmly in old lime plaster, and pierced in its center by a wide entrance-way. Over the entrance there still remained a massive grill of Italian wrought iron, and a battered capital of marble surmounted each of the lofty gate-posts. The court itself was paved with large flag-stones, which even beneath the accumulated grime of a century, glimmered with faint and varying pastel shades in direct sunlight. The south wall, which was always in shadow, was lichened from pavement to rotting gutter; and opposite the northern face, unbroken except by rows of small-paned windows, showed every color through its flaking stucco, and, in summer a steady blaze of scarlet from rows of geraniums that bloomed in old vegetable tins upon every window-sill.

Within the high-ceilinged rooms, with their battered colonial mantels and broken decorations of Adam designs in plaster, governors had come and gone, and ambassadors of kings had schemed and danced. Now before the gaping entrance lay only a narrow, cobbled street, and beyond, a tumbled wharf used by negro fishermen. Only the bay remained unchanged. Beyond the litter of the wharf, it stretched to the horizon, taking its mood from the changing skies; always different—invariably the same.

Directly within the entrance of the Row, and having upon the street a single bleary window, wherein were displayed plates of fried fish, was the "cook-shop" which catered to the residents of the tenement.

Porgy's room was opposite the shop and enjoyed the great advantage of having a front window that commanded the street and harbor, and an inner door where he could sit and enter into the life of the court. To him, the front window signified adventure, the door—home.

IT WAS PORGY'S CUSTOM, when the day's work was done and he had exchanged a part of his collections for his evening meal of fish and bread, to sit at his front window and watch the world pass by. The great cotton wharves lay up the river, beyond the Row; and when the cotton season was on, he loved to sit in the dusk and see the drays go by. They would sweep into view with a loud thunder of wheels on the cobbles; and from his low seat they loomed huge and mysterious in the gathering dark. Sometimes there would be twenty of them in a row, with great swiftly-stepping mules, crouched figures of drivers, and bales piled toweringly above them. Always Porgy experienced a vague and not unpleasant fear when the drays swung past. There was power, vast, awe-inspiring; it could so easily crush him were he in its path. But here, safe within his window, he could watch it with perfect safety. At times when the train was unusually long, the sustained, rhythmic thunder and the sweep of form after form past his window produced an odd pleasurable detachment in his mind, and pictures of strange things and places would brighten and fade. But the night following the killing, the window was closed, and through the open door behind him beat the rhythm of a dirge from Robbins' room.

"What de matter, chillen?" came the strophe. And the antistrophe swelled to the answer:

"Pain gots de body, an' I can't stan' still."

Porgy sat upon his floor counting the day's collection: one dollar and twenty cents. It had been a good day. Perhaps the sorrow that had brooded over his spirit had quickened the sympathy of the passer-by.

"What de matter, Sister?"

"Jesu gots our brudder, an' I can't stan' still."

Ever since Porgy had come home the air had swung to the rhythm of the chant. He divided his pile into equal portions, and commenced to pocket one. The burden swayed out again.

"Pain gots de body, an' I can't stan' still."

He hesitated a moment, poured all the coins together again, selected a twenty-five-cent piece which he put into his pocket, and, taking the remainder in his hand, went out and drew himself across the short distance to the room of mourning.

The body lay upon a bed in the corner of the room, sheeted to the eyes, and upon its breast rested a large blue saucer. Standing in a circle about the bed, or seated upon the floor, backs to the wall, were a score of negroes, some singing, and others swaying, patting the floor with their feet. For not a single moment since the body had been laid out had the rhythm slackened. With each hour it gathered weight until it seemed to swing the massive structure.

Porgy had heard that Robbins had left no burial insurance, the customary Saturday night festivities having consumed the slender margin between daily wage and immediate need. Now, at sight of the saucer, he knew the rumor had not erred. It had been an old custom among penniless negroes to prepare the corpse thus, then to sing dirges until neighborhood sympathy provided the wherewithal for proper interment. Recent years had introduced the insurance agent and the "buryin' lodge," and the old custom had fallen into disuse. It had even become a grievous reproach to have a member of the family a "saucer-buried nigger."

At the foot of the bed, bowed by the double weight of sorrow and disgrace, the widow sat swaying to the rhythm like a beach palm in the ebb and flow of a bleak sea wind.

The sight of her grief, the close room, the awful presence beneath the sheet, and the unceasing pulse of sound that beat against his ears, all contributed to stir a strange desire into being within Porgy. Suddenly he threw his head back and wailed long and quaveringly. In rushed a vast feeling of relief. He wailed again, emptied his handful of small coins into the saucer, and sank to the floor at the head of the bed. Presently he commenced to croon with the others, and a sense of exaltation flooded his being, compelling him from the despair of the dirge to a more triumphant measure.

"Oh, I gots a little brudder in de new grabe-yahd. What outshine de sun," he sang.

Without missing the beat the chorus shifted: "An' I'll meet um in the primus lan'."

Then came a rude interruption. A short yellow negro bustled into the room. His voice was low, oily, and penetrating. He was dressed entirely in black, and had an air of great importance. The song fell away to scarcely more than a throbbing silence. The man crossed the room to where the widow sat huddled at the foot of the bed, and touched her shoulder. She raised a face like a burned out ember.

"How de saucer stan' now, my sister?" he whispered, at the same time casting an appraising glance toward the subject of his inquiry.

"Dere ain't but fifteen dollar," she replied in a flat, despairing voice.

"An' he gots tuh git buried termorrer," called an awed voice, "or de boahd ob healt' will take um, an' give um tuh de students."

The widow's scream shrilled wildly. She rose to her knees and clutched the man's hand between both of hers. "Oh, fuh Gawd's sake bury um in de grabe-yahd. I goin' tuh pay yuh ebery cent."

For a second even the rhythm ceased, leaving an aching suspense in the air. Watchers waited tensely. Wide eyes, riveted on the man's face, pleaded silently. Presently his professional manner slipped from him. "All right, Sister," he said simply. "Wid de box, an' one ca'age it will cost me more dan twenty-five. But I'll see yuh t'rough. Yuh can all be ready at eight tumorruh. It's a long trip tuh de cemetery."

The woman relaxed silently across the foot of the bed, her head between her outflung arms. Then from the narrow confines of the room, the song beat up and out triumphantly:

"Oh, I gots a little brudder in de new grabe-yahd. What outshine de sun!"

The rhythm swelled, and voices in the court and upper rooms took it up, until the deeply-rooted old walls seemed to rock and surge with the sweep of it.

In the cool of the early morning, the procession took its departure for the cemetery that lay beyond the city limits to the north. First went the dilapidated hearse, with its rigid wooden plumes, and faded black velvet draperies that nodded and swayed inside the plate glass panels. Then followed the solitary carriage, in which could be seen massed black accentuated by several pairs of white cotton gloves held to lowered eyes. Behind the carriage came the mourners in a motley procession of wagons and buggies that had been borrowed for the occasion.

Porgy drove with Peter, and four women, seated on straight chairs in the wagon behind them, completed their company. From time to time a long-drawn wail would rise from one of the conveyances, to be taken up and passed back from wagon to wagon like a dismal echo.

Moving from the negro district into the wide thoroughfare of Meeting House Road, with its high buildings and its white faces that massed and scattered on the pavement, the cortège appeared almost grotesque, with the odd fusion of comedy and tragedy so inextricably a part of negro life in its deep moments.

The fat German who kept the shop on the corner of King Charles Street and Summer Road, called his clerk from the depths of the building, and their stomachs shook with laughter. But the little, dark Russian Jew in the next shop, who dealt in abominably smelling clothing, gave them a reproving look, and disappeared indoors.

The cemetery lay several miles beyond the city limits. The lot was bare of trees, but among the graves many bright flowering weeds masked the ugliness of the troubled earth. To the eastward a wide marsh stretched away to a far, bright line of sea. Westward, ploughed fields swept out to a distant forest of yellow pine. From the sea to the far tree tops, the sky swung a dizzy arch of thin blue, high in the center of which several buzzards hung motionless, watching.

In the vast emptiness of the morning the little procession crawled out to the edge of the broken wooden fence that marked the enclosure, and stopped.

By the time the last wagon had arrived, the cheap pine casket was resting upon battens over the grave, and the preacher, robed in white, was preparing to commence the service.

The mourners gathered close about the grave.

"Death, ain't yuh gots no shame?" called a clear, high, soprano voice; and immediately the mortal embodiment of infinite sorrow broke and swayed about the grave in the funeral chant. Three times the line swung its curve of song, shrill, keen, agonizing; then it fell away to a heart-wrenching minor on the burden:

> "Take dis man an' gone—gone.
> Death, ain't yuh gots no shame?"

When the singing ceased, the burial service commenced, the preacher extemporizing fluently. Taking his rhythm from the hymn, he poured his words along its interminable reiteration until the cumulative effect rocked the entire company.

The final moment of the ritual arrived. The lid was removed from the casket, and the mourners were formed into line to pass and look upon the face of the dead. A very old, bent negress went first. She stooped, then suddenly, with a shriek of anguish, cast herself beside the coffin.

"Tell Peter tuh hold de do' open fuh me. I's comin' soon!" she cried.

"Yes, Gawd, goin' soon," responded a voice in the crowd. Others pressed about the grave, and the air was stabbed by scream on scream. Grief spent itself freely, terrifyingly.

Slowly the clashing sounds merged into the regular measure of a spiritual. Beautiful and poignant it rose, swelling out above the sounds of falling earth as the grave was filled:

> "What yuh goin' ter do when yuh
> come out de wilderness,
> Come out de wilderness,

Come out de wilderness;
What yuh goin' ter do when yuh
Come out de wilderness
Leanin' on my Lord.

"Leanin' on my Lord,
Leanin' on my Lord,
Leanin' on my Lord
Who died on Calvary."

The music faded away in vague, uncertain minors. The mood of the crowd changed almost tangibly. There was an air of restless apprehension. Nervous glances were directed toward the entrance. Peter, always sagacious, unless taken unawares, had conferred in advance with Porgy about this moment. When he had helped him from the wagon, he had stationed him just inside the fence, where he could be lifted quickly into the road.

"De las' man in de grabe-yahd goin' tuh be de nex' one tuh git buried," he had reminded his friend.

Now, as the final shovelful of earth was thrown upon the grave, he came running to Porgy, and lifted him quickly into the road. Behind them broke a sudden earth-shaking burst of sound, as of the stampeding of many cattle, and past them the mourners swept, stumbling, fighting for room; some assisting weaker friends, others fighting savagely to be free of the enclosure. In the center of the crowd, plunging forward with robes flying, was the preacher. In an incredibly short time the lot was cleared. Then, from a screening bush near the grave, arose the old negress who had been the first to wail out her grief. She had lain there forgotten, overcome by the storm of her emotion. She tottered feebly in to the road. "Nebber you min', Sister," the preacher assured her comfortingly. "Gawd always lub de righteous."

Dazed, and much pleased at the attention that she was receiving, while still happily unmindful of its cause, the old woman smiled a vaguer smile, and was hoisted into the wagon.

During the funeral the sun had disappeared behind clouds that had blown in swiftly from the sea, and now a scurry of large drops swept over the vehicles, and trailed away across the desolate graves.

"Dat's all right now fer Robbins," commented Porgy. "Gawd done sen' he rain already fuh wash he feet-steps offen dis eart'."

"Oh, yes, Brudder!" contributed a woman's voice; and, "Amen, my Jedus!" added another.

IN THE EARLY afternoon of the day of the funeral, Porgy sat in his doorway communing with Peter. The old man was silent for awhile, his grizzled head bowed, and an expression of brooding tenderness upon his lined face.

"Robbins war a good man," he reflected at length, "an' dat nigger, Crown, war a killer, an' fuhebber gettin' intuh trouble. Yet, dere lie Robbins, wid he wife an' fadderless chillen; an' Crown done gone he ways tuh do de same t'ing ober again somewheres else."

"Gone fuh true. I reckon he done loose now on Kittiwar Islan', in dem palmettuh t'icket; an' de rope ain't nebber make fuh ketch um an' hang um." Porgy stopped suddenly, and motioned with his head toward someone who had just entered the court. The new arrival was a white man of stocky build, wearing a wide-brimmed hat, and a goatee. He was swinging a heavy cane, and he crossed the court directly and paused before the two. For a moment he stood looking down at them with brows drawn fiercely together. Then he drew back his coat, exhibiting a police badge, and a heavy revolver in a breast holster.

Peter shook violently, and his eyes rolled in his head. He made an ineffectual effort to speak, tried again, and finally said, "'Fore Gawd, Boss, I ain't nebber done it."

Like a flash, the pistol was out of its holster, and pointing between his eyes. "Who did it, then?" snapped the man.

"Crown, Boss. I done see him do um," Peter cried in utter panic.

The man laughed shortly. "I thought so," he said. Then he turned to Porgy. "You saw it too, eh?"

There was panic in Porgy's face, and in his lap his hands had clinched upon each other. But his eyes were fixed upon the paving. He drew a deep breath, and waited.

A flare of anger swept the face above him. "Come. Out with it. I don't want to have to put the law on you."

Porgy's only answer was a slight tremor that shook the hands in his lap. The detective's face darkened, and sweat showed under his hat-brim. Suddenly his temper bolted.

"Look at me, you damned nigger!" he shouted.

Slowly the sitting figure before him relaxed, almost it seemed, muscle by muscle. At last the hands fell apart, and lay flexed and idle. Finally Porgy raised eyes that had become hard and impregnable as onyx. They met the angry glare that beat down upon them without flinching. After a long moment, he spoke slowly, and with great quietness.

"I ain't know nuttin' 'bout um. I been inside, asleep on my bed, wid de do' closed."

"You're a damn liar," the man snapped.

He shrilled a whistle, and two policemen entered.

"He saw the killing," the detective said, indicating Peter. "Take him along, and lock him up as a material witness."

"How about the cripple?" asked one of the officers.

"He could not have helped seeing it," the man said sourly. "That's his room right there. But I can't make him come through. But it don't matter. One's enough to hang Crown, if we ever get him. Come, get the old man in the wagon."

The policeman lifted the shaking old negro to his feet. "Come along, Uncle. It ain't going to be as bad for you as Crown, anyway," encouraged one of them. Then the little party passed out of the entrance, leaving Porgy alone.

From the street sounded the shrill gong of the patrol wagon, followed by the beat of swiftly receding hoofs upon the cobbles.

TEN DAYS had passed since the detective had taken Peter away. For a week the wagon had waited under the tottering shed, and the dejected old horse had subsisted upon a varied diet brought to him by the friends of his absent master. Then a man had come and taken the outfit away. In answer to the protests of the negroes, he had exhibited a contract, dated three years previous, by which Peter was to pay two dollars a week for an indefinite period, on an exorbitant purchase price. Failure to pay any installment would cause the property to revert to the seller. It all looked thoroughly legal. And so the dilapidated old rig rattled over the cobbles and departed.

Then the man from the installment furniture house came. He was a vile-mouthed, bearded Teuton, and swore so fiercely that no one dared to protest when he loaded Peter's furniture on his truck and drove away.

Now there remained in a corner of Porgy's room, where he had taken them into custody, only a battered leather trunk, a chromo of "The Great Emancipator," and a bundle of old clothes; mute reminders of their kindly and gentle old owner.

From Part III

[Porgy, Bess, and Sportin' Life]

[The cotton season has passed and it is now summer. Peter has been freed from jail and "Crown's Bess" has returned to Catfish Row. Porgy falls in love with her and takes her in.]

THE CHANGE IN PORGY, which Peter had been first to notice, was now apparent to all who knew him. The defensive barrier of reserve that he had built about his life was down. The long hours when he used to sit fixed and tense, with the look of introspection upon his face, were gone. Even the most skeptical of the women were beginning to admit that Bess was making him a good mate. Not that they mingled freely with other residents of the court. On the contrary, they seemed strangely sufficient unto themselves in the midst of the intensely gregarious life that was going on about them. Porgy's earnings were adequate to their modest needs, and Bess was always up and out with the first of the women, and among them all there was none who could bargain more shrewdly with the fishermen and hucksters who sold their wares on the wharf.

Like Porgy, Bess had undergone a subtle change that became more evident from day to day. Her gaunt figure had rounded out, bringing back a look of youthful comeliness, and her face was losing its hunted expression. The air of pride that had always shown in her bearing, which had amounted almost to disdain, that had so infuriated the virtuous during her evil days, was heightened, and, in her bettered condition forced a resentful respect from her feminine traducers.

One morning while she was doing her marketing on the wharf, one of the river men who had known her in the past, hailed her too familiarly. He was at that moment stepping from the top round of a ladder on to the wharf.

"How 'bout ternight?" he asked with a leer.

She was holding a string of whiting in her left hand, and was hanging upon the final penny of a bargain with the fisherman. She half turned, and delivered a resounding slap with her right hand. The man staggered backward, hung for a moment, then vanished. There was a tremendous splash from the shallow water.

"Twenty cent fuh dis string, an' not one cent mo'," Bess continued coolly to the fisherman.

He accepted the price. Bess gave him eighteen cents and a hard look. He counted the money, glanced at the hand that had flung innocently against her apron, then laughed.

"Just as yuh say, Sister. I ain't quarrelin' none wid *yuh dis* mornin'."

Bess gave him one of the faint, cryptic smiles that always made men friends and women enemies for her, and departed for Catfish Row, as if nothing had happened to break the dull routine of the morning's chores.

SATURDAY NIGHT, and the court had flung off its workaday clothes and mood. In the corner by Serena's washbench a small intimate circle had gathered about a smoking kerosene lamp. Several women sat on the bench with drowsy little negroes in their laps. A man near the light leaned over a guitar, with a vague wistfulness in his face, and plucked successive chords with a swift, running vibrance of sound. Then a deep baritone hummed for a second and raised an air:

> "Ain't it hahd tuh be a nigger;
> Ain't it hahd tuh be a nigger;
> Ain't it hahd tuh be a nigger;
> 'Cause yuh can't git yo' rights w'en yuh do.
>
> "I was sleepin' on a pile ob lumber,
> Jus' as happy as uh man kin be,
> W'en a w'ite man come wake me from my slumber,
> An' he say, 'Yuh gots tuh work now, 'cause yuh free!'"

Then they were all in on the chorus:

> "Ain't it hahd tuh be a nigger,"

and the gloom hummed with the low, close harmonies.

In another corner the crap circle had gathered. Porgy's delight in the game had not waned with his increasing interests, and he sat fondling the white cubes, and whispering to them in his old confidential manner.

"Little w'ite babies," he crooned, "come sing fuh di nigger."

He cast—and won.

Gathering the heap of pennies and nickels, he passed them behind him to Bess, who squatted in the shadows. She took the money in silence, counted

it, dropped it into her apron pocket, and continued to watch the game intently, smiling her cryptic smile when Porgy won, but saying scarcely anything at all.

The negro known as Sportin' Life had come in just as the game was commencing, and had sat in. That he was not altogether above suspicion was evidenced by the fact that the circle of men refused to allow him to use his own
dice, and told him so frankly. He scowled at them, dropped the dice back into
his pocket, and started to leave. Then he seemed to think better of it, and
joined the circle.

As the game proceeded it became evident that Porgy's luck was with him;
he was the most consistent winner, and Sportin' Life was bearing most of the
burden. But the mulatto was too good a gambler to evince any discomfiture.
He talked steadily, laughed much, and missed no opportunity to drop in a
sly word of suspicion when Porgy drew in a pot. There was nothing that
could be taken up and resented, but Porgy was mystified, and Bess's face
was dark with anger more than once. He had a way of leaning over just as
Porgy cast, and placing his face almost on the flags so he could see under the
dice when they struck. Then he would look up, laugh meaningly in Porgy's
face, and clap his hands as though the cripple had managed something very
cleverly.

When the game finally broke up it was clear that he had poisoned the
minds of the company, and the good nights lacked their usual warmth.

Bess reached into her apron pocket, and drew out the evening's winnings.
The coins made quite a little weight in her hand. A late fragment of moon
swung over the wall and poured its diminished light into her open palm. She
commenced to count the money. Porgy left her, and drew himself into his
room. She proceeded to count, absorbed in her task.

"PORGY LUCKY," said a low voice beside her. "Mus' be yer gots two dollar
dere fer um." Sportin' Life lifted his elegant trousers, so that the knees would
not bag, and squatted on the flags at her side. He removed his stiff straw hat,
with its bright band, and spun it between his hands. The moonlight was full
upon his face, with its sinister, sensuous smile.

She looked at him squarely a moment, then said in a cold, level voice:

"I can't 'member ebber meetin' a nigger dat I like less dan I does you."

"Thank yer kindly," he replied, not in the least degree daunted. "But jus'
de same, I wants ter be frien' wid yer. Me and you ain't usen ter dese small-

town slow ways. We ain't been above seein' night-life what is night-life, an' I jus' wants ter talk to you now and den; dat's all."

"I gots no time fuh talk," she told him. "an' wut mo', I t'rough wid de kin' ob nights you is t'inking 'bout."

"No mo' red-eye; none 'tall?" he queried. "Nebber gits t'irsty, eh?"

"Yes, Gawd knows, I does git t'irsty now and den," she said impulsively; then added sharply, "But I done t'rough now, I tells yer; I done t'rough."

She arose to go. "Yo' kin' mek me sick," she told him; "an' I ain't wants tuh hab no mo' talk wid yuh."

He got spryly to his feet, and stood beside her. "Oh, come on, le's let by-gone be bygone, an' be frien'." Then his voice became low and ingratiating: "Come; gimme yer han', Sister," he said.

Acquiescent, but mystified, she held out her open palm.

He poured a little pile of white powder into it. There it lay in the moon-light, very clean and white on her dark skin. "Hapy dus'!" she said, and her voice was like a gasp. "Take dat t'ing away, nigger. I t'rough wid um, I tells yuh." But she did not turn her hand over and let it fall upon the ground.

"Jus' a little touch fer ole time sake," he whispered. "'Tain't 'nough ter hurt er fly. An' it ain't goin' ter cos' yer one cent."

She stood a moment longer, and her hand trembled, spilling a few grains between her fingers. Then suddenly she clapped her palm over her mouth. Whern she took it away it was quite empty.

Sportin' Life heaved a sigh of relief, turned and leant against the wall—and waited.

In the corner by Serena's bench the party was breaking up. Only a few women were left, and instead of the blur of general talk, remarks leapt clear. They were discussing the crap game that had just closed.

"Dey is some'ting berry queer 'bout de way de money always go tuh de same place," a voice was saying.

The moonlight ebbed from the corner where Bess and Sportin' Life stood. Five minutes had passed since she had made her sudden decisive gesture. She stood oddly rigid, with her hands clenched at her sides.

Abruptly she spun around. "Yuh gots mo' ob dat?" Her voice was low and taut.

"Sho' I has!" came the answer, with a confident laugh. "But it don't come cheap. Gimme dat money yer got dere."

Silently she held out her hand, and poured the coins into his palm.

He gave her a small folded paper.

"I got more ob dat when yer needs it," he said, as he turned away.

But she did not hear him. She snatched the paper, opened it, and threw the contents into her mouth.

The court was sinking to sleep. One by one the lighted windows went blank. The women at the washbench got to their feet. One yawned noisily, and another knocked her clay pipe out on the flags in a shower of sparks. Then a voice came clearly—the one that had complained before about the crap game.

"I ain't sayin' ef it conjer, er jus' plain loaded dice. All I gots tuh say is dat dam nigger, Porgy, steal my Sam' wages off him now t'ree week runnin'."

Out of the shadows and across the moonlit square a figure flashed, gesturing wildly.

The women leapt back. The one who had done the talking screamed once, the shrill not echoing around the walls. The advancing figure closed convulsive hands upon her shoulders and snatched her body forward. Wide, red-lit eyes glared into her face. A voice half sobbed, half screamed, "Yuh say dat 'bout Porgy? Yuh say Porgy is t'ief?"

The victim was young and strong. She tore the hands from her shoulders and raised her arms before her face. One of the other women reached out to seize the intruder, but was met with a glare so insanely malignant that she retreated screaming.

Above them windows were leaping to light. Dark bodies strained from sills. Feet sounded, running down dilapidated stairways. A shrill, long, terrifying shriek cut across the growing noise, and the women clenched and fell. Bystanders rushed to intervene and became involved. Always in the center of the storm a mad woman whirled like a dervish and called horribly upon her God, striking and clawing wildly.

The babel became terrific. The entire population of the court contributed to the general confusion. In the rooms above, children wailed out a nameless terror.

Suddenly over the tumult sounded the gong of the patrol wagon, and through the gateway half-a-dozen policemen advanced with pistols out, and clubs ready.

The uproar stopped suddenly at its peak. Shadows dropped back and were gulped by deeper shadow. Feet made no sound in retreating. Solid bodies became fluid, sliding. Yawning doorways drew them in. Miraculously the court was transformed into a vacant, walled square, in which stood six erect figures, looking a little theatrical and foolish with their revolvers and clubs, and a woman who shook menacing hands at nothing at all and swore huskily at phantoms.

"No trouble finding the cause of disturbance," said an authoritative voice. "Get her, men. Better use bracelets. Can't tell about dope cases."

The squad closed quickly. For a moment a grotesque shadow tumbled and shifted in the center of the court; then a voice said, "Steady now." The mass broke into individual figures, and, under the ebbing moonlight, moved toward the entrance with a manacled woman in their midst.

Porgy had opened his door at the first outcry and sat on the sill trying to get the import of the disturbance. Now, as the group passed close to him he looked up. The woman had ceased her outcry, and was looking about with vague, unseeing eyes. As they walked past his doorway, so close that he could have touched the nearest officer with his hand, she looked down, and her gaze focused upon the sitting figure. Her body stiffened, and her head lifted with the old, incongruous gesture of disdain.

"Bess!" called Porgy once very loudly; and again, in a voice that sagged, "Bess!"

One of the policemen paused and looked down upon the speaker. But the woman turned deliberately away, and he hastened to rejoin the party. Then the wagon clanged down the darkened street.

UNDER THE GAS LIGHT that supplemented a far, dusty window in the Recorder's Court, stood Bess. She swayed, and her face twitched occasionally; but her glance was level, and her head erect.

Behind a high desk sat a man well past middle age. His florid complexion caused his long grey mustache to appear very white. His eyes were far apart and suggested a kindness that was born of indolence rather than of wide compassion. His hands were slender and beautifully made, and he sat with elbows on desk, and finger-tips touching. When he spoke it was in a drawl that suggested weariness.

"What is the charge, Officer?" he asked.

"Bein' under the influence of dope, an' creatin' a disturbance in Catfish Row, yer Honor," replied the policeman who stood by the prisoner.

"Anybody hurt?"

"Not as we was able to see, yer Honor."

The judge turned to the prisoner.

"Have you ever been here before?"

"No, suh," came the reply in a low, clear tone.

"The officer of the day thinks she has, yer Honor," put in the policeman, "but he can't swear to it. She looks like a hundred others, he says, scar and all; an' they change names so fast you get nothing from the records."

The judge regarded the prisoner with amiability. The thermometer on the wall registered ninety. It was asking too much of good-nature to require it to subvert itself in such heat.

"I suppose we will have to give you the benefit of the doubt," he said. Then he turned to the officer.

"After all, it's the man who sold her the poison we want. I was kept here three hours yesterday by dope cases. I want it put a stop to."

He contracted his brows at a weak attempt at sternness, and directly a steady gaze at Bess.

"Who sold you that dope?"

She met his eyes squarely.

"I don't t'ink I know um again," she said in a low, even tone. "I buy from um in de dark, las' night, an' he gone off right away."

"It's no use, Your Honor," put in the policeman. "They won't give each other away."

The judge fixed the culprit with a long scrutiny. Then he asked:

"Have you any money to pay a fine?"

"No, suh. Yuh'll jus' hab tuh gib' me my time."

A man entered the room.

"I beg your pardon, Your Honor," he said, "but there is a cripple outside in a goatcart who says he is prepared to pay the woman's fine."

"Eh; what's that?" exclaimed the judge. "Is it that black scoundrel, Porgy, the beggar?"

"That's him, Yer Honor," replied the man, with a grin.

"Why, the highwayman takes a dime from me every time I venture on King Charles Street. And here he has the audacity to come and offer to pay a fine."

"Don't tek he money, Boss."

The prisoner said the words steadily, then caught her lower lip with her strong, white teeth.

"Address the Court as 'Your Honor,' not 'Boss,'" ordered the judge.

"Yo' Honuh," amended the culprit.

For a long moment the Recorder sat, his brow contracted. Then he drew a large, cool, linen handkerchief from his pocket and mopped his face.

"Go out and take ten dollars from the beggar," he told the policeman. "It's a small fine for the offence." Then turning to the woman, he said:

"I am going to lock you up for ten days; but any time you give the name of that dope peddler to the jailor you can leave. Do you understand?"

Bess had nothing to say in reply, and after a moment the policeman took her by the arm.

"This way to the wagon," he directed, and led her from the court room.

The street was a blaze of early morning sun, and the woman covered her eyes with her hand. The wagon stood, step to curb, and the officer hurried her across the narrow pavement and into the conveyance.

The bell clanged, and the heavy horse flung its weight against the collar.

Something impelled Bess to remove her hand and to look down.

Below the high side of the patrol, looking rather like a harbor tug beside an ocean liner, stood the goat-cart. For a moment she looked into Porgy's face. It told her nothing, except that he seemed suddenly to have grown older, and that the real Porgy, who had looked out at her from the eyes for a little while, had gone back into his secret places and closed the door.

The wagon lunged forward.

Then Porgy spoke.

"How long?" he called.

The incessant clamor of the gong commenced, and the hoofs beat their noisy tattoo upon the stones.

Bess raised both hands with fingers extended.

The wagon rounded a corner and disappeared.

The jail in which Bess was incarcerated was no better, and no worse, than many of the others of its period, and the score of negro women with whom she found herself could not be said to suffer acutely under their imprisonment. When life reaches a certain level of misery, it envelops itself in a protective anesthesia which deadens the senses to extremes; and having no tasks to perform, the prisoners awaited the expiration of their brief sentences with sodden patience, or hastened the passage of time with song.

By day they were at liberty to exercise in the jail yard, a square of about half an acre surrounded by a high brick wall, containing not so much as a single blade of grass. Like a great basin, the yard caught and held the heat which poured from the August sun until it seemed to overflow the rim, and

quiver, as though the immense vessel had been jarred from without. But the
soaring walls gave always a narrow strip of shade to which the prisoners clung,
moving around the sides as the day advanced, with the accuracy of the hand
of a sundial.

Before nightfall the prisoners were herded into the steaming interior of the
building, and Bess and the other women were locked in a steel cage, which
resembled a large dog-pound and stood in the centre of a high, square room,
with a passageway around it. A peculiarly offensive moisture clung to the ceil-
ing, and streamed in little rivulets down the walls. An almost unbreathable
stench clogged the atmosphere.

The jailers were not vindictive. They were not even unkind. Some of them
evidenced a mild affection for their charges, and would pause to exchange
greetings with them on their rounds. But it would have meant effort to better
the living conditions, and effort on the part of a white warden in August was
not to be considered. They locked them up, gave them a sufficiency of hominy
and white pork to sustain life, allowed them to see their visitors, talk, and sing
to their heart's content. If they were suffering from tuberculosis, or one of a
hundred nameless and communicable diseases, when they entered, it was
none of the County's affair. And if they left showing that ash-pallor so unmistakable in a negro, it was as lamentable as it was unavoidable. But when all
was said and done, what must one expect if one added to the handicap of a
dark skin the indiscretion of swallowing cocaine and indulging in a crap game?

Bess received but one visitor during her imprisonment. When the callers
were admitted, on the day following her arrival, Maria loomed in the centre
of the small, timid group. She went directly to Bess where she sat by the wall,
with her eyes closed against the glare. The big negress wore an expression of
solicitude, and her voice was low and surprisingly gentle as she said:

"Porgy ask me tuh bring yer dis blanket fuh lie on, an' dese fish an' bread.
How yuh is feelin' now?" Then she bent over and placed a bundle in the prisoner's lap.

Bess opened her eyes in surprise.

"I ain't been expectin' no fabors off none ob you folks," she replied. "How
come yuh tuh care ef I lib er die, attuh dat row I mek?"

Maria lowered herself to a seat beside her.

"I lubs dat nigger, Porgy, lak he been my chile," she told her. "An' wut mo',
I t'ink I know what happen tuh yuh."

"Wut yuh know?"

"I been in my do' dat night; an' I seen dat skunk, Sportin' Life, sell yuh dat stuff. Ef I had er known den wut it wuz, I'd a been hyuh long side ob yuh now fuh murder."

After a moment, she asked: "Wut mek yuh don't tell de jailluh who done um, an' come on home?"

Bess remained silent for a moment; then she raised her head and looked into the eyes of the older woman.

"I's a 'oman grown. Ef I tek dope, dat muh own business. Ef I ebber gits muh han' on dat nigger, I goin' fix um so he own mammy ain't know um! But I ain't gib um 'way tuh de w'ite folks."

The hard lines about her mouth softened, and, in scarcely more than a whisper, she added:

"I gots tuh be decent 'bout somet'ing, 'less I couldn't go back an' look in Porgy face."

Maria got heavily to her feet. The other visitors were leaving, and she longed to be free of the high, brick walls. She dropped a hand on Bess's shoulder.

"Yuh do right, Sister. But ef dat yalluh nigger come tuh Catfish Row agin—leabe him fuh me—dat's all!" Then the big negress joined the departing group, and passed out through the small steel doorway that pierced the massive gate.

Bess sat for a long while without moving. The sun lifted over the high wall, and drove its white-hot tide into her lap, and upon her folded hands.

"Wut mek yuh ain't mobe intuh de shade?" a neighbor asked curiously.

Bess looked up and smiled.

"I jes' settin' hyuh t'inkin' 'bout muh frien'," she said. "Yuh done hear um call me 'Sister,' ain't yuh? Berry well den. Dat mean me and she is frien'."

From Part V

[The Hurricane]

[Bess has given in to the temptation offered by Sportin' Life in the form of cocaine, has been arrested, and in withdrawal-induced delirium nursed back to health by Porgy and Black Maria, the matriarch of Catfish Row. However, at a picnic on Kittawah Island in part IV, Crown is discovered hiding out. He tells Bess he will come for her "when de cotton come tuh town." Catfish Row senses Bess's weakness and tries to protect her; when Sportin' Life reappears in the tenement Black Maria bodily ejects him from the courtyard, out onto the street. It is now September, the start of fishing season.]

"FISH RUNNIN' well outside de bar, dese days," remarked Jake one evening to several of his seagoing companions.

A large, bronze-colored negro paused in his task of rigging a line, and cast an eye to sea through the driveway.

"An' we mens bes' make de mores ob it," he observed. "Dem Septumbuh storm due soon, an' fish ain't likes eas' win' an' muddy watuh."

Jake laughed reassuringly.

"Go 'long wid yuh. Ain't yuh done know we hab one stiff gale las' summer, an' he nebber come two yeah han' runnin'."

His wife came toward him with a baby in her arms, and, giving him the child to hold, took up the mess of fish which he was cleaning in a leisurely fashion.

"Ef yuh ain't mans enough tuh clean fish no fastuh dan dat, yuh bes' min' de baby, an' gib um tuh a 'oman fuh clean!" she said scornfully, as she bore away the pan.

The group laughed at that, Jake's somewhat shamefaced merriment rising above the others. He rocked the contented little negro in his strong arms, and followed the retreating figure of the mother with admiring eyes.

"All right, mens," he said, returning to the matter in hand. "I'm all fuh ridin' luck fer as he will tote me. Turn out at fo' tuhmorruh mornin', and we'll push de *Seagull* clean tuh de blackfish banks befo' we wets de anchor. I gots er feelin' in my bones dat we goin' be gunnels undeh wid de pure fish when we comes in tuhmorruh night."

The news of Jake's prediction spread through the negro quarter. Other crews got their boats hastily in commission and were ready to join the "Mosquito Fleet" when it put to sea.

On the following morning, when the sun rose out of the Atlantic, the thirty or forty small vessels were mere specks teetering upon the water's rim against the red disc that forged swiftly up beyond them.

Afternoon found the wharf crowded with women and children, who laughed and joked each other as to the respective merits of their men and the luck of the boats in which they went to sea.

Clara, Jake's wife, sought the head of the dock long before sundown, and sat upon the bulkhead with her baby asleep in her lap. Occasionally she would exchange a greeting with an acquaintance; but for the most part she gazed toward the harbor mouth and said no word to any one.

"She always like dat," a neighbor informed a little group. "A conjer 'oman once tell she Jake goin' git drownded; an' she ain't hab no happiness since, 'cept when he feet is hittin' de dirt."

Presently a murmur arose among the watchers. Out at the harbor mouth, against the thin greenish blue of the horizon, appeared the "Mosquito Fleet." Driven by a steady breeze, the boats swept toward the city with astonishing rapidity.

Warm sunlight flooded out of the west, touched the old city with transient glory, then cascaded over the tossing surface of the bay to paint the taut, cupped sails salmon pink, as the fleet drove forward directly into the eye of the sun.

Almost before the crowd realized it, the boats were jibing and coming about at their feet, each jockeying for a favorable berth.

Under the skillful and daring hand of Jake, the *Seagull* took a chance, missed a stern by a hairbreadth, jibed suddenly with a snap and boom, and ran in, directly under the old rock steps of the wharf.

A cheer went up from the crowd. Never had there been such a catch. The boat seemed floored with silver which rose almost to the thwarts, forcing the crew to sit on gunnels, or aft with the steersman.

Indeed the catch was so heavy that as boat after boat docked, it became evident that the market was glutted, and the fishermen vied with each other in giving away their surplus cargo, so that they would not have to throw it overboard.

BY THE FOLLOWING MORNING the weather had become unsettled. The wind was still coming out of the west; but a low, solid wall of cloud had replaced the promising sunset of the evening before, and from time to time the wind would wrench off a section of the black mass, and volley it with great speed across the sky, to accumulate in unstable pyramids against the sunrise.

But the success of the day before had so fired the enthusiasm of the fishermen that they were not easily to be deterred from following their luck, and the first grey premonition of the day found the wharf seething with preparation.

Clara, with the baby in her arms, accompanied Jake to the pier-head. She knew the futility of remonstrance; but her eyes were fearful when the heavy, black clouds swept overhead. Once, when a wave slapped a pile, and threw a handful of spray in her face, she moaned and looked up at the big negro by her side. But Jake was full of the business in hand, and besides, he was growing a little impatient at his wife's incessant plea that he sell his share of the *Seagull* and settle on land. Now he turned from her, and shouted:

"All right, mens!"

He bestowed a short, powerful embrace upon his wife, with his eyes looking over her shoulder into the Atlantic's veiled face, turned from her with a quick, nervous movement, and dropped from the wharf into his boat.

Standing in the bow, he moistened his finger in his mouth, and held it up to the wind.

"You mens bes' git all de fish yuh kin tuhday," he admonished. "Win' be in de eas' by tuhmorruh. It gots dat wet tas' ter um now."

One by one the boats shoved off, and lay in the stream while they adjusted their spritsails and rigged their full jibs abeam, like spinnakers, for the free run to sea. The vessels were similar in design, the larger ones attaining a length of thirty-five feet. They were very narrow, and low in the waist, with high, keen bows, and pointed sterns. The hulls were round-bottomed, and had beautiful running lines, the fishermen, who were also the designers and builders, taking great pride in the speed and style of their respective craft. The boats were all open from stem to stern and were equipped with tholepins for rowing, an expedient to which the men resorted only in dire emergency.

Custom had reduced adventure to commonplace; yet it was inconceivable that men could put out, in the face of unsettled weather, for a point beyond sight of land, and exhibit no uneasiness or fear. Yet bursts of loud, loose laughter, and snatches of song, blew back to the wharf long after the boats were in mid-stream.

The wind continued to come in sudden flaws, and, once the little craft had gotten clear of the wharves, the fleet made swift but erratic progress. There were moments when they would seem to mark time upon the choppy waters of the bay; then suddenly a flaw would bear down on them, whipping the water as it came, and, filling the sails, would fairly lift the slender bows as it drove them forward.

By the time that the leisurely old city was sitting down to its breakfast, the fleet had disappeared into the horizon, and the sun had climbed over its obstructions to flood the harbor with reassuring light.

The mercurial spirits of the negroes rose with the genial warmth. Forebodings were forgotten. Even Clara sang a lighter air as she rocked the baby upon her lap.

But the sun had just lifted over the eastern wall, and the heat of noon was beginning to vibrate in the court, when suddenly the air of security was shattered. From the center of town sounded the deep, ominous clang of a bell.

At its first stroke life in Catfish Row was paralyzed. Women stopped their tasks, and, not realizing what they did, clasped each others' hands tightly, and stood motionless, with strained, listening faces.

Twenty times the great hammer fell, sending the deep, full notes out across the city that was holding its breath and counting them as they came.

"Twenty!" said Clara, when it had ceased to shake the air.

She ran to the entrance and looked to the north. Almost at the end of vision, between two buildings, could be seen the flagstaff that surmounted the custom-house. It was bare when she looked—just a thin, bare line against the intense blue, but even as she stood there, a flicker of color soared up its length; then fixed and flattened, showing a red square with a black center.

"My Gawd!" she called over her shoulder. "It's de trut'. Dat's de hurricane signal on top de custom-house."

Bess came from her room, and stood close to the terrified woman.

"Dat can't be so," she said comfortingly. "Ain't yuh 'member de las' hurricane, how it tek two day tuh blow up. Now de sun out bright, an' de cloud all gone."

But Clara gave no sign of having heard her.

"Come on in!" urged Bess. "Ef yuh don't start tuh git yuh dinner, yuh won't hab nuttin' ready fuh de mens w'en dey gits in."

After a moment the idea penetrated, and the half-dazed woman turned toward Bess, her eyes pleading.

"You come wid me, an' talk a lot. I ain't like tuh be all alone now."

"Sho' I will," replied the other comfortingly. "I min' de baby fuh yuh, an' yuh kin be gittin' de dinner."

Clara's face quivered; but she turned from the sight of the far red flag and opened her door for Bess to pass in.

After the two women had remained together for half an hour, Bess left the room for a moment to fetch some sewing. The sun was gone, and the sky presented a smooth, leaden surface. She closed the door quickly so that Clara might not see the abrupt change, and went out of the entrance for a look to sea.

Like the sky, the bay had undergone a complete metamorphosis. The water was black, and strangely lifeless. Thin, intensely white crests rode the low, pointed waves; and between the opposing planes of sky and sea a thin westerly wind roamed about like a trapped thing and whined in a complaining treble key. A singularly clear half-light pervaded the world, and in it she could see the harbor mouth distinctly, as it lay ten miles away between the north and south jetties that stretched on the horizon like arms with the finger-tips nearly touching.

Her eyes sought the narrow opening. Guiltless of the smallest speck, it let upon the utter void.

"It'd take 'em t'ree hour tuh mek harbor from de banks wid good win'," said a woman who was also watching. "But dere ain't no powuh in dis breeze, an' it a head one at dat."

"Dey kin row it in dat time," encouraged Bess. "An' de storm ain't hyuh yit."

But the woman hugged her forebodings, and stood there shivering in the close, warm air.

EXCEPT FOR the faint moan of the wind, the town and harbor lay in a silence that was like held breath.

Many negroes came to the wharf, passed out to the pier-head, and sat quietly watching the entrance to the bay.

At one o'clock the tension snapped. As though it had been awaiting St. Christopher's chimes to announce "Zero Hour," the wind swung into the east, and its voice dropped an octave, and changed its quality. Instead of the complaining whine, a grave, sustained note came in from the Atlantic, with an undertone of alarming variations, that sounded oddly out of place as it traversed the inert waters of the bay.

The tide was at the last of the ebb, and racing out of the many rivers and creeks toward the sea. All morning the west wind had driven it smoothly before it. But now, the stiffening eastern gale threw its weight against the water, and the conflict immediately filled the bay with large waves that leapt up to angry points, then dropped back sullenly upon themselves.

"Choppy water," observed a very old negro who squinted through half-closed eyes. "Dem boat nebbuh mek headway in dat sea."

But he was not encouraged to continue by the silent, anxious group.

Slowly the threatening undertone of the wind grew louder. Then, as though a curtain had been lowered across the harbor mouth, everything beyond was blotted by a milky screen.

"Oh, my Jedus!" a voice shrilled. "Here we come, now! Le's we go!"

Many of the watchers broke for the cover of buildings across the street. Some of those whose men were in the fleet crowded into the small wharf-house. Several voices started to pray at once, and were immediately drowned in the rising clamor of the wind.

With the mathematical precision that it had exhibited in starting, the gale now moved its obliterating curtain through the jetties, and thrust it forward in a straight line across the bay.

There was something utterly terrifying about the studied manner in which the hurricane proceeded about its business. It clicked off its moves like an automaton. It was Destiny working nakedly for the eyes of men to see. The watchers knew that for at least twenty-four hours it would stay, moving its tides and winds here and there with that invincible precision, crushing the life from those whom its preconceived plan had seemed to mark for death.

With that instant emotional release that is the great solace of the negro, the tightly packed wharf-house burst into a babblement of weeping and prayer.

The curtain advanced to the inner bay and narrowed the world to the city, with its buildings cowering white and fearful, and the remaining semi-circle of the harbor.

And now from the opaque surface of the screen came a persistent roar that was neither of wind or water, but the articulate cry of the storm itself. The curtain shot forward again and became a wall, grey and impenetrable, that sunk its foundations into the tortured sea and bore the leaden sky upon its soaring top.

The noise became deafening. The narrow strip of water that was left before the wharves seemed to shrink away. The buildings huddled closer and waited.

Then it crossed the strip, and smote the city.

From the roofs came the sound as though ton after ton of ore had been dumped from some great eminence. There was a dead weight to the shocks that could not conceivably be delivered by so unsubstantial a substance as air, yet which was the wind itself, lifting abruptly to enormous heights, then hurling its full force downward.

These shocks followed the demoniac plan, occurring at exact intervals, and were succeeded by prying fingers, as fluid as ether, as hard as steel, that felt for cracks in roofs and windows.

One could no longer say with certainty, "This which I breathe is air, and this upon which I stand is earth." The storm had possessed itself of the city and made it its own. Tangibles and intangibles alike were whirled in a mad, inextricable nebula.

The waves that moved upon the bay could be dimly discerned for a little distance. They were turgid, yellow, and naked; for the moment they lifted a crest, the wind snatched it and dispersed it, with the rain, into the warm semi-fluid atmosphere with which it delivered its attack upon the panic-stricken city.

Notch by notch the velocity increased. The concussions upon the roofs became louder, and the prying fingers commenced to gain a purchase, worrying small holes into the large ones. Here and there the wind would get beneath the tin, roll it up suddenly, whirl it from a building like a sheet of paper, and send it thundering and crashing down a deserted street.

Again it would gain entrance to a room through a broken window, and, exerting its explosive force to the full, would blow all of the other windows outward, and commence work upon the walls from within.

It was impossible to walk upon the street. At the first shock of the storm, the little group of negroes who had sought shelter in the wharf-house fled to the Row. Even then, the force of the attack had been so great that only by bending double and clinging together were they able to resist the onslaughts and traverse the narrow street.

Porgy and Bess sat in their room. The slats had been taken from the bed and nailed across the window, and the mattress, bundled into a corner, had been pre-empted by the goat. Bess sat wrapped in her own thoughts, apparently unmoved by the demoniac din without. Porgy's look was one of wonder, not unmixed with fear, as he peered into the outer world between two of the slats. The goat, blessed with an utter lack of imagination, revelled in the comfort and intimacy of his new environment, expressing his contentment in suffocating waves, after the manner of his kind. A kerosene lamp without a chimney, smoking straight up into the unnatural stillness of the room, cast a faint, yellow light about it, but only accentuated the heavy gloom of the corners.

From where Porgy sat, he could catch glimpses of what lay beyond the window. There would come occasional moments when the floor of the storm would be lifted by a burrowing wind, and he would see the high, naked breakers racing under the sullen pall of spume and rain.

Once he saw a derelict go by. The vessel was a small river sloop, with its rigging blown clean out. A man was clinging to the tiller. One wave, larger than its fellows, submerged the little boat, and when it wallowed to the surface again, the man was gone, and the tiller was kicking wildly.

"Oh my Jedus, hab a little pity!" the watcher moaned under his breath.

Later, a roof went by.

Porgy heard it coming, even above the sound of the attack upon the Row, and it filled him with awe and dread. He turned and looked at Bess, and was reassured to see that she met his gaze fearlessly. Down the street the roar advanced, growing nearer and louder momentarily. Surely it would be the final instrument of destruction. He held his breath, and waited. Then it thundered past his narrow sphere of vision. Rolled loosely, it loomed to the second story windows, and flapped and tore at the buildings as it swept over the cobbles.

When a voice could be heard again, Porgy turned to his companion.

"You an' me, Bess," he said with conviction. "We *sho'* is a little somet'ing attuh all."

After that, they sat long without exchanging a word. Then Porgy looked out of the window and noticed that the quality of the atmosphere was becoming denser. The spume lifted for a moment, and he could scarcely see the tormented bay.

"I t'ink it mus' be mos' night," he observed. "Dey ain't much light now on de outside ob dis storm."

He looked again before the curtain descended, and what he saw caused his heart to miss a beat.

He knew that the tide should be again at the ebb, for the flood had commenced just after the storm broke. But as he looked, the water, which was already higher than a normal flood, lifted over the far edge of the street, and three tremendous waves broke in rapid succession, sending the deep layers of water across the narrow way to splash against the wall of the building.

This reversal of nature's law struck terror into the dark places of Porgy's soul. He beckoned to Bess, his fascinated eyes upon the advancing waves.

She bent down and peered into the gloom.

"Oh, yes," she remarked in a flat tone. "It been dis way in de las' great storm. De win' hol' de watuh in de jetty mout' so he can't go out. Den he pile up annoder tide on him."

Suddenly an enormous breaker loomed over the backs of its shattered and retreating fellows. The two watchers could not see its crest, for it towered into, and was absorbed by, the low-hanging atmosphere. Yellow, smooth, and with a perpendicular, slightly concave front, it flashed across the street, and smote the solid wall of the Row. They heard it roar like a mill-race through the drive, and flatten, hissing in the court. Then they turned, and saw their own door give slightly to the pressure, and a dark flood spurt beneath it, and debouch upon the floor.

Bess took immediate command of the situation. She threw an arm about Porgy, and hurried him to the door. She withdrew the bolt, and the flimsy panels shot inward. The court was almost totally dark. One after another now the waves were hurtling through the drive and impounding in the walled square.

The night was full of moving figures, and cries of fear; while, out of the upper dark, the wind struck savagely downward.

With a powerful swing, Bess got Porgy to a stairway that providentially opened near their room, and, leaving him to make his way up alone, she rushed back, and was soon at his heels with an armful of belongings.

They sought refuge in what had been the great ball-room of the mansion, a square, high-ceilinged room on the second story, which was occupied by a large and prosperous family. There were as many refugees there before them. In the faint light cast by several lanterns, the indestructible beauty of the apartment was evident, while the defacing effects of a century were absorbed in shadow. The noble open fireplace, the tall, slender mantel, with its Grecian frieze and intricate scrollwork, the high panelled walls were all there. And then, huddled in little groups on the floor, or seated against the walls, with eyes wide in the lantern-shine, the black, fear-stricken faces.

Like the ultimate disintegration of a civilization—there it was; and upon it, as though to make quick work of the last, tragic chapter, the scourging wrath of the Gods—white, and black.

The night that settled down upon Catfish Row was one of nameless horror to the inhabitants, most of whom were huddled on the second floor in order to avoid the sea from beneath, and deafening assaults upon the roof above their heads.

With the obliteration of vision, sound assumed an exaggerated significance, and the voice of the gale, which had seemed by day only a great roar, broke up in the dark into its various parts. Human voices seemed to cry in it; and there were moments when it sniffed and moaned at the windows.

Once, during a silence in the room, a whinny was distinctly heard.

"Dat my ole horse!" wailed Peter. "He done dead in he stall now, an' dat he woice goin' by. Oh, my Gawd!"

They all wailed out at that; and Porgy, remembering his goat, whimpered and turned his face to the wall.

Then someone started to sing:

"I gots uh home in de rock, don't yuh see?"

WITH A FEELING of infinite relief, Porgy turned to his Jesus. It was not a charm that he sought now for the assuaging of some physical ill, but a benign power, vaster perhaps even than the hurricane. He lifted his rich baritone above the others:

"Oh, between de eart' an' sky,
I kin see my Sabior die.
I gots uh home in de rock,
Don't yuh see!"

Then they were all in it, heart and soul. Those who had fallen into a fitful sleep, awoke, rubbed their eyes, and sang.

Hour after hour dragged heavily past. Outside, the storm worked its will upon the defenceless city. But in the great ball-room of Catfish Row, forty souls sat wrapped in an invulnerable garment. They swayed and patted, and poured their griefs and fears into a rhythm that never missed a beat, which swept the hours behind it into oblivion, and that finally sang up the faint grey light that penetrated the storm, and told them that it was again day.

At about an hour after daybreak the first lull came. Like the other moves of the hurricane, it arrived without warning. One moment, the tumult was at its height. The next, there was utter suspension. Abruptly, like an indrawn breath, the wind sucked back upon itself, leaving an aching vacuum in its place. Then from the inundated waterfront arose the sound of the receding flood.

The ebb-tide was again overdue, and with the second tide piled upon it, the whole immeasurable weight of the wind was required to maintain its height. Now, with the pressure removed, it turned and raced beneath the low-lying mist toward the sea, carrying its pitiful loot upon its back.

To the huddled figures in the great room of the Row came the welcome sound, as the court emptied itself into the street. The negroes crowded to the windows, and peered between the barricades at the world without.

The water receded with incredible speed. Submerged wreckage lifted above the surface. The street became the bed of a cataract that foamed and boiled on its rush to the sea. Presently the wharf emerged, and at its end even a substantial remnant of the house could be descried. How it had survived that long was one of the inexplicable mysteries of the storm.

Suddenly Peter, who was at one of the windows, gave a cry, and the other negroes crowded about him to peer out.

The sea was still running high, and as a large wave lifted above the level of the others, it thrust into view the hull of a half-submerged boat. Before the watchers could see, the wave dropped its burden into a trough, but the old man showed them where to look, and presently a big roller caught it up, and swung it, bow on, for all to see. There was a flash of scarlet gunnel, and, beneath it, a bright blue bird with open wings.

"De *Seagull!*" cried a dozen voices together. "My Gawd! dat Jake' boat!"

All night Clara had sat in a corner of the room with the baby in her arms, saying no word to anyone. She was so still that she seemed to be asleep, with her head upon her breast. But once, when Bess had gone and looked into her face, she had seen her eyes, wide and bright with pain.

Now the unfortunate woman heard the voices, and sprang to the window just in time to see the craft swoop into a hollow at the head of the pier.

She did not scream out. For a moment she did not even speak. Then she spun around on Bess with the dawn of a wild hope in her dark face.

"Tek care ob dis baby 'til I gits back," she said, as she thrust the child almost savagely into Bess's arms. Then she rushed from the room.

The watchers at the window saw her cross the street, splashing wildly through the knee-deep water. Then she ran the length of the wharf, and disappeared behind the sheltering wall of the house.

It was so sudden, and tired wits move slowly. Several minutes had passed before it occurred to anyone to go with her. Finally Peter turned from the window.

"Dat 'oman ain't ought tuh be out dey by sheself," he said. "Who goin' out dey wid me, now?"

One of the men volunteered, and they started for the door.

A sound like the detonation of a cannon shook the building to its foundations. The gale had returned, smashing straight downward from some incredible height to which it had lifted during the lull.

The men turned and looked at one another.

Shock followed shock in rapid succession. Those who stood by the windows felt them give inward, and instinctively threw their weight against the frames. The explosions merged into a steady roar of sound that surpassed anything that had yet occurred. The room became so dark that they could no longer see one another. The barricaded windows were vaguely discernible in bars of muddy grey and black. Deeply rooted walls swung from the blows, and then settled slowly back on the recoil.

A confused sound of praying filled the room. And above it shrilled the terror of the women.

For an appreciable space of time the spasm lasted. Then, slowly, as though by the gradual withdrawing of a lever, the vehemence of the attack abated. The muddy grey bars at the windows became lighter, and some of the more courageous of the negroes peered out.

The wharf could be seen dimly extending under the low floor of spume and mist. The breakers were higher than at any previous time, but instead of smashing in upon the shore, they raced straight up the river and paralleled the city. As each one swung by it went clean over the wharf, obliterating it for the duration of its passage.

Suddenly from the direction of the lower harbor a tremendous mass appeared, showing first only a vast distorted stain against the grey fabric of the mist. Then a gigantic wave took it, and drove it into fuller view.

"Great Gawd A'mighty!" some one whispered. "It's dat big lumbuh schooner bruck loose in de harbor."

The wave hunched its mighty shoulders under the vessel and swung it up—up, for an interminable moment. The soaring bow-sprit lifted until it was lost in mist. Tons of water gushed from the steep incline of the deck, and poured over the smooth, black wall of the side, as it reared half out of the sea. Then the wave swept aft, and the bow descended in a swift, deadly plunge.

A crashing of timbers followed that could be heard clearly above the roaring of the storm. The hull had fallen directly across the middle of the wharf. There was one cataclysmic moment when the whole view seemed to disintegrate. The huge timbers of the wharf up-ended, and were washed out like straws. The schooner rolled half over, and her three masts crashed down with their rigging. The shock burst the lashings of the vessel's deck load, and as the hull heeled, an avalanche of heavy timbers took the water. The ruin was utter.

Heavy and obliterating, the mist closed down again.

Bess turned from the window holding the sleeping infant in her arms, raised her eyes and looked full at Porgy.

With an expression of awe in his face, the cripple reached out a timid hand and touched the baby's cheek.

THE WINDOWS of the great ball-room were open to the sky, and beyond them, a busy breeze was blowing across its washed and polished expanse, gathering cloud-remnants into little heaps, and sweeping them in tumbling haste out over the threshold of the sea.

Most of the refugees had returned to their rooms, where sounds of busy salvaging could be heard. Porgy's voice arose jubilantly announcing that the goat had been discovered, marooned upon the cook-stove; and that Peter's old horse had belied his whinny, and was none the worse for a thorough wetting.

Serena Robbins paused before Bess, who was gathering her things preparatory to leaving the room, placed her hands upon her hips, and looked down upon her.

"Now, wut we all goin' do wid dis po' mudderless chile?" she said, addressing the room at large.

The other occupants of the room gathered behind Serena, but there was something about Bess's look that held them quiet. They stood there waiting and saying nothing.

Slowly Bess straightened up, her face lowered and pressed against that of the sleeping child. Then she raised her eyes and met the gaze of the complacent older woman.

What Serena saw there was not so much the old defiance that she had expected, as it was an inflexible determination, and, behind it, a new-born element in the woman that rendered the scarred visage incandescent. She stepped back, and lowered her eyes.

Bess strained the child to her breast with an elemental intensity of possession, and spoke in a low, deep voice that vested her words with sombre meaning.

"Is Clara come back a'ready, since she dead, an' say somet'ing 'bout 'we' tuh yuh 'bout dis chile?"

She put the question to the group, her eyes taking in the circle of faces as she spoke.

There was no response; and at the suggestion of a possible return of the dead, the circle drew together instinctively.

"Berry well den," said Bess solemnly. "Ontell she do, I goin' stan' on she las' libbin' word an' keep dis chile fuh she 'til she do come back."

Serena was hopelessly beaten, and she knew it.

"Oh, berry well," she capitulated. "All I been goin' tuh do wuz jus' tuh puhwide um wid er propuh Christian raisin'. But ef she done gib um tuh yuh, dere ain't nuttin mo' I kin do, I guess."

From Part VI

[Porgy's Heroism and His Loss]

[It is October, and with the rumored return of Crown, "a vague prescience of disaster" darkens Porgy's spirit. With the intense upper body strength that has come from being a cripple, Porgy stabs Crown in the dark of Catfish Row, and the police come to investigate.]

A GROUP OF THREE white men stood over the body. One was the plain-clothes man with the goatee and stick who had investigated the Robbins murder. Behind him stood a uniformed policeman. The third, a stout, leisurely individual, was stooping over the body, in the act of making an examination.

"What do you make of it, Coroner?" asked the plain-clothes man.

"Knife between the fifth and sixth ribs; must have gone straight through the heart."

"Well, he had it comin' to him," the detective observed. "They tell me he is the nigger, Crown, who killed Robbins last April. That gives us the widow to work on fer a starter, by the way; and Hennessy tells me that he used to run with that dope case we had up last August. She's livin' in the Row, too. Let's go over and have a look."

The Coroner cast an apprehensive glance at the forbidding structure across the way.

"Can't be so sure," he cautioned. "Corpse might have been washed up. Tide's on the flood."

"Well, I'm goin' to have a look at those two women, anyway," the plain-clothes man announced. "That place is alive with crooks. I'd like to get something on it that would justify closing it up as a public nuisance, and throwing the whole lot of 'em out in the street. One murder and a happy-dust riot already this summer; and here we are again."

Then turning to the policeman, he gave his orders.

"Get the wagon and take the body in. Then you had better come right back. We might have some arrests. The Coroner and I'll investigate while you're gone."

He turned away toward the Row, assuming that he would be followed.

"All right, Cap; what do you say?" he called.

The Coroner shook his ponderous figure down into his clothes, turned with evident reluctance, and joined him.

"All right," he agreed. "But all I need is a couple of witnesses to identify the body at the inquest."

Across the street a small negro boy detached himself from the base of one of the gateposts and darted through the entrance.

A moment later the white men strode into an absolutely empty square. Their heels made a sharp sound on the flags, and the walls threw a clear echo down upon them.

A cur that had been left napping in the sun woke with a start, looked about in a bewildered fashion, gave a frightened yelp, and bolted through a doorway.

It was all clearly not to the taste of the Coroner, and he cast an uneasy glance about him.

"Where do we go?" he asked.

"That's the widow's room over there, if she hasn't moved. We'll give it a look first," said the detective.

The door was off the latch, and, without knocking, he kicked it open and walked in.

The room was small, but immaculately clean. Beneath a patched white quilt could be seen the form of a woman. Two other women were sitting in utter silence beside the bed.

The form under the covers moaned.

"Drop that," the detective commanded. "And answer some questions."

The moaning stopped.

"Where were you yesterday and last night?"

The reply came slowly, as though speaking were great pain.

"I been sick in dis bed now t'ree day an' night."

"We been settin' wid she, nursin' she, all dat time," one of the women said.

And the other supplemented. "Dat de Gawd' trut'."

"You would swear to that?" asked the Coroner.

Three voices answered in chorus:

"Yes, Boss, we swear tuh dat."

"There you are," said the Coroner to the plain-clothes man, "an air-tight alibi."

The detective regarded him for a moment with supreme contempt. Then he stepped forward and jerked the sheet from Serena's face, which lay upon the pillow as immobile as a model done in brown clay.

"You know damn well that you were out yesterday!" he snapped. "I have a good mind to get the wagon and carry you in."

Silence followed.

"What do you say to that?" he demanded.

But Serena had nothing to say, and neither had her handmaidens.

Then as he turned a menacing frown upon them, as they sat motionless with lowered eyes.

"Well!"

They jumped slightly, and their eyes showed white around the iris. Suddenly they began to speak, almost in unison.

"We swear tuh Gawd, we done been hyuh wid she t'ree day."

"Oh, Hell!" said the exasperated detective. "What's the use? You might as well argue with a parrot-cage."

"That woman is just as ill at this moment as you are," he said to his unenthusiastic associate when they were again in the sunlight. "Her little burlesque show proves that, if nothing else. But there is her case all prepared. I don't believe she killed Crown; she doesn't look like that kind. She is either just playing safe, or she has something entirely different on her chest. But there's her story; and you'll never break in without witnesses of your own; and you'll never get 'em."

The Coroner was not a highly sensitized individual; but as he moved across the empty court, he found it difficult to control his nerves under the scrutiny which he felt leveled upon him from behind a hundred shuttered windows. Twice he caught himself looking covertly over his shoulders; and, as he went, he bore hopefully away toward the entrance.

But the detective was intent upon his task, and presently called him back.

"This is the cripple's room," he said. "He ain't much of a witness. I tried to break him in the Robbins case; but he wouldn't talk. I want to have a look at the woman, though."

He kicked the door open suddenly. Porgy and Bess were seated by the stove, eating breakfast from tin pans. On the bed in the corner the baby lay.

Porgy paused, with his spoon halfway to his mouth and looked up. Bess kept her eyes on the pan, and continued to eat.

The Coroner stopped in the doorway, and made a businesslike show of writing in a notebook.

"What's your name?" he asked Porgy.

The cripple studied him for a long moment, taking in the ample proportions of the figure and the heavy, but not unsympathetic, face. Then he smiled one of his fleeting, ingenuous smiles.

"Jus' Porgy," he said. "Yuh knows me, Boss. Yuh is done gib me plenty ob penny on King Charles Street."

"Of course, you're the goat-man. I didn't know you without your wagon," he said amiably. Then, becoming businesslike, he asked:

"This nigger, Crown. You knew him by sight. Didn't you?"

Porgy debated with himself for a moment, looked again into the Coroner's face, was reassured by what he saw there, and replied:

"Yes, Boss; I 'member um w'en he usen tuh come hyuh, long ago."

"You could identify him, I suppose?"

Porgy looked blank.

"You'd know him if you saw him again?"

"Yes, Boss; I know um."

The Coroner made a note in his book, closed it with an air of finality, and put it in his pocket.

During the brief interview, the detective had been making an examination of the room. The floor had been recently scrubbed, and was still damp in the corners. He gave the clean, pine boards a close scrutiny, then paused before the window. The bottom of the lower sash had been broken, and several of the small, square panes were missing.

"So this is where you killed Crown, eh?" he announced.

The words fell into silence and were absorbed by it, causing them to seem theatrical and unconvincing. Neither Porgy nor Bess spoke. Their faces were blank and noncommittal.

After a full moment, the woman said:

"I ain't onduhstan', Boss. Nobody hyuh ain't kill Crown. My husban' he fall t'rough dat winduh yisterday when he leg gib' way. He er cripple."

"Any one see him do it?" enquired the Coroner from the door.

"Oh, yes, Boss," replied Bess, turning to him. "T'ree or four ob de mens was in de street; dey will tell yuh all 'bout um."

"Yes, of course; more witnesses," sneered the detective. Then turning to the Coroner, he asked with a trace of sarcasm in his tone:

"That satisfies you fully, I suppose?"

The Coroner's nerves were becoming edgy.

"For God's sake," he retorted, "do you expect me to believe that a cripple could kill a two-hundred pound buck, then tote him a hundred yards? Well, I've got what I need now anyway. As far as I'm concerned, I'm through."

They were passing the door of Maria's shop when the detective caught sight of something within that held his gaze.

"You can do as you please," he told his unwilling companion. "But I'm going to have a look in here. I have never been able to get anything on this woman; but she is a bad influence in the neighborhood. I'd trust her just as far as I could throw her."

The Coroner heaved a sigh of resignation, and they stepped back, and entered the shop.

Upon the flooring, directly before the door, and not far from it, was a pool of blood. Standing over the pool was a table, and upon it lay the carcass of a shark. Maria sat on a bench behind the table. As the men entered she swung an immense cleaver downward. A cross-section of the shark detached itself and fell away on a pile of similar slices. A thin stream of blood dribbled from the table, augmenting the pool upon the floor.

Maria did not raise her eyes from her task. Again the cleaver swung up, and whistled downward.

From the street sounded the clatter of the returning patrol.

"I'll wait for you in the wagon," said the Coroner hastily, and stepped back into the sunlight.

But he was not long alone. The uninterrupted swing of the dripping cleaver was depressing, and the enthusiasm of his associate waned.

The bell clanged. Hoofs struck sparks from the cobbles, and the strong but uncertain arm of the law was withdrawn, to attend to other and more congenial business.

THE SOUND from the retreating wagon dwindled and ceased.

For a moment Catfish Row held its breath; then its windows and doors flew open, and poured its life out into the incomparable autumn weather. The crisis had passed. There had been no arrests.

Serena stepped forth, her arms filled with the morning's wash.

"'Ain't it hahd tuh be er nigger!'" someone sang in a loud, clear voice. And everybody laughed.

Down the street, like an approaching freight train, came the drays, jarring the building and rattling the windows, as the heavy tires rang against the cobbles.

Bess and Porgy came out with the others, and seated themselves against the wall in the gracious sunlight. Of the life, yet apart from it, sufficient unto each other, they did not join in the loud talk and badinage that was going on about them. Like people who had come on a long, dark journey, they were content to sit, and breathe deeply of the sun. The baby was sleeping in Bess's arms, and from time to time she would sing a stave to it in a soft, husky voice.

Into the court strode a group of stevedores. Their strong white teeth flashed in the sunshine, and their big, panther-like bodies moved easily among the women and children that crowded about them.

"Wey all de gals?" called one in a loud, resonant voice. "Mus' be dey ain't know dat dis is pay-day."

Two women who were sitting near Porgy and Bess rose and went forward, with their arms twined about each other's waists. In a few minutes they were out of the crowd again, each looking up with admiring eyes into the face of one of the men.

"Mens an' 'omans ain't de same," said Porgy. "One mont' ago dem gals been libbin' wid dey own mens. Den de storm tek um. Now dey is fuhgit um a'ready, an' gibbin' dey lub tuh de nex'."

"No; dey is diff'rent fuh true," replied Bess. "An' yuh won't nebber on-duhstan'. All two dem gal gots baby fuh keep alibe." She heaved a deep sigh; and then added, "Dey is jus' 'oman, an' nigger at dat. Dey is doin' de bes' dey kin—dat all."

She was looking down at the baby while she spoke, and when she raised her eyes and looked at Porgy, he saw that they were full of tears.

"But you, Bess; you is diff'rent f'om dat?" he said, with a gently interrogating note in his voice.

"Dat 'cause Gawd ain't mek but one Porgy!" she told him. "Any 'oman gots tuh be decent wid you. But I gots fuh tell yuh de trut', widout Porgy I is jus' like de res'."

A shadow drifted across their laps, and they lifted their faces to the sky.

A solitary buzzard had left the circle that had hung high in the air all morning, and was swinging back and forth over the Row, almost brushing the parapet of the roof as it passed. While Porgy and Bess looked, it suddenly raised the points of its wings, reached tentative legs downward, spread its feet wide, and lit on the edge of the roof directly over their room.

"My Gawd!" exclaimed Maria, who was standing near. "Crown done sen' he buzzud back fuh bring trouble. Knock um off, Porgy. Fer Gawd' sake, knock um off befo' he settle!"

The cripple reached out and picked up a brick-bat. The happiness had left his face, and his eyes were filled with fear. With a swing of his long, powerful arm, he sent the missile on its errand.

It struck the parapet directly beneath the bird.

With a spasmodic flap of wings, the black body lifted itself a few feet from the building, then settled suddenly back. For a moment it hopped awkwardly about, as though the roof were red hot beneath its feet, then folded its wings, drew its nude head in upon its breast, and surveyed the court with its aloof, malevolent eyes.

"T'row agin," Maria called, handing Porgy another brick-bat. But he seemed not to hear. His face quivered, and he hid it in his hands.

"Sonny," the big negress called to a small boy who was standing near, looking at the bird with his mouth open. "Git out on de roof wid uh stick, an' run dat bird away."

But Porgy plucked at her skirt, and she looked down.

"Let um be," he said in a hopeless voice. "It too late now. Ain't yuh see he done settle, an' he pick my room fuh light ober? It ain't no use now. Yuh knows dat. It ain't no use."

THE NEXT MORNING Porgy sat in his accustomed place by Archdale's door. Autumn had touched the oaks in the park across the way, and they brushed the hard, bright sky with a slow circling motion, and tossed handfuls of yellow leaves down upon the pedestrians who stepped briskly along.

King Charles Street was full of hurrying men on their way to the cotton offices and the big wholesale warehouses that fronted on the wharves. Like the artery of a hale old man who has lain long asleep, but who wakens suddenly and springs into a race, the broad thoroughfare seemed to pound and sing with life.

The town was in a generous mood. Again and again the bottom of Porgy's cup gave forth its sharp, grateful click as a coin struck it and settled. But the cripple had not even his slow glance of thanks for his benefactors on that flashing autumn morning. Always he kept veiled, apprehensive eyes directed either up or down the street, or lifted frightened glances to the sky, as though fearing what he might see there.

At noon a white man stopped before him. But he did not drop a coin and pass on.

After a moment, Porgy brought his gaze back, and looked up.

The white man reached forward, and handed him a paper.

"Dat fuh me?" asked Porgy, in a voice that shook.

"You needn't mind takin' it," the man assured him with a laugh. "It's just a summons as witness to the Coroner's inquest. You knew that nigger, Crown, didn't you?"

He evidently took Porgy's silence for assent, for he went on.

"Well, all you got to do is to view the body in the presence of the Coroner, tell him who it is, and he'll take down all you say."

Porgy essayed speech, failed, tried again, and finally whispered:

"I gots tuh go an' look on Crown' face wid all dem w'ite folks lookin' at me. Dat it?"

His voice was so piteous that the constable reassured him:

"Oh, cheer up; it's not so bad. I reckon you've seen a dead nigger before this. It will all be over in a few minutes."

"Dey ain't goin' be no nigger in dat room 'cept me?" Porgy asked.

"Just you and Crown, if you still call him one."

After a moment Porgy asked:

"I couldn't jus' bring a 'oman wid me? I couldn't eben carry my—my 'oman?"

"No," said the white man positively. "Now I've got to be gettin' along, I reckon. Just come over to the Court House in half an hour, and I'll meet you and take you in. Only be sure to come. If you don't show up it's jail for you, you know."

For a moment after the man had gone, Porgy sat immovable, with his eyes on the pavement. Then a sudden change swept over him. He cast one glance up and down the hard, clean street, walled by its uncompromising, many-eyed buildings. Then in a panic he clambered into his cart, gave a cruel twist to the tail of his astonished goat, and commenced a spasmodic, shambling race up Meeting House Road in the direction in which he knew that, miles away, the forests lay.

To MANY, the scene which ensued on the upper Meeting House Road stands out as an exquisitely humorous episode, to be told and retold with touching up of high lights and artistic embellishments. To these, in the eyes of whom the negro is wholly humorous, per se, there was not the omission of a single conventional and readily recognizable stage property.

For, after all, what could have been funnier than an entirely serious race between a negro in a dilapidated goat-cart, and the municipality's shining new patrol wagon, fully officered and clanging its bell for the crowd to hear as it came.

The finish took place in the vicinity of the railway yards and factories, and the street was filled with workmen who smoked against the walls, or ate their lunch, sitting at the pavement's edge—grand-stand seats, as they were quite accurately described in the telling.

The street cars ran seldom that far out; and Porgy had the thorough-fare almost entirely to himself. His face wore a demented look, and was working pitifully. In his panic, he wrung the tail of his unfortunate beast without mercy. The lunchers along the pavement saw him coming, and called to friends further along; so that as he came, he was greeted with shouts of laughter and witty sallies from the crowd.

Then the wagon appeared, a mere speck in the distance, but sending the sound of its bell before it as an advertisement of its presence. It grew rapidly until it reached the cheering crowds. Then it seemed that even the sedate officers of the law were not above a sly humor of their own, for the vehicle slackened its pace perceptibly and prolonged the final moment of capture.

The big buildings had been left behind, and there lay before Porgy only the scattered, cheap bungalows of the labor quarters; and beyond, as elusive and desirable as the white man's heaven, glimmered the far line of the woods, misty and beautiful in the pink autumn haze.

The patrol forged ahead and came to a clanging stop. The officers leapt out and, amid shouts of laughter from the crowd, lifted wagon, goat and man into the vehicle. The driver jerked the horse back into its breechings, swung

the wagon with a dramatic snap that was not wasted upon his gallery, and sent
it clanging and rocking back in the direction from which it had come.

Porgy fell forward, with his arms thrown out upon the back of the goat,
and buried his face between them in the shaggy, evil-smelling hair.

The workmen upon the sidewalks cheered and shouted with mirth. Surely
it had been a great day. They would not soon have another laugh to match it.

WHEN THE WAGON reached the down-town district, the inquest was over.
It had been a simple matter to secure another witness for the identification of
the body. The jury had made short work of their task, and had found that
Crown had come to his death as the result of a chest wound at the hands of
person or persons unknown.

Porgy was taken at once to the station house, where the charge of "Contempt of Court" was formally entered against him on the blotter, and he was
locked up to await trial early the following morning.

Under the wheezing gas jet, the Recorder looked Porgy over with his
weary glance, brought the tips of his slender fingers together; gave him "five
days," in his tired drawl, and raised his eyes to the next negro on the morning's list.

They hoisted the outfit, goat and all, into the patrol for the trip to the jail,
thus again brightening a day for a group of light-hearted Nordics upon the
pavement.

A large, red-faced policeman took his seat at the rear of the wagon.

"You sure beat all!" he confided to Porgy, with a puzzled frown. "Runnin'
away like the devil was after you, from bein' a witness; an' now goin' to jail
with a face like Sunday mornin'."

IN THE FRESH BEAUTY of an early October morning, Porgy returned
home. There were few of his friends about, as work was now plentiful, and
most of those who could earn a day's wage were up and out. He drove through
the entrance, pulled his goat up short, and looked about him.

Serena was seated on her bench with a baby in her arms.

Porgy gave her a long look, and a question commenced to dawn in his eyes.
The child turned in her arms, and his suspicions were confirmed. It was his
baby—his and Bess's.

Then Serena looked up and saw him. She arose in great confusion, clasped
the infant to her ample bosom, and, without a word of greeting, stepped

through her doorway. Then, as though struck by an afterthought, she turned, thrust her head back through the opening, and called loudly:

"Oh, Maria! hyuh Porgy come home."

Then she disappeared and the door slammed shut.

Mystified and filled with alarm, Porgy turned his vehicle toward the cook-shop and arrived at the door just as Maria stepped over the threshold.

She seated herself on the sill and brought her face level with his. Then she looked into his eyes.

What Porgy saw there caused him to call out sharply:

"Where's Bess? Tell me, quick, where's Bess?"

The big negress did not answer, and after a moment her ponderous face commenced to shake.

Porgy beat the side of his wagon with his fist.

"Where, where—" he began, in a voice that was suddenly shrill.

But Maria placed a steadying hand over his frantic one and held it still.

"Dem dutty dogs got she one day w'en I gone out," she said in a low, shaken voice. "She been missin' yuh an' berry low in she min' 'cause she can't fin' out how long yuh is lock up fuh. Dat damn houn' she knock off de wharf las' summer fin' she like dat an' git she tuh tek er swalluh ob licker. Den half a dozen of de mens gang she, an' mek she drunk."

"But wuh she now?" Porgy cried. "I ain't keer ef she wuz drunk. I want she now."

Maria tried to speak, but her voice refused to do her bidding. She covered her face with her hands, and her throat worked convulsively.

Porgy clutched her wrist. "Tell me," he commanded. "Tell me, now."

"De mens all carry she away on de ribber boat," she sobbed. "Dey leabe word fuh me dat dey goin' tek she all de way tuh Sawannah, an' keep she dey. Den Serena, she tek de chile, an' say she is goin' gib um er Christian raisin'."

Deep sobs stopped Maria's voice. For a while she sat there, her face buried in her hands. But Porgy had nothing to say. When she finally raised her head and looked at him, she was surprised at what she saw.

The keen autumn sun flooded boldly through the entrance and bathed the drooping form of the goat, the ridiculous wagon, and the bent figure of the man in hard, satirical radiance. In its revealing light, Maria saw that Porgy was an old man. The early tension that had characterized him, the mellow mood that he had known for one eventful summer, both had gone; and in their place she saw a face that sagged wearily, and the eyes of age lit only by a faint reminiscent glow from suns and moons that had looked into them, and had already dropped down the west.

She looked until she could bear the sight no longer; then she stumbled into her shop and closed the door, leaving Porgy and the goat alone in an irony of morning sunlight.

THE END

The Half Pint Flask

I PICKED UP THE BOOK and regarded it with interest. Even its format suggested the author: the practical linen covered boards, the compact and exact paragraphing. I opened the volume at random. There he was again: "There can be no doubt," "An undeniable fact," "I am prepared to assert." A statement in the preface leaped from the context and arrested my gaze:

"The primitive American Negro is of a deeply religious nature, demonstrating in his constant attendance at church, his fervent prayers, his hymns, and his frequent mention of the Deity that he has cast aside the last vestiges of his pagan background, and has unreservedly espoused the doctrine of Christianity."

I spun the pages through my fingers until a paragraph in the last chapter brought me up standing:

"I was hampered in my investigations by a sickness contracted on the island that was accompanied by a distressing insomnia, and, in its final stages, extreme delirium. But I already had sufficient evidence in hand to enable me to prove—"

Yes, there it was, fact upon fact. I was overwhelmed by the permanence, the unanswerable last word of the printed page. In the face of it my own impressions became fantastic, discredited even in my own mind. In an effort at self-justification I commenced to rehearse my *impressions* of that preposterous month as opposed to Barksdale's *facts*; my feeling for effects and highly developed fiction writer's imagination on the one hand; and on the other, his cold record of a tight, three dimensional world as reported by his five good senses.

Sitting like a crystal gazer, with the book in my hand, I sent my memory back to a late afternoon in August, when, watching from the shore near the landing on Ediwander Island, I saw the *General Stonewall Jackson* slide past a

SOURCE: *The Half Pint Flask* (New York: Farrar and Rinehart, 1929).

frieze of palmetto trees, shut off her steam, and nose up to the tenuous little wharf against the ebb.

Two barefooted Negroes removed a section of the rail and prepared to run out the gang plank. Behind them gathered the passengers for Ediwander landing: ten dozen Negroes back from town with the proceeds of a month's labor transformed into flaming calico, amazing bonnets, and new flimsy, yellow luggage; and trailing along behind them, the single white passenger.

I would have recognized my guest under more difficult circumstances and I experienced that inner satisfaction that comes from having a new acquaintance fit neatly into a preconceived pattern. The obstinacy of which I had been warned was evident in the thin immobile line of the mouth over the prognathous jaw. The eyes behind his thick glasses were a bright hard blue and moved methodically from object to object, allowing each its allotted time for classification then passing unhurriedly on to the next. He was so like the tabloid portrait in the letter of the club member who had sent him down that I drew the paper from my pocket and refreshed my memory with a surreptitious glance.

"He's the museum, or collector type," Spencer had written; "spends time collecting facts—some he sells—some he keeps to play with. Incidentally his hobby is American glass, and he has the finest private collection in the state."

We stood eyeing each other over the heads of the noisy landing party without enthusiasm. Then when the last Negro had come ashore he picked up his bag with a meticulousness that vaguely exasperated me, and advanced up the gang plank.

Perfunctory introductions followed; "Mr. Courtney?" from him, with an unnecessarily rising inflection; and a conventional "Mr. Barksdale, I presume," from me in reply.

The buckboard[1] had been jogging along for several minutes before he spoke.

"Very good of Mr. Spencer to give me this opportunity," he said in a close clipped speech. "I am doing a series of articles on Negroid Primates, and I fancy the chances for observation are excellent here."

"Negroid Primate!" The phrase annoyed me. Uttered in that dissecting voice, it seemed to strip the human from the hundred or more Negroes who were my only company except during the duck season when the club members dropped down for the shooting.

"There are lots of Negroes here," I told him a little stiffly. "Their ancestors were slaves when the island was the largest rice plantation in South Carolina, and isolation from modern life has kept them primitive enough, I guess."

"Good!" he exclaimed. "I will commence my studies at once. Simple souls, I fancy. I should have my data within a month."

We had been traveling slowly through deep sand ruts that tugged at the wheels like an undertow. On either side towered serried ranks of virgin long-leaf pine. Now we topped a gentle rise. Before us was the last outpost of the forest crowning a diminishing ridge. The straight columned trees were bars against a released splendor of sunset sky and sea.

Impulsively I called his attention to it:

"Rather splendid, don't you think?"

He raised his face, and I was immediately cognizant of the keen method-ical scrutiny that passed from trees to sea, and from sea back to that last wooded ridge that fell away into the tumble of dunes.

Suddenly I felt his wire-tight grasp about my arm.

"What's that?" he asked, pointing with his free hand. Then with an air of authority, he snapped: "Stop the cart. I've got to have a look at it."

"That won't interest you. It's only a Negro burying ground. I'll take you to the quarters tomorrow, where you can study your 'live primates.'"

But he was over the wheel with surprising alacrity and striding up the slight ascent to the scattered mounds beneath the pines.

The sunset was going quickly, dragging its color from the sky and sea, rolling up leagues of delicately tinted gauze into tight little bales of primary color, then draping these with dark covers for the night. In sharp contrast against the light the burying ground presented its pitiful emblems of the de-parted. Under the pine needles, in common with all Negro graveyards of the region, the mounds were covered with a strange litter of half-emptied medi-cine bottles, tin spoons, and other futile weapons that had failed in the final engagement with the last dark enemy.

Barksdale was puttering excitedly about among the graves, peering at the strange assortment of crockery and glass. The sight reminded me of what Spencer had said of the man's hobby and a chill foreboding assailed me. I jumped from the buckboard.

"Here," I called, "I wouldn't disturb those things if I were you."

But my words went unheeded. When I reached Barksdale's side, he was holding a small flat bottle, half filled with a sticky black fluid, and was rubbing the earth from it with his coat sleeve. The man was electric with excitement. He held the flask close to his glasses, then spun around upon me.

"Do you know what this is?" he demanded, then rushed on triumphantly with his answer: "It's a first issue, half pint flask of the old South Carolina state dispensary. It gives me the only complete set in existence. Not another one in America. I had hoped that I might get on the trail of one down here. But to fall upon it like this!"

The hand that held the flask was shaking so violently that the little palmetto tree and single X that marked it described small agitated circles. He drew out his handkerchief and wrapped it up tenderly, black contents and all.

"Come," he announced, "we'll go now."

"Not so fast," I cautioned him. "You can't carry that away. It simply isn't done down here. We may have our moral lapses, but there are certain things that—well—can't be thought of. The graveyard is one. We let it alone."

He placed the linen covered package tenderly inside his pocket and buttoned his coat with an air of finality; then he faced me truculently.

"I have been searching for this flask for ten years," he asserted. "If you can find the proper person to whom payment should be made I will give a good price. In the meantime I intend to keep it. It certainly is of no use to anyone, and I shan't hesitate for a silly superstition."

I could not thrash him for it and I saw that nothing short of physical violence would remove it from his person. For a second I was tempted to argue with him; tell him why he should not take the thing. Then I was frustrated by my own lack of a reason. I groped with my instinctive knowledge that it was not to be done, trying to embody the abstract into something sufficiently concrete to impress him. And all the while I felt his gaze upon me, hard, very blue, a little mocking, absolutely determined.

Behind the low crest of the ridge sounded a single burst of laughter, and the ring of a trace chain. A strange panic seized me. Taking him by the arm I rushed him across the short distance to the buckboard and into his seat; then leaped across him and took up the lines.

Night was upon us, crowding forward from the recesses of the forest, pushing out beyond us through the last scattered trees, flowing over the sea and lifting like level smoke into the void of sky. The horse started forward, wrenching the wheels from the clutching sand.

Before us, coming suddenly up in the dusk, a party of field Negroes filled the road. A second burst of laughter sounded, warm now, volatile and disarming. It made me ashamed of my panic. The party passed on both sides of the road. The vestiges of the day brought out high lights on their long earth-polished hoes. Teeth were a white accent here and there. Only eyes, fallen sockets under the brows of the very old, seemed to defy the fading glimmer, bringing the night in them from the woods. Laughter and soft Gullah words were warm in the air about us.

"Howdy, Boss."

"Ebenin', Boss."

The women curtsied in their high tucked up skirts; the men touched hat brims. Several mules followed, grotesque and incredible in the thickening dark, their trace chains dangling and chiming faintly.

The party topped the rise, then dropped behind it.

Silence, immediate and profound, as though a curtain had been run down upon the heels of the last.

"A simple folk," clipped out my companion. "I rather envy them starting out at zero, as it were, with everything to learn from our amazing civilization."

"Zero, hell!" I flung out. "They had created a Congo art before our ancestors drugged and robbed their first Indian."

The first few days at the club were spent by my guest in going through the preliminary routine of the systematic writer. Books were unpacked and arranged in the order of study, looseleaf folders were laid out, and notes made for the background of his thesis. He was working at a table in his bedroom which adjoined my own, and as I also used my sleeping apartment as a study for the fabrication of the fiction which, with my salary as manager of the club, discharged my financial obligations, I could not help seeing something of him.

On the morning of the second day I glanced in as I passed his door, and surprised him gloating over his find. It was placed on the table before him, and he was gazing fixedly at it. Unfortunately, he looked up; our glances met and, with self-consciousness that smote us simultaneously, remained locked. Each felt that the subject had better remain closed—yet there the flask stood evident and unavoidable.

After a strained space of time I managed to step into the room, pick up a book and say:

"I am rather interested in Negroes myself. Do you mind if I see what you have here?"

While I examined the volume he passed behind me and put the flask away, then came and looked at the book with me. *"African Religions and Superstitions,"* he said, reading the title aloud; then supplemented:

"An interesting mythology for the American Negro, little more. The African Gullah Negro, from whom these are descended, believed in a God, you know, but he only created, then turned his people adrift to be preyed upon by malign spirits conjured up by their enemies. Really a religion, or rather a superstition, of senseless terror."

"I am not so sure of the complete obsoleteness of the old rites and superstitions," I told him, feeling as I proceeded that I was engaged in a useless mission. "I know these Negroes pretty well. For them, Plat-eye, for instance, is a very actual presence. If you will notice the cook you will see that she seems to get along without a prayer book, but when she goes home after dark she sticks a sulphur match in her hair. Sulphur is a charm against Plat-eye."

"Tell me," he asked with a bantering light in his eyes, "just what is Plat-eye?"

I felt that I was being laughed at and floundered ahead at the subject, anxious to be out of it as soon as possible.

"Plat-eye is a spirit which takes some form which will be particularly apt to lure its victims away. It is said to lead them into danger or lose them in the woods and, stealing their wits away, leave them to die alone."

He emitted a short acid laugh.

"What amusing rot. And I almost fancy you believe it."

"Of course I don't," I retorted, but I experienced the feeling that my voice was over-emphatic and failed to convince.

"Well, well," he said, "I am not doing folklore but religion. So that is out of my province. But it is amusing and I'll make a note of it. Plat-eye, did you say?"

The next day was Thursday. I remember that distinctly because, although nearly a week's wages were due, the last servant failed to arrive for work in the morning. The club employed three of them; two women and a man. Even in the off season this was a justifiable expense, for a servant could be hired on Ediwander for four dollars a week. When I went to order breakfast the kitchen was closed, and the stove cold.

After a makeshift meal I went to find the yard boy. There were only a few Negroes in the village and these were women hoeing in the small garden patches before the cabins. There were the usual swarms of lean mongrel hounds, and a big sow lay nourishing her young in the warm dust of the road. The women looked up as I passed. Their soft voices, as they raised their heads one after another to say "Mornin', Boss," seemed like emanations from the very soil, so much a part of the earth did they appear.

But the curs were truculent that morning: strange, canny, candid little mongrels. If you want to know how you stand with a Negro, don't ask him—pat his dog.

I found Thomas, the hired boy, sitting before his cabin watching a buzzard carve half circles in the blue.

"When are you coming to work?" I demanded. "The day's half done."

"I gots de toot' ache, Boss. I can't git ober 'fore termorrer." The boy knew that I did not believe him. He also knew that I would not take issue with him on the point. No Negro on the island will say "no" to a white man. Call it "good form" if you will, but what Thomas had said to me was merely the code for "I'm through." I did not expect him and I was not disappointed.

Noon of the following day I took the buckboard, crossed the ferry to the mainland, and returned at dark with a cheerful wholesome Negress, loaned to me by a plantation owner, who answered for her faithfulness and promised that she would cook for us during the emergency. She got us a capital supper, retired to the room adjoining the kitchen that I had prepared for her, as I did not wish her to meet the Negroes in the village, and in the morning had vanished utterly. She must have left immediately after supper, for the bed was undisturbed.

I walked straight from her empty room to Barksdale's sanctum, entered, crossed to the closet where he had put the flask, and threw the door wide. The space was empty. I spun around and met his amused gaze.

"Thought I had better put it away carefully. It is too valuable to leave about."

Our glances crossed like the slide of steel on steel. Then suddenly my own impotence to master the situation arose and overwhelmed me. I did not admit it even to myself, but that moment saw what amounted to my complete surrender.

We entered upon the haphazard existence inevitable with two preoccupied men unused to caring for their own comfort: impossible makeshift meals, got when we were hungry; beds made when we were ready to get into them; with me, hours put into work that had to be torn up and started over the next day; with Barksdale, regular tours of investigation about the island and two thousand words a day, no more, no less, written out in longhand and methodically filed. We naturally saw less and less of each other—a fact which was evidently mutually agreeable.

It was therefore a surprise to me one night in the second week to leap from sleep into a condition of lucid consciousness and find myself staring at Barksdale who had opened the door between our rooms. There he stood like a bird of ill omen, tall and slightly stooping, with his ridiculous nightshirt and thin slightly bowed shanks.

"I'll leave this open if you don't mind," he said with a note of apology in his voice. "Haven't been sleeping very well for a week or so, and thought the draft through the house might cool the air."

Immediately I knew that there was something behind the apparently casual action of the man. He was the type who could lie through conviction; adopt some expedient point of view, convince himself that it was the truth, then assert it as a fact; but he was not an instinctive liar, and that new apologetic note gave him away. For a while after he went back to bed, I lay wondering what was behind his request.

Then for the first time I felt it; but hemmed in by the appalling limitations of human speech, how am I to make the experience plain to others!

Once I was standing behind the organ of a great cathedral when a bass chord was pressed upon the keys; suddenly the air about me was all sound and movement. The demonstration that night was like this a little, except that the place of the sound was taken by an almost audible silence, and the vibrations were so violent as to seem almost a friction against the nerve terminals. The wave of movement lasted for several minutes, then it abated slowly. But this was the strange thing about it: the agitation was not dissipated into the air; rather it seemed to settle slowly, heavily, about my body, and move upon my skin like the multitudinous crawling of invisible and indescribably loathsome vermin.

I got up and struck a light. The familiar disorder of the room sprang into high relief, reassuring me, telling me coolly not to be a fool. I took the lamp into Barksdale's room. There he lay, his eyes wide and fixed, braced in his bed with every muscle tense. He gave me the impression of wrenching himself out of invisible bonds as he turned and sat up on the edge of the bed.

"Just about to get up and work," he said in a voice that he could not manage to make casual. "Been suffering from insomnia for a week, and it's beginning to get on my nerves."

The strange sensation had passed from my body but the thought of sleep was intolerable. We went to our desks leaving the door ajar, and wrote away the four hours that remained until daylight.

And now a question arises of which due cognizance must be taken even though it may weaken my testimony. Is a man quite sane who has been without sleep for ten days and nights? Is he a competent witness? I do not know. And yet the phenomena that followed my first startled awakening entered into me and became part of my life experience. I live them over shudderingly when my resistance is low and memory has its way with me. I know that they transpired with that instinctive certainty which lies back of human knowledge and is immune from the skepticism of the cynic.

After the first night the house was filled with the vibrations. I closed the door to Barksdale's room, hoping a superstitious hope that I would be immune. After an hour I opened it again, glad for even his companionship. Only while I was wide awake and driving my brain to its capacity did the agitation cease. At the first drowsiness it would commence faintly, then swell up and up, fighting sleep back from the tortured brain, working under leaden eyelids upon the tired eyes.

Ten days and nights of it! Terrible for me: devastating for Barksdale. It wasted him like a jungle fever.

Once when I went near him and his head had dropped forward on his desk in the vain hope of relief, I made a discovery. He was the *center*. The moment I bent over him my nerve terminals seemed to become living antennae held out to a force that frayed and wasted them away. In my own room it was better. I went there and sat where I could still see him for what small solace there was in that.

I entreated him to go away, but with his insane obstinacy he would not hear it. Then I thought of leaving him, confessing myself a coward—bolting for it. But again, something deeper than logic, some obscure tribal loyalty, held me bound. Two members of the same race; and out there the palmetto jungle, the village with its fires bronze against the midnight trees, the malign, beleaguering presence. No, it could not be done.

But I did slip over to the mainland and arrange to send a wire to Spencer telling him to come and get Barksdale, that the man was ill.

During that interminable ten days and nights the fundamental difference between Barksdale and myself became increasingly evident. He would go to great pains to explain the natural causes of our malady.

"Simple enough," he would say, while his bloodshot eyes, fixed on me, shouted the lies to his words. "One of those damn swamp fevers, Livingstone complained of them, you will remember, and so did Stanley. Here in this subtropical belt we are evidently subject to the plague. Doubtless there is serum. I should have inquired before coming down."

To this I said nothing, but I confess now, at risk of being branded a coward, that I had become the victim of a superstitious terror. Frequently when Barksdale was out I searched for the flask without finding the least trace of it. Finally I capitulated utterly and took to carrying a piece of sulphur next to my skin. Nothing availed.

The strange commotion in the atmosphere became more and more persistent. It crowded over from the nights into the days. It came at noon; any time that drowsiness fell upon our exhausted bodies it was there, waging a battle with it behind the closed lids. Only with the muscles tense and the eyes wide could one inhabit a static world. After the first ten days I lost count of time. There was a nightmare quality to its unbreakable continuity.

I remember only the night when I saw *her* in Barksdale's doorway, and I think that it must have been in the third week. There was a full moon, I remember, and there had been unusual excitement in the village. I have always had a passion for moonlight and I stood long on the piazza watching the great disc change from its horizon copper to gold, then cool to silver as it swung up into the immeasurable tranquility of the southern night. At first I thought that Negroes must be having a dance, for I could hear the syncopation of sticks on a cabin floor, and the palmettos and moss-draped live oaks that grew about the buildings could be seen the full quarter of a mile away, a ruddy bronze against the sky from a brush fire. But the longer I waited listening the less sure I became about the nature of the celebration. The rhythm became strange, complicated; and the chanting that rose and fell with the drumming rang with a new, compelling quality, and lacking entirely the abandon of the dancers.

Finally I went into my room, stretched myself fully dressed on the bed, and almost achieved oblivion. Then suddenly I was up again, my fists clenched, my body taut. The agitation exceeded anything that I had before experienced. Before me, across Barksdale's room, were wide open double doors letting on the piazza. They molded the moonlight into a square that plunged through the darkness of the room, cold, white, and strangely substantial among the half-obliterated familiar objects. I had the feeling that it could be touched. That hands could be slid along its bright surface. It possessed itself of the place. It was the one reality in a swimming, nebulous cube. Then it commenced to tremble with the vibrations of the apartment.

And now the incredible thing happened. Incredible because belief arises in each of us out of the corroboration of our own life experience; and I have met no other white man who has beheld Plat-eye. I have no word, no symbol which can awaken recognition. But who has not seen heat shaking upward from hot asphalt, shaking upward until the things beyond it wavered and quaked? That is the nearest approach in the material world. Only the thing that I witnessed was colored a cold blue, and it was heavy with the perfume of crushed jasmine flowers.

I stood, muscle locked to muscle by terror.

The center of the shaft darkened; the air bore upon me as though some external force exerted a tremendous pressure in an effort to render an abstraction concrete: to mold moving unstable elements into something that could be seen—touched.

Suddenly it was done—accomplished. I looked—I saw *her*.

The shock released me, and I got a flare from several matches struck at once. Yellow light bloomed on familiar objects. I got the fire to a lamp wick, then looked again.

The shaft of moonlight was gone. The open doors showed only a deep blue vacant square. Beyond them something moved. The lamplight steadied, grew. It warmed the room like fire. It spread over the furniture, making it real again. It fell across Barksdale's bed, dragging my gaze with it. *The bed was empty.*

I got to the piazza just as he disappeared under a wide armed live oak. The Spanish moss fell behind him like a curtain. The place was a hundred yards away. When I reached it, all trace of him had vanished.

I went back to the house, built a rousing fire, lit all the lamps, and stretched myself in a deep chair to wait until morning.

Then! An automobile horn on Ediwander Island. Imagine that! I could not place it at first. It crashed through my sleep like the trump of judgment. It called me up from the abysses into which I had fallen. It infuriated me. It reduced me to tears. Finally it tore me from unutterable bliss, and held me blinking in the high noon, with my silly lamps still burning palely about me.

"You're a hell of a fellow," called Spencer. "Think I've got nothing to do but come to the jungle in summer to nurse you and Barksdale."

He got out of a big muddy machine and strode forward laughing. "Oh, well," he said, "I won't row you. It gave me a chance to try out the new bus. That's why I'm late. Thought I'd motor down. Had a hell of a time getting over the old ferry; but it was worth it to see the niggers when I started up on Ediwander. Some took to trees—one even jumped overboard."

He ended on a hearty burst of laughter. Then he looked at me and broke off short. I remember how his face looked then, close to mine, white and frightened.

"My God, man!" he exclaimed, "what's wrong? You aren't going to die on me, are you?"

"Not today," I told him. "We've got to find Barksdale first."

We could not get a Negro to help us. They greeted Spencer, who had always been popular with them, warmly. They laughed their deep laughter—were just as they had always been with him. Mingo, his old paddler, promised to meet us in half an hour with a gang. They never showed up; and later, when we went to the village to find them, there was not a human being on the premises. Only a pack of curs there that followed us as closely as they dared and hung just out of boot reach, snapping at our heels.

We had to go it alone: a stretch of jungle five miles square, a large part of it accessible only with bush hooks and machetes. We dared not take the time to go to the mainland and gather a party of whites. Barksdale had been gone over twelve hours when we started and he would not last long in his emaciated condition.

The chances were desperately against us. Spencer, though physically a giant, was soft from office life. I was hanging on to consciousness only by a tremendous and deliberate effort. We took food with us, which we ate on our feet during breathing spells, and we fell in our tracks for rest when we could go no farther.

At night, when we were eating under the high, white moon, he told me more of the man for whom we were searching.

"I ought to have written you more fully at the start. You'd have been sorry for him then, not angry with him. He does not suggest Lothario now, but he was desperately in love once.

"She was the most fantastically imaginative creature, quick as light, and she played in circles around him. He was never dull in those days. Rather handsome, in the lean Gibson manner; but he was always—well—matter of fact. She had all there was of him the first day, and it was hers to do as she pleased with. Then one morning she saw quite plainly that he would bore her. She had to have someone who could *play*. Barksdale could have died for her, but he could not play. Like that," and Spencer gave a snap of his fingers, "she jugged him. It was at a house party. I was there and saw it. She was the sort of surgeon who believes in amputation and she gave it to Barksdale there without an anaesthetic and with the crowd looking on.

"He changed after that. Wouldn't have anything he couldn't feel, see, smell. He had been wounded by something elusive, intangible. He was still scarred; and he hid behind the defenses of his five good senses. When I met him five years later he had gone in for facts and glass."

He stopped speaking for a moment. The August dark crowded closer, pressing its low, insistent nocturne against our ears. Then he resumed in a musing voice: "Strange the obsession that an imaginative woman can exercise over an unimaginative man. It is the sort of thing that can follow a chap to the grave. Celia's living in Europe now, married—children—but I believe that if she called him today he'd go. She was very beautiful, you know."

"Yes," I replied, "I know. Very tall, blonde, with hair fluffed and shining about her head like a madonna's halo. Odd way of standing, too, with her head turned to one side so that she might look at one over her shoulder. Jasmine perfume, heavy, almost druggy."

Spencer was startled: "You've seen her!"

"Yes, here. She came for Barksdale last night. I saw her as plainly as I see you."

I turned to Spencer with a sudden resolve: "You've heard the Negroes here talk of Plat-eye?"

He nodded.

"Well, I've got to tell you something whether you believe it or not. Barksdale got in wrong down here. Stole a flask from the graveyard. There's been hell turned loose ever since: fires and singing every night in the village and a lot more. I am sure now what it all meant—conjuring, and Plat-eye, of course, to lead Barksdale away and do him in, at the same time emptying the house so that it could be searched for the flask."

"But Celia; how could they know about her?"

"They didn't. But Barksdale knew. They had only to break him down and let his old obsession call her up. I probably saw her on the reflex from him, but I'll swear she was there."

Spencer was leaning toward me, the moon shining full upon his face. I could see that he believed.

"Thank God you see it," I breathed. "Now you know why we've got to find him soon."

In the hour just before dawn we emerged from the forest at the far side of the island. The moon was low and reached long fingers of pale light through the trees. The east was a swinging nebula of half light and vapor. A flight of immense blue heron broke suddenly into the air before us, hurling the mist back into our faces from their beating wings. Spencer, who was ahead of me, gave a cry and darted forward, disappearing behind a palmetto thicket.

I grasped my machete and followed.

Our quest had ended. Barksdale lay face downward in the marsh with his head toward the east. His hands flung out before him were already awash in the rising tide.

We dragged him to high ground. He was breathing faintly in spasmodic gasps, and his pulse was a tiny thread of movement under our finger tips. Two saplings and our coats gave us a makeshift litter, and three hours of stumbling, agonizing labor brought us with our burden to the forest's edge.

I waited with him there, while Spencer went for his car and some wraps. When he returned his face was a study.

"Had a devil of a time finding blankets," he told me, as we bundled Barksdale up for the race to town. "House looks as though a tornado had passed through it; everything out on the piazza, and in the front yard."

With what strength I had left I turned toward home. Behind me lay the forest, dark even in the summer noon; before me, the farthest hill, the sparse pines, and the tumble of mounds in the graveyard.

I entered the clearing and looked at the mound from which Barksdale had taken the flask. There it was again. While it had been gone the cavity had filled with water; now this had flooded out when the bottle had been replaced and still glistened gray on the sand, black on the pine needles.

I regained the road and headed for the club.

Up from the fields came the hands, dinner bound; fifteen or twenty of them; the women taking the direct sun indifferently upon their bare heads. Bright field hoes gleamed on shoulders. The hot noon stirred to deep laughter, soft Gullah accents:

"Mornin', Boss—howdy, Boss."

They divided and flowed past me, women curtsying, men touching hat brims. On they went; topped the bridge; dropped from view.

Silence, immediate and profound.

FROM

Mamba's Daughters

A NOVEL OF CHARLESTON

From Part II

[Hagar and Bluton]

[In this excerpt from part II, Hagar has taken a job at a phosphate mining camp far
outside the city in order to help finance her daughter Lissa's ambitions for a career
in music, away from Charleston and above the low social plateau to which her race
has consigned her. Brutish and illiterate, Hagar (who has taken the name Baxter)
cares deeply for her daughter and for her fellow Gullahs. In this scene, she risks imprisonment by taking Gilly Bluton, a scoundrel who is wounded in a knife fight, into
town to get medical help, knowing that if she is found with Bluton, police will assume it was she who wounded him. In an ironic reversal, Hagar later will kill Bluton
when she learns that he has tried to force himself on Lissa and, in a mirror image of
this scene, carries his corpse out into the woods to bury it.]

IT WAS TIME for the love feast. The committee had the refreshments
ready—gaudy little factory-made cakes from the commissary, cherry bounce,
thinned economically with lemonade. But the spirit of song had seized the
bodies of the congregation, and the gross appetites of the stomachs were
forgotten. They passed the plates to a few, but the singers would have none
of them. Benches were being thrown back and the floor cleared for a shout.
Already splay feet were slapping the loose boards of the floor. The spiritual
rang out:

SOURCE: Mamba's Daughters (New York: Farrar and Rinehart, 1929), 100–112, 205–39, and
305–11.

> "Oh, mornin' star is in de West—
> Honour de Lamb, honour de Lamb!
> An' I wish dat star was in my breast.
> Honour de Lamb, honour de Lamb . . ."

Now the shouters were in full swing, bodies that could give themselves utterly to a rhythm swayed and bent; here two facing each other, the rest forgotten; there several together with a more concerted interplay. But always the feet hit the same time, swaying and rattling the whole building.

> "Oh, way down yonder in de Harbes' Fiel'—
> Honour de Lamb, honour de Lamb!
> Angel workin' on de cha'iot wheel.
> Honour de Lamb, honour de Lamb!"

One of the larger groups started to circle, and a ring shout was under way. The refreshment committee knew that this could last until morning. They put their plates aside to be eaten by those who would drop out later from exhaustion.

Shrill and piercing above the more measured rhythm of the spiritual, with its worship of the new Christ, cut the voice of a soprano in the Gullah shouting rhythm:

> "Simmi yubba leaba, simmi uyh,
> Ronda bohda simmi yuh . . ."

Only the two lines, but repeated interminably in a heavily syncopated measure, with the concerted stamping of the feet crashing through it like the thunder of a tribal tom-tom.

Some of the older people began to drop out and reach gratefully for the cooling drink. But, with the younger, the excitement mounted. Women screamed. Men emptied their flasks openly, their feet holding the rhythm the while.

Ned was there. He had tried to persuade Dolly to come, but she never went out with him now, and had said she was ill and would go to bed. They had a sort of understanding now. He did not ask much of her—except not to go around openly with Bluton. She was not to shame him before everybody. Now he looked up from his shouting and saw them in the door. Dolly was good-looking, the best-looking woman in the room. Her full figure was pressed close to the man to whose arm she clung. Gilly had been drinking, and the beast that he was looked unguarded out from his face. The cunning, bestiality, hypocrisy—there they were. His eyes were fixed on Ned, gloating with insolent amusement. The man and woman left the doorway and sauntered into the room. Then, with the rhythm of the shouters, who were so rapt that they were dazed, rushing it up to a swift dramatic climax, tragedy was upon them.

Ned had his razor out, holding it as the old razor fighters used to, the handle clenched lightly in his hand, and the blade with back resting against the closed fingers of his fist. Held so, it could not close on its owner and could be hurled downward with the full weight of the fist behind it. Some one snatched up one lamp and hurled it from a window, but one remained hanging from a beam and could not be reached. There was a rush for doors and windows. When the crowd gained the open and looked back, it was over. Ned had vanished as if by magic. Dolly was gone. Of the three principals in the drama Bluton alone remained. He lay under the lamp that was swinging slightly, casting his shadow eerily from side to side, creating a terrifying illusion of movement. He was not alone. Baxter loomed above him. She stood as though hypnotised, looking down at the dark venous blood that flowed out of the slashed clothing and sent the arc of its sinister circle rapidly toward her. Now it was under one of her great bare feet. She moved. A foot slid sickeningly and waked her suddenly from her trance.

"Sweet Jedus!" she ejaculated and dropped to her knees.

Knife wounds were nothing new to her. She opened a slashed sleeve and examined the cut. It was as clean and incisive as surgery—but, God! she didn't know a man had so much blood to spill. She hoisted her shirt, snatched off her petticoat and tore it into strips. She saw the windows and doors, then, filled with wide eyes and sullen faces.

"Gimme a han', somebody," she called. "Can't be yo' goin' stan' dere an' let a man dead!"

No one moved. Their hatred of Bluton seemed to make the air dark and thick about the kneeling woman. Ned had done it for them. They had only to go away and leave him. But no one could muster the courage to call her off. They could only watch and see which way the dice would fall—"Good luck Gilly"—or the rest of them. He lay with his face toward her. There was a slash across the forehead close to the hair and, below it, the yellow skin had gone a ghastly grey. Alone—he was worse off than she, for all his money and his dubious good luck. His hand lay flung open beside her. It was long-fingered, sensual, soft, with that beauty of modelling so often found in the hand of a negro. The palm was scarcely lighter than the outer skin. She took it in both of hers, his plight forgotten for the moment. Her brain had been cloudy with liquor, but the excitement had charged across it like an electric storm and left it clear and ringing, but it was a thing separate from herself, working irresistibly from premises of its own choosing. The slender hand lying between her strong, dark ones held her fascinated gaze. It dissociated itself from the personality of Bluton. The touch of it made her flinch, but she could not release it. Then she knew why: it was an enlarged replica of Lissa's, shaped and coloured the same. A warm smothering sensation took her suddenly, making her senses lurch and waver. Then her starved maternity took Bluton in. It was instinctive but it was utter. For that night, while he lay alone and near to death, she gave him all that she could have given to her own flesh and blood.

She worked with frantic haste. A band tied above a wound and drawn tight with her bare hands was as effectual as a tourniquet. He was deeply slashed in both arms as he had shielded his face with them, and there was that gash across the forehead. After the uproar in the room its poisoned atmosphere now hung in a dead and ominous quiet. The silent watchers at the window waited, their eyes following Baxter's every movement. No arteries had been cut, but the veins had poured out the man's life until he was in desperate straits. The ghastly visage thrown up toward the light showed that something must be done immediately. Baxter bound the wounds, staunching the bleeding. Then she stood up and met the eyes that were fixed on her.

"We gots to get um to town quick," she said. "If we can get um in de hospital, maybe dey can pull um t'rough."

Not a body moved. They kept on standing there staring at her inimically. She faced them desperately. Oh, if she only had Mamba now! Mamba who always made plans, pushed things through. She turned back on her own resources, and a plan began to form. She met old Drayton's eyes peering in a window, and in a second she had him by the arm.

"Listen!" she shot into his face. "Yo' go an' break in de commissary stable an' get de wagon here soon as yo' can. Ah'll fix it wid Mr. Saint." The old man hesitated. "If dat wagon ain't here in fibe minute I ain't nebber goin' dig anoder pit wid yo'. Onnerstan'!"

She loosed him and he started for the stable at an unsteady run.

A voice that was unable to conceal its satisfaction called out, "Dat ain't no use. Dey ain't le's nuthin' but city niggers free to de hospital. Country nigger gots to pay in exvance."

"Dat all right," Baxter answered. "Gilly always gots money."

She dropped on her knees and went through Bluton's pockets. Not a penny. Then they all remembered at once. The man had stripped the settlement of every cent on the whiskey sale and had carried the money away to hide. The irony of the situation struck the negro humour and they began to laugh.

"Sarve um right," some one called. "Can't trus' we—now he can dead. Ain't nuttin' but a low white-folks nigger nohow."

The big woman glared at them.

"He ain't goin' dead. Yo' hear dat, yo' dirty passel ob yellow-liver nigger?—He ain't goin' dead. 'Cause Ah's goin' see um t'rough."

The wagon rattled up. Baxter heard it, stooped, lifted her charge in her arms, and, taking him from the building, lay him on the floor of the vehicle. There was an old tarpaulin on the seat. She spread it carefully over him and climbed in. Then she looked down at the sullen crowd about the wagon and lashed them with her parting words.

"Yo' gawd-damned low-livered niggers. Yo' fair mak' me 'shamed tuh be black."

No one answered, and the vehicle started off under the live oaks with the horse moving soundlessly between the deep sandy ruts and the passenger lying, awful in his immobility, under the tarpaulin.

BAXTER BROUGHT all of her faculties to bear on the problem of getting him into the hospital. If she could only have Mamba here now—she would know what to do. Then, slowly, under the urge of necessity, her brain began to evolve a scheme. What if he were found near the hospital—lying unconscious in the street—who would know that he was not a town nigger? She had had friends who had been found so by the police and carried to the hospital, where they were cared for. She knew the city well. The police were few in the quiet part of the town. Perhaps she could slip through the darkened streets and leave Bluton on one of the beats.

They had covered several miles before she finally decided to risk the plan. She had been so intent upon it that no other consideration had entered her mind. Now she was aware of a menacing shadow—a prescience that all was not right. Then it came down upon her like a physical blow—what if she were caught? Two years in jail. Immediately the horror elaborated itself in her quickened imagination. What would Mamba say? Lissa!—All the young girl's toney friends—her music—and her ma in the jail! They would throw Lissa out—she knew it. Instantly it loomed insurmountable before her. But here was Bluton—she could not let him die now. Sweat burst out on her face, cold and clammy in the night air.

With the odd instinct of dumb animals, the horse had sensed her hesitation and stopped in the middle of the road. She mopped her streaming face. Then, with a decisive gesture, she slapped the animal's back with the slack lines. She'd have to gamble on her luck. Maybe it had changed. Anyway, she'd have to see it through.

She was on the main road now, and the going was good. In the distance she could see the taut thread of the bridge, white under the moonlight, and the red light at the draw glowing like a single ruby at its centre. Then came a short drive over the flats, with the marsh talking to her in its soft plopping monosyllables.

On the planking now, the loose timbers making a thunder of sound in her apprehensive ears as the shod hoofs fell rhythmically against them. The draw was closed. That made it final. She must go ahead now. Had it been left open to-night, as was sometimes done, fate would have turned her back. A high tide ran under the bridge, sweeping the moon's silver under it in a shining flood. Overhead the luminous disk—no longer brass, but a cold platinum— was so brilliant that its light had drowned out all of the lesser stars. The vehicle, with its silent passenger and the great hunched figure of its driver, moved toward the dark clustered buildings of the city as though it advanced beneath a vast flood light upon a gargantuan stage.

The toll office was closed for the night, but Baxter's approach had been heralded by the noise of the vehicle, and as she left the bridge she saw the night watchman waiting. He was a very old, bent man, and he stood swinging his stick and peering up in surprise.

"Where you goin' this hour of the night?" he called querulously, with the pettishness of one who has just been awakened. Then Baxter remembered that she had no money to pay toll.

"Jus' takin' some truck[1] to town," she said lamely. "I'll pay comin' back when de office open."

But the persistent old creature would not let it go at that. She had stopped the wagon, and he now came up and peered over the side. He was standing there, undecided what to do. Baxter's mind was in panic. Should she risk bolting for it with the old horse and heavy wagon? They were both silent, trying to make up their minds. Bluton became the deciding factor. There was movement beneath the canvas and a low, agonized groan. With an instinctive reflex action, Baxter's foot shot out and caught the horse full on the rump. An astonished spring jerked the vehicle clear of the watchman. Then the animal gathered himself together and set off with the vehicle clattering and jouncing over the cobbles. The din would bring the whole town about her ears if it continued, and so, as soon as the driver collected her wits, she threw her weight on the right line with the result that they were plunged into the immediate peace of an unpaved side street. She pulled the animal down to a walk and listened with her heart thumping heavily in her throat. There was no sound of pursuit. Evidently the watchman had gone back to his nap and the policeman had been at the remote end of his beat.

She waited a moment under a shade tree to quiet the trembling animal and to gather courage for the plunge from the pool of shadow into the relentless moonlight. Confidence that her luck had changed began to come. She had won the first break. The horse was quiet now. She must get on with it.

She moved out of the shadow, driving slowly and soundlessly in the soft deeply rutted earth. Now her whole being seemed concentrated in her sense of hearing. In the remote residential section through which she was passing the stillness was so absolute that she even heard faint snoring in one of the houses. Then, with a sudden intrusion of humour into tragedy, came a fretful female voice waking the offender and telling him to lie on his side. Then came footsteps on the pavement of a side street, indolent, heavy, maddening in their deliberation. Baxter pulled the wagon under the wide-flung branches of a tree and waited. Around the corner a half block away came a policeman. He was swinging his club by its thong, and his head was thrown back while he gazed up into the wonder of the night. Without looking down, he pursued his leisurely way down the street past where Baxter was waiting.

She saw his broad back receding ahead of her and knew that for the second time luck had been with her. Now she had only to wait until he was out of earshot, then follow, discharge her passenger near the hospital, and the officer would find him on his next round. Presently she was under way again and covered the three blocks to her destination without adventure.

She pulled the wagon into the shadow of a palmetto. A faint air was talking to the tree, and it was answering in its harsh gutturals, so different from the voices of other trees. The sound frightened Baxter, but she conquered her qualms. She climbed down and removed the canvas from Bluton's form. Then she saw that his eyes were open and fixed upon her.

"Oh, dat yo', Baxter?" he said in a weak voice. "What de hell is all dis about, anyhow?" Then he moved, became aware of his wounds, and groaned loudly.

"Shut yo' damn' mout'," she answered fiercely; then gathered him up, carried him into the light, and placed him on the pavement. Bending down, she spoke almost savagely into his face.

"Yo' want fuh dead?"

"Fuh Gawd's sake, no! You wouldn't—"

She cut him off. "Berry well, den. Listen! Keep yo' eye an' yo' mout' shet. Don't tell nobody who yo' is or whar yo' come from. Got dat straight?"

He nodded. Then she saw that the exertion had caused him to faint again.

She drove the rig down a side street, tied the horse beneath a tree, and crept back to watch. She had not long to wait. The deliberate steps were coming back. She saw the figure now, a black, solid bulk in the white light.

Now he was fairly on the supine form of Bluton. Had he gone blind? Then, "Well, I'll be god damned!"

He stooped, made a swift examination, then rose quickly, trotted to a box on the corner, and put in a call. Scarcely had he got back to the inert form before the wagon came. Two alert figures sprang out and lifted the wounded man in. Then, with a single clang of the bell, the vehicle lunged away toward the hospital.

BAXTER SLIPPED BACK around the corner of the fence that had been shielding her and returned to the wagon. There, suddenly, in her moment of triumph, she knew that she had lost. The bridge was the only way back, and the irate watchman would be waiting for her there. There would be no disguising her great body that always got her into trouble. She was caught in a trap. The realisation came with a numbing shock and paralysed her initiative. Mamba! She must get to her and ask her what to do. The recklessness generated by the whiskey had gone from her blood; the maternal impulse that had driven her blindly into her danger was passing. She was suddenly terribly afraid; a little whimpering sound escaped her.

Then she heard a human voice, casually conversational, expressing amused surprise. "Well, if here ain't the big un back in town!"

She looked down and knew the man instantly. He had called for her more than once in the room on East Bay, and he had been the officer who had carried her off that last fateful night.

She was speechless, sitting massively above him, sobbing freely now into the crook of her arm. Down on the pavement the Celtic intuition in the big square body was beginning to put two and two together.

"So, it's you that just dumped the high yaller on Calhoun Street? Well, I got to hand it to you; you ain't fergot how to take 'em to pieces! Reckon you better drive back there to the box while I call a special to take you in."

"I swear to Gawd, chief, I ain't cut dat nigger up. Listen 'fore yo' call, fuh Gawd' sake! an' lemme tell yo' how 'tis!"

He led the horse out into the light where he could see the woman plainly and told her to go ahead. When she had finished her story he stood silent a moment. Then he said, "You know, Big Un, it's funny, but I don't believe you're lying. I think you're just about that damned a fool." Then he asked, "This the first time you been in town?"

"Yes, Boss. I swear tuh Gawd."

He fairly snapped his answer at her: "Well, git out o' it damn quick! An' I ain't seen no woman nor wagon since suppertime, I don't care what the hell anybody says."

He turned and walked briskly away. In a moment he had rounded the nearest corner, and his footfalls were fading into silence.

Hagar must get to Mamba now. That was the only thing to do. Her own mind had stopped working. She had to cross the city in a diagonal direction, and it was more instinct than conscious judgment that selected the deserted byways and alleys for her passage. But luck was with her—luck and a sharp retrenchment in the police department with a reluctant cut in personnel— and she traversed the distance without being again in jeopardy. Finally, just before the day, she drove the wagon into the court in East Bay Street.

She routed out a startled friend and sent her to wake and fetch Mamba; then sat waiting like a child who knows that she has done wrong and will be punished.

An hour after the old woman came cursing into the court arrangements were complete. The wagon had been washed down until it was scarcely recognisable as the mud-covered country vehicle; a half-grown boy had been engaged at an honorarium of two dollars to drive it over and deliver it to the commissary, and a fisherman had contracted, for the sum of three dollars, to row Baxter around the city and across the river where she would be within safe walking distance of the mines.

Mamba peered from the gateway and scanned the street. It was absolutely empty, its air astir with that indefinable thrill of expectancy which is the precursor of dawn. There was silence save for the far panting of a freight engine. Growling bitterly over the injustice of a fate that had imposed such a daughter upon her, the old woman conducted the culprit across the street and to the pier head. At the foot of a ladder a boat could be discerned, its rower waiting with oars ready.

Silently Baxter descended and took her seat. In the moment of departure, the old face, hanging above her against the thinning night, softened, and the deep-timbred voice said gently, "Good-bye, Daughter. Fuh Gawd' sake take care ob yo'self an' keep out ob trouble."

The oars dipped, and Baxter was once again out of the city. Behind her the night seemed to cower suddenly down into the narrow streets and beneath the dock. Far out beyond Fort Sumter a new day lifted, washed and shining, from the Atlantic. The oarsman pulled steadily ahead. Above the crouching woman, and looming fabulously into the morning skies, hung the great Battery mansions, their high-flung columns and façades showing rose and saffron in the young day. To her left the "mosquito fleet" was putting to sea for its day at the fishing banks, sailing straight into the eye of the rising sun, and, under Baxter's dazzled gaze, seeming to founder and vanish eastward in a flood of intolerable glory. Close by her now, where she could touch them with her hand, small, plangent waves sprang up and caught the light. She looked for a long moment, lifted out of herself by the splendour; then her large bullet head fell forward on her crossed arms.

"Sweet Jedus," she muttered, "in a worl' like dis, why Yo' gots to make me such a damn' fool!"

The oarsman pulled doggedly ahead toward the distant line of trees.

From Part IV

[Lissa and the Black Elite]

[In this section from part IV, Lissa gains admittance to the society of Charleston's brown elite and learns that class stratification and color prejudice exist in this quar-

ter of the city as well. The contrast between this culture and her mother's and grandmother's is made clear in the way in which the mulattos sing and play music—
technically perfect, but without emotion. Here she also goes "slumming" with one
of her new acquaintances to a country roadhouse and meets "Prince," a.k.a. Gilly
Bluton, who tries (and later succeeds in) taking her away with him.]

MAMBA SAT in her window over the old carriage house in the rear of the
Atkinsons'[2] garden. About her everywhere the spring was busy with its splendid occupation of the old city. At the pavement's edge it had captured a
gnarled oak that had not yet waked from its winter sleep, and had buried it
beneath the headlong rush of a wistaria vine. Now, from this vantage point,
flying columns were being flung to right and left to whelm the chrome and
madder[3] of a winter wall beneath invading mauve and purple. During the
night the wind had changed. It no longer lashed in from the sea with its win-
try tang of salt, but swept across the city from the southwest in a broad languorous tide, heavy with earthy smells from the waking sea islands. It was the
season when youth strains forward with racing pulses; when age, disturbed
and saddened, takes stock of the past and draws solace from such philosophy
as the years may have brought. With elbows on the sill and her face propped
between her palms, Mamba looked upon the alarming visage of spring with
an expression in which the spirit was still unvanquished but in which fear was
held at bay by her old indomitable look of determination.

Under her feet the years were gathering speed alarmingly now. There were
black moments when she would wonder whether she had it in her to hold on
until Lissa could take care of herself and make her own way in that strange
new world of hers. The Atkinson children were growing too, and no longer
needed her care. But she had made no mistake when she had elected the family as her white folk and bound them to herself by an illusory mutual past. As
the boy and girl achieved emancipation from her watchful eyes and became
absorbed by school, athletics, and the social diversion of the ultra-social old
city, she felt herself gradually taking rank as a pensioner of the family. Now
the thousand-and-one odd jobs that had engaged her time when she first in-
sinuated herself into the lives of the Wentworths were again her lot. She no
longer carried the slipper bags to dances, for Jack, now a breezy lad of seventeen, resplendent in his first dinner jacket, and his sister, who was being beautifully finished at an expensive school, went rolling out of the gate in the big
new car that had come to live under Mamba's room in the old carriage house.

But there were still shoes to be shined, flowers to be found, and the front door to be tended on Mrs. Atkinson's afternoons. She knew that as long as she could hold on, could successfully substitute the illusion of being valuable for actual value, Lissa would fare well. Her large clean room over the garage gave the girl a good home, and her white folks fed her, just as they did Mamba, in their kitchen. But if she failed, now at this most critical of all times for her grandchild, the girl would have no claim on the Atkinsons—and her mother would be less than useless as a guiding hand. Sometimes now on Sundays, after the long hot walk to meet Hagar, there would be moments when she would forget names and faces and the steady light of her purpose would be obscured by blowing mists. Then she would summon her forces and pull her faculties together again, but it was an effort that always left her shaken.

Had she spared herself in any particular in her sacrifices for Lissa, her hardness to Hagar would have been quite without justification, but she had given everything that she had looked forward to in her old age for the girl, and so, as a matter of course, should the mother. When Lissa reached the age of seventeen, so long had it been since she had seen her mother that the figure had first grown vague and then been remodelled in her imagination into at least partial conformity with her new standards. To her friends Ma, who was now "Mamma," was employed "up state" and sent her the money for clothes, music, and all of the things that enabled her to hold her head up in the Reformed Church set. The girl's voice was beginning to attract attention. She was doing solos in church, and in programmes given at the new coloured Y.W.C.A. rooms. In appearance she was unforgettable. A large girl for her age, her figure was well developed and straight as an Indian's, and that almost obscured strain of Indian in Mamba had flared up in the grandchild, as it so often will, and given her a skin of pale lustred bronze through which the colour beat in her cheeks and her full-lipped small mouth. Her hair, fine and straight, was worn after the fashion of the Mona Lisa, and beneath it she held in reserve small close-set ears, which, like her beautifully modelled hands, were a heritage from her mother's people. But her glory lay in her eyes, which under stress of emotion would deepen and brighten until they glowed like dark amber in sunlight. She had the negro's faculty of giving her whole being to an emotion, so that under stress every gesture became a graphic interpretation, but her years of hard drilling in music, and her teacher's directions for posture and platform presence were in danger of overdisciplining the emotions as well as the body. Her early natural charm was becoming a studied attitude. Now, only when she was singing for fun, as she would say, could she let herself go and forget herself in music. But the cultivated air of well-bred restraint was the charm that presently admitted her to the most exclusive circle of negro society in the city.

Among the girls that she knew it was said by many that she was hard—that what she wanted she took regardless of others. But in a set rife with jealousies, and with her conspicuous attainments, talk of this sort was no more than was to be expected.

In the old city that was so strong in its class consciousness among the whites it was singular that there was so little realisation of the fact, that, across the colour line, there existed much the same state of affairs. There were, in the opinion of most of the white residents, two general classes of negroes—those who knew their place, and those who did not—and of late years the latter class was drawing upon the former in lamentably large numbers. If they thought at all of the innumerable distinct segments that comprised negro society it was apt to be with mild and, on the whole, indulgent amusement. For it was well known that the sharp cleavages between full-blooded negroes and mulattoes, between the waning power of the ministerial union and the new secular leaders, the labour element and the young but powerful business class, all served to make any dangerous concerted negro movement improbable.

In the set in which Lissa moved she seldom met a full-blooded negro—the barrier of mistrust and prejudice that rose between her fellow members of the Reformed Church and Mamba's friends on East Bay was scarcely less formidable than that separating white from black. The atmosphere that she breathed was that of the Victorian drawing room. Music, which had always found a spontaneous outlet in the spiritual and work chant, colour which was flung with a lavish hand over the house fronts and clashed and rang in the women's dresses down in the waterfront district, had, in that rarer air, become "culture," and found expression in the Monday Night Music Club, and exhibitions of paintings. The untrammelled hilarity and broad humour of Mamba's friends was here muted to the restrained mirth of the late 'nineties. The pendulum had swung with a vengeance and was then at the limit of its range. Far above, in the life of the aristocracy, the new freedom was beginning to be manifest, smashing conventional usage; talking its Freud and Jung—rearranging moral standards, and explaining lapses in its pat psychoanalytical jargon. But in the Monday Night Music Club ladies were ladies, those who were pale enough blushed, a leg was still a limb—and gentlemen asked permission to smoke cigarettes.

It was all a little absurd, one might say—copybook gentility with its middle-class taboos and reticences. Neither the one thing nor the other in the amazing old city of colourful extremes on the one hand and interesting tradition on the other. But it must always be remembered as a beginning. It was establishing standards, putting a premium on chastity. Drawing-room pioneers, perhaps, but adventurers none the less, and leading the way into a terrain that was new and strange.

THE MONDAY NIGHT CLUB held its meeting at the home of Thomas Broaden, a fine old frame building of the conventional Charleston type with piazzas along its south façade, overlooking a square of garden on upper Coming Street.

Seen about the street Broaden was an inconspicuous figure, of middle height and age and light in colour. He habitually wore a soft felt hat pulled well down over his eyes, and always walked, although he was known to be exceedingly well-to-do, and a number of his friends now owned machines. In his office of the new negro bank, however, and facing a caller across his desk, he emerged as an individual. Immediately one would notice the high broad structure of the forehead and the deep thoughtful eyes. Mrs. Broaden was a perfect partner—small and delicately made, she carried her fifty years as though they were thirty and managed the home with that consummate skill which conceals itself in its work and gives an effect of effortlessness and ease. Both Mary and Thomas Broaden had taken degrees, but his was from Tuskegee, while she was a graduate of Howard University.

On the first night that Lissa attended a meeting of the club, such was her eagerness that she was the first member to arrive at the Broaden residence. Her hostess greeted her affectionately. "I am so glad that you have come early," she exclaimed. "Now I'll have a chance to make you feel at home before the others arrive." Explaining that her husband had been detained at the bank, she took the girl by the hand and led her over the lower floor of the house, through large, high-ceilinged rooms in which periods gave the impression of being superimposed upon each other like geological strata—red plush—horsehair—down to several pieces of beautiful old Hepplewhite and Chippendale—for the Broadens had always been free negroes, and some of the furniture had been in the family for more than a century. Lissa was amazed at all that she saw and heard. Here was a life among her own people that she never knew existed. Finally her hostess stopped before a picture. It exhibited a group of mansions on East Battery at the time of the earthquake, porticos down, and great fissures zigzagging across the walls. She spoke of it sadly as one might of a friend who has received a hurt.

"Say," said Lissa with a note of surprise, "you really love this old town, don't you?"

"Why not?" she replied with a smile. "It's home."

"That's funny: most of the crowd in the choir and at the Y. talk of nothing now but a chance to go to New York. That's where the money is these days—that's where coloured people have a chance."

"I wonder," said Mary Broaden wistfully; then, with a kind earnestness, added, "You mustn't say coloured people, my dear—that doesn't mean anything—Japanese, Indian—all are coloured. You are a negro—doesn't it make you proud to say it?"

Lissa looked at her closely to see whether she was serious.

"No," she replied; "my friends don't like that word. It's a new idea, being proud of it."

Her hostess gave a light indulgent laugh and patted her on the shoulder. "I am glad that you didn't wait to say that when the others are here. Frank North, for one, would have withered you with a look."

"Frank North?"

"Yes; he's the painter, you know—and he plays the violin too."[4]

THERE WAS A SHARP RING at the bell. Mrs. Broaden stepped to the door and opened it. From the drawing room Lissa heard several voices pleasantly blended in a composite greeting. Then they drew apart and she distinguished a suave low-pitched man's voice, a higher one with a bright vital quality that she decided must belong to the artist, and several women's voices still interwoven in talk.

When they entered, the owner of the higher man's voice was at once presented, confirming her guess as to his identity. He was pale and slender, with an eager look in his sensitive face. Not more than twenty, Lissa thought as he held out his hand. Bowing slightly from the hips, he said, "I am delighted to make your acquaintance, Miss Atkinson."

Nella Taylor, her music teacher, was there, and she put her arm around the girl's waist and faced the others. "This is my star pupil," she said, "and we're going to give you a treat this evening—aren't we, Lissa?"

She felt by the sudden stiffening of the girl that she was embarrassed, and she hurried on with the introductions. They proved to be an interesting group. There was Dr. Vincent, a short motherly woman in late middle life, a graduate of a Northern university who had turned her back on a promising practice in a large city above the line and had come back home to the old town to work at a minimum income among the women and children of her own race.

The owner of the deep, suave voice proved to be Frederick Gerideau, a contractor and builder who was an authority on colonial architecture and who had restored most of the old dwellings in the lower part of the city. He placed a 'cello on the sofa and greeted the girl warmly.

Gardinia Whitmore Lissa already knew—she was the soprano in the Reformed Church choir, a large girl with a magnificent voice and a bold mulatto beauty that she flaunted like a battle flag. Lissa liked Gardinia, and her youth and obvious good-fellowship helped her to feel at ease in an atmosphere that was commencing to have an overpowering effect upon her.

They fell into groups, standing about in the large rooms. Others entered: the secretary of the Y.W.C.A. and a young social worker from the new civic bureau; both were young mulatto women, and both exhibited the flawless approach of the trained worker.

In spite of the fact that Lissa was standing with her teacher, to whom she was devoted, and young North, who was obviously interested in her, she found herself talking in a constrained half whisper. She felt as though they were all playing parts and that she alone was not letter perfect.

North said, "I heard you sing the aria the other night at the Y. concert and have been wanting to congratulate you. The performance was entrancing."

She could only manage an embarrassed "Thank you very much." Then she was relieved to see that the performers were gathering at the piano. One of the young women was playing first violin, North second. Gerideau seated himself with his 'cello against his knee, and Miss Taylor was at the piano.

"Shall we start with Beethoven?" she inquired with a crisp professional accent. "How about the 'Moonlight Sonata'?"

There was a turning of sheets on the stands—silence—then they launched into an excellent rendition of the piece. Lissa could see that they were all highly trained musicians, and that technically the performance was of a very high order. But they played with their eyes on the notes, and instead of releasing the music that was prisoned there to fill the room with its magic, they seemed to hold the performance down to a technical demonstration.

Some one asked for Chopin, and Miss Taylor beckoned to Lissa. The girl rose unhesitatingly and crossed the room. Her teacher had been drilling her in the fifth nocturne, and she felt confident of her ability to acquit herself well. The piece was open, ready. She made a striking picture seated before the grand piano.

"Ready?" she asked, then, after a moment, commenced to play. She knew the nocturne by heart, and she loved it, but there was something in the air about her that kept her from throwing herself into it. This wasn't playing for fun. There was a weighty seriousness about it. She found herself, like the others, reading the page, desperately intent on a finished technical performance, thinking with an intensity that almost hurt, conscious of notes—notes. Bound together by the relentless exactitude of the score they advanced toward its conclusion with a precision that evoked a round of applause. Later Lissa sang Gounod's "Serenade," and although it was enthusiastically received she knew that the restraint under which she laboured had rendered it a colourless performance.

Mrs. Broaden called the girl to her and made a place on the sofa beside her.

"We shall be very proud of you some day, my dear," she said. "You have genius, and we will all be telling that we knew you when you were a young girl."

Some one suggested spirituals. Lissa had learned dozens of them from Mamba, and still sang them with the old woman in their room. She saw the ice breaking at last and rose impulsively. "Oh, do let's sing them," she cried. "Do you know 'Play On Your Harp, Little David'?"

"You will find the Burleigh arrangements[5] at the back of the piano, Nella," Mrs. Broaden called. "There is a quartette of 'Swing Low, Sweet Chariot' that is quite charming."

North, Gerideau, and two of the young women took the parts, and Miss Taylor accompanied.

Lissa took a seat beside her hostess and told herself quite positively that she was realising a cherished ambition, that this life was the thing that she most greatly desired, and, finally, almost argumentatively, that she was enjoying the evening immensely. She wondered about the others. They were so different from her childhood associates. What were they thinking, feeling, behind their drawing-room reserve? North, for instance. She raised her eyes and met his singularly intense, bright gaze. It gave her a faint pleasurable shock, and for a moment they sat with the breadth of the room between them, and a tingling sense of each other's presence bridging the distance, drawing them subtly together. Then he smiled and dropped his eyes to the music. Lissa's face grew hot, she looked quickly away and noticed Gardinia Whitmore observing her with open and mocking amusement. Gardinia was seated alone in a shadowed corner and with her full, dark body held in forced inertia seemed literally to smoulder in the gloom. But her smile was not only for Lissa, the girl noticed. From her retreat it took in all of them one by one. There could be no doubt about it—she was deliberately laughing at them all. The eyes of the two girls met, Gardinia's openly inviting Lissa to share her amusement. For a fraction of a second there was an instinctive response, then Lissa's look changed. It became deliberately unresponsive, obtuse, ranging her definitely on the defensive and with the club. What right had Gardinia Whitmore to be pretending a superiority? she thought angrily. She was lucky to have been taken up by them. She ought to be thanking her stars.

When the music ceased Mrs. Broaden smiled upon Lissa.

"You see, my dear," she said, "what our race is accomplishing artistically—when we have Burleigh, a poet like Paul Laurence Dunbar, and in painting, Tanner, to speak for us, we have something to be proud of; and, by the way, you must ask Frank to tell you about Tanner. He has some photographic reproductions of his pictures, I believe."

They lingered awhile over ice cream and cakes, and then, to her relief, the girl found herself out under soft spring stars with the April night cool against her face. North had asked to see her home, and they took their way downtown through the deserted streets. Lissa sighed and stretched her arms in a wide and deliberately undignified gesture. Then she stole a glance at her companion. He seemed to have brought the atmosphere of the room with him, and was regarding her with polite inquiry in his face.

She said, "If I ask you a straight question, will you give me a straight answer?"

"Why, of course," he assured her.

"This evening—was that your idea of a good time?"

North was mildly shocked. "I thought the evening was a great success," he said on a note of reproof. "What's your idea of a good time?"

"Oh, I don't know—I thought I'd rather sing than anything else, but it doesn't seem to be the fun that it used to. Don't let's talk about it any more. Tell me about yourself and who was it?—oh, yes, Tanner."

"You know his work?" he said eagerly, taking up the end of her request first. Then, without waiting for an affirmative, he plunged into a description of the artist's triumphs and methods.

Lissa was sorry that she had started him, it kept the drawing-room atmosphere tagging along with them. When he paused she asked, "Now tell me about yourself."

"Oh, there isn't much to tell," and she was relieved to notice that he was embarrassed. "Graduated from Avery here in town[6] and Dad gave me two years in an art school in New York. Now I am going in for portraiture. I want to paint my own people, and they are good about sitting for me."

Their way had led them through wide unpaved back streets under large shade trees. A faint air smelling of the sea moved through the young leaves and made them whisper. At a far street intersection a big double-truck trolley passed. Lissa heard the clank-clank—clank-clank and the hum of the motors as it drew away in the distance. Then she became cognizant of another sound: the unmistakable rhythm of a spiritual. "Where is that coming from?" she asked.

"I believe I heard that a church near the jail was having a revival this week," he said without interest. "We can go that way if you want," and he turned into a dark and rather forbidding byway.

Beyond her Lissa saw the menacing battlemented tower of the jail against the soft stars. Soon they arrived at the church, a small frame building behind a fence of whitewashed palings. The door and windows were wide to the spring night, and the building was jammed with black humanity. The service was well advanced, and the congregation was swaying to "Swing Low, Sweet Chariot." This was not the Burleigh arrangement. Thought had little to do with this performance. The air rocked to a deep solid chorus, yet a chorus of individuals each creating his own part—shaving harmonies with fractional notes so fine and so spontaneous that no written page could ever capture and prison the sound.

Lissa gripped the palings with her hands. She was trembling with excitement. "There," she said, "that's what I mean. They're having fun when they sing. They don't care whether the notes are right or not. They are just naturally cutting loose, can't you feel the difference?"

The rhythm beat in waves against the soft spring night—the air was heady with the faint, indefinable, yet intoxicating odour of untamed bodies rocking in a close mass, one with the song that they were creating.

North's voice, held on a deliberately casual note, cut across the music. "Oh, that's all right for these ignorant negroes, I suppose, but where'd we be if we stopped at that? We've got to go beyond it. We've living in a civilised community."

"Oh, hell!" the girl cried, "forget it, will you?" She caught him by the arm and urged him forward. He was so amazed at the change in her that he went a step before he collected himself. Then he stopped and looked at her. But she kept on tugging at his arm and pleaded, "Oh, let's step in and cut loose just once—listen to that," and she started to hum the tune. "How can you stand there like a dummy with a chance to sing like that?"

She felt his arm relax for a moment in her fingers. "Good boy," she said, "here we go."

Suddenly he pulled back sharply. "No," he said sternly. "It won't do—we've got to get away from here. I must get you home. This isn't our sort of crowd, and we must stand for something, you know. Think what Mrs. Broaden would say if she heard that we were seen at a revival—shouting our heads off with a lot of dirty negroes."

He took her firmly by the arm and was surprised at her sudden and complete capitulation. She turned away and walked without a word by his side. Only a few more steps and they were passing the jail. Above them the high buttressed wall soared, cutting the sky away almost to the zenith, and above the wall the loom of the battlemented tower hanging dizzily in sharp outline against the milky way.

Lissa looked up, and the black wall seemed to swoop forward and hang poised above them. The night was suddenly dank with the suffering of the thousands who had lain there in the cages—slaves, freemen, her own people. Her mother's face sprang vividly up before her, and she thought that she must go to see her with Mamba next Sunday morning.

Then they were under a bleary gas lamp. She had not said a word since leaving the church, and now North looked at her curiously. "Why, you're crying," he exclaimed. "What in the world's the matter?"

"I am lonely," she said in a trembling voice. "I'm the loneliest girl in the world, I reckon. Just let's hurry, please: I want to get home."

BUT THE FOLLOWING Sunday found Lissa at church as usual, where she had a small solo part in the offertory selection. She had forgotten all about it that night when she had that strange brainstorm near the jail and had decided to cut church and go to see her mother. She would go some time, of course, but this was her career. Mamba said that her mother would be the last person to want her to miss an opportunity to sing.

The solo went well, she did not feel the restraint in church that she had experienced at the Broadens, and she let herself go into the music. Everybody spoke about it when service was over and the congregation went streaming out into the spring sunshine. Absurd, that fancy of hers that she was lonely. Why, no girl ever had more friends.

North came and asked her to join a party that was going to his studio to see his pictures, and she found herself stepping into a closed car with several well-dressed men and women. North introduced her to Mrs. Prescott, and then, with punctilious observance of the social code, presented Mr. Prescott to her. His introductions were always ceremonious.

The Prescotts occupied the front seat, and the man's large, faultlessly gloved hands lay in an attitude of easy familiarity upon the wheel.

Lissa had never touched such luxury before. The handsomely dressed woman gave her a welcoming smile over a cloudy fur collar. The car exhaled a faint but pervasive violet perfume.

North and Lissa crowded into the rear seat with another young couple, and while the car glided smoothly over the asphalt he told her how their hosts had made their money. Prescott had started out as a carpenter, then climbed into a small contracting business, and now owned several blocks of negro tenant houses which yielded him a handsome income. They had just returned from a visit to New York where they had heard Roland Hayes[7] in a recital, and had seen Paul Robeson in an O'Neill play, and North asked Mrs. Prescott to tell them about it. Lissa listened greedily while she told of the successes of the new negro artists, and the life in Harlem with the theatres and concert halls, its dances, and its emerging intellectual group.

"Some day I am going there to have my try," the girl said with flashing eyes.

"Of course you are, my dear," Mrs. Prescott assured her; "you can't bury a voice like yours here forever, you know."

North pressed her arm and smiled. "That's what I've been telling her," he said, "but she wouldn't believe me."

The studio was a large airy second-story room, and a number of portraits were already hung, while many more were stacked against the walls. The group scattered, examining the paintings and exclaiming over them. Lissa was left standing alone before two portraits, a man and a woman in middle life. Then she recognised them as the Broadens. She wondered why she had been so slow in knowing them. The likenesses were good, she could see that the features were those of her host and hostess of a few nights ago. What was the difference? She turned and examined other portraits that hung near, puzzling out the problem as she looked from one to another. Then in a swift reveal-ing moment she had the answer. In spite of the fact that the drawing was well done and the features characteristically negro, they gave an effect of not be-ing negroes at all, but white people painted in darker shades—some subtle racial element was lacking. While she pondered, this inexplicable lack com-menced to associate itself with other impressions in her mind—the Broad-ens' drawing room, the music that she had heard there that night.

North came and stood beside her, looking eagerly at her face for her ver-dict. She tried to find words for her inchoate impressions.

"I can see you know a heap about painting. Those pictures are just like Mr. and Mrs. Broaden, only they don't look just like coloured people and the Broadens do." North was slightly dashed in spirit. "That's a matter of artis-tic technique," he explained. "You learn to paint in the academy by a certain method, a method that has been used by great artists, then you apply that technique to your own subjects. After all, if the pictures look like them, that's about all we can do isn't it?"

The girl noticed a defensive tone in his voice and hastened to reassure him. "Oh, I think they're fine. And I know what you mean about technique. It's the same with music. You are awfully smart to catch them so well."

They were joined by Mrs. Prescott, and the girl returned at once to the subject of New York.

"I wish you'd tell me some more about the coloured people up North," she begged.

"Certainly, my dear. And Frank must listen too. Things have changed a lot even in the three years since he has been there." She stepped between the young people and slipped her arms through theirs. "Come and sit down," she said. "Frank can leave his pictures to entertain his guests for him. That's the good of being a painter."

"Those men you told me about. Do white people go to hear them sing?" Lissa asked.

The older woman laughed. "Do they? Why, my dear child, if a negro wants to hear one of his own colour he has to get a seat in the gallery. We are not good enough to sit in the orchestra yet, but they will pay three dollars a piece to hear us sing or act."

North said, "When I was there Charles Gilpin was about the only one. I saw him in Emperor Jones."

"That's ancient history," she asserted. "Why, there are a dozen or more top-liners now, and lots of capable artists earning handsome incomes."

"I suppose it would take an awful lot of money to go on and study?" Lissa queried.

"Yes, that's the big trouble with us here in the South. It takes so much to even reach a starting point, and there is so little to do it with."

Lissa hesitated on the edge of a vital question, then framed it, with her wide warm gaze on the woman's sympathetic face:

"How much money do you think it would take?"

Mrs. Prescott considered a moment. "Oh, I suppose it would take at least a couple of years to do it properly—even to get a good start, and living is high up there, somewhere between two and three thousand dollars, I imagine."

Lissa received the information in blank silence. The older woman saw the disappointment in her face and patted her hand sympathetically. "But don't you worry about that. Something is sure to turn up sooner or later."

They were joined by several others, and the talk turned on North's paintings. Presently the party commenced to break up and leave, and Lissa's new acquaintance asked if she would like to be dropped at home, as they were driving downtown and would pass near the Atkinsons'.

In the privacy of the comfortable sedan the girl seemed wrapped around with an atmosphere of security and luxury. Looking out upon the familiar streets from such a vantage point anything seemed possible, even a New York career, even two thousand dollars. She talked to the others, a light answer here, an inconsequent question there, but beneath the surface, her mind hung blinded in a dazzle of radiance, possessed by a dream and deluded by a dreamer's illusion of actuality.

The car came to a standstill at the curb, and Lissa met the questioning eyes of her friend. "Yes, this is the house," she said, "and thank you so very much for bringing me home."

She stepped out and closed the door behind her, then stood for a moment waving farewell as the car drew away. Across the street a group of white people were standing before a handsome Georgian dwelling. Lissa looked up and caught their gaze fixed upon her with that frank amusement which in the old city is always provoked by the sight of a negro attempting what they would have described as putting on airs. There was nothing inimical in their regard. The girl was merely very amusing.

The effect on Lissa was actually physical, like that produced by the violent awakening of a hypnotic subject. She swayed slightly, pulled herself together with an effort, and climbed the stairs to the room over the garage.

Mamba was sitting on a large chair, her eyes fixed on a sundrenched roof across the way upon which pigeons were strutting and making soft drowsy talk. Her hands lay on her lap, and between the thumb and forefinger of her right hand, much as a reader might pause and rest, spectacles on lap, she held Judge Harkness's large gleaming teeth.[8]

Lissa flung herself down beside the old woman, buried her face in her lap, and burst into a storm of weeping. The paroxysm was so violent and so unexpected from the habitually self-restrained girl that Mamba was frightened. She patted Lissa's head with her gnarled brown hands and begged her with tremulous urgency to tell her of her trouble.

Finally Lissa looked up into the familiar face that was dimming a little now with the advancing years. The girl was getting herself in hand again. The sobs ceased, and a bitter little smile thinned and stiffened her full lips.

"It's no use, Grandma," she said, and there was a new hard tone in the low-timbered voice. "I've just been wanting something like hell that I'm never going to get. There's no use breaking our hearts over it. You better forget it, and not let it fret you."

"But all dem new frien' yo' got—ain't dey yo' kind? What's de matter wid dem?"

"Oh, I don't know," Lissa said wearily. "They seem to spend all their time saying how glad they are to be negroes and all the time they're trying their damnedest to be white."

"Hush yo' mout' chile," Mamba chided. "Ain't yo' knows swearin' ain't fuh ladies?"

"I'm not so sure I want to be a lady, after all," Lissa exclaimed. She got to her feet and strode to the open window, then turned and faced Mamba again. Her body was drawn taut against the brilliance of the Southern noon, her fists were clenched at her sides and shaking slightly from their muscular tension.

"Oh, I don't know what the hell I want," she flung out in a reckless voice, "but if I don't find out soon and get it I'm going crazy."

LISSA HAD NEVER been on intimate terms with Gardinia Whitmore. This was strange, because their music had thrown them together constantly, and as their voices were perfectly suited to each other's they were always in demand for duets at recitals and concerts. The explanation probably lay in Lissa's instinctive good taste. She was not herself aware that she possessed such a characteristic. But she realised that, while she was attracted by the flamboyant personality of the popular soprano, she experienced an involuntary withdrawal into herself at the other's frank advances. She knew also that Gardinia did not hold the same position in society that she did, for while Gardinia was accepted everywhere on account of her voice, it was obvious that she did not belong.

Seen in the Broadens' drawing room Gardinia immediately made one think of a Bengal tigress in a zoo. She was magnificently proportioned, with a slack sinuousness of body and dark, heavy-lidded eyes in which the banked fires of desire smouldered and glowed. She seemed at times to move among the furniture with a desperate and scarcely veiled hostility. By turns she would be seized by a gaiety so reckless that it seemed almost violent; or sit watching the others with her sardonic and sultry gaze. But over her lay, like a transparent gauze, a surface sleekness which, while it did not in the least disguise her essential self, gave her hostesses something upon which to fix their attention while they introduced her to their friends. But when Gardinia sang, everything was forgotten, and people ceased explaining her even to themselves.

It would have been difficult to find a more interesting contrast than that which the two girls presented in one of their appearances in a duet. They were of the same height, but Lissa was more slender and showed a greater refinement of form and feature. She gave the impression of holding her powers in reserve, and there was behind her art an indefinable suggestion of tragedy that made even her lighter numbers poignant. Gardinia, on the other hand, was an emotional geyser, and except when she was under the rigid discipline of the

Monday Night Musical Club, she captured her listeners with a power that was almost physical.

The Sunday following Lissa's outburst to Mamba she found herself on the pavement before the Reformed Church, with the congregation from the morning service streaming past her. The week had increased rather than diminished her feeling of unrest. In spite of Mamba's entreaties, she had not confided in her. In the first place her own feelings were too vague to put into words. There was no use to tell her grandmother that she wanted two thousand dollars with which to go away. She knew that the old woman had been putting something aside for her every week, every cent that she could spare, in fact. It was to be hers to help her along when she no longer had the loving care of the shrewd old head and busy hands. She had never let herself think of it, for to do so brought the tragic prescience of the human loss that it would imply. And what would that pitiful sum amount to, anyway? No, she could not ask Mamba for money, and what the other things were that she wanted she did not know.

Overhead, the portico of the church hung against a soft grey-blue sky, and the air was voluptuous with the warmth of early summer. About her many feet shuffled on the pavement, friendly greetings filled the air. A girl slipped an arm through hers—"Going my way?" Lissa shook her head, and the girl moved on.

The crowd was thinning, breaking away in ones and twos, laughing in the bright summer weather that the negroes loved, bound for Sunday dinner, or long idle walks through the quiet street. Lissa saw the Prescotts getting into their car. North was with them again, and Nella Taylor, her music teacher. They all saw her together and beckoned and waved. Lissa shook her head and watched them drive off with a feeling akin to relief. Then she heard Gardinia's voice behind her. She had a heavy, rather husky speaking voice. "What's the kid waiting for?" she asked. "Got a date?"

"No, I am going home. Just waiting for the crowd to scatter. I hate crowds." Then she gave Gardinia a faint smile and added, "But I am surprised not to see you with a feller. Thought you always had one on a string."

"Did, but I forgot my umbrella and had to go back for it. Now he's gone. I bet that yeller cat Lila snitched him while I was inside."

"Well, I guess I'll be going," Lissa opined.

"Say, you ain't so chummy, are you?—regular chilly sister. But I'm going downtown too, and I just as lief trot along with you."

"Sure, glad to have you."

They walked in silence for a while, then Gardinia turned and looked with frank curiosity into Lissa's face.

"Do you know," she said, "I can't somehow make you out. You look just like a human bein'—got hands and feet 'n everything, but you don't seem to get no kick out o' life. All bus' out with the blues all the time. Say, what do you do nights, anyway?"

Thus challenged Lissa gave the matter thought. "Oh, I don't know," she answered. "Of course, there's the Monday Night Musical—"

"Good Gawd!" her companion exploded. "You don't call that life, do you?"

"Well, most nights, when I am not singing, I just sit round with Grandma and talk."

"You little hell-raiser," Gardinia mocked. "Aren't you 'fraid the cops'll get you?"

"Sometimes Frank North comes around, and we walk out."

"Frank North—so that's it! Don't you know, bright eyes, if you keep that up you'll end highbrow?"

Lissa drew away and regarded her companion coldly. "Look here," she challenged. "You've a great way of throwing off on my friends. Frank's the only boy I know who's got something to talk about. You could learn a lot from him yourself."

Gardinia refused to accept the challenge. She remained silent for a moment, then yielded to an impulse.

"Say, kid, wouldn't you like to try just one real party? You think you're gettin' life with that highbrow crowd, just because you don't know what life's like. What you say I fix up a date for a dance with a coupla fellows for next Saturday night? What you say? You jus' try it once, life with a red lining, and night turned on bright—"

Gardinia shocked Lissa's sensibilities, as she always did when she let herself go, but the girl was conscious of a vague excitement over the idea. Also she was acutely aware of the physical attraction of the girl at her side, whose sheer animal spirits called to something hidden deep within herself.

"I wonder," she whispered.

"Oh, hell, don't wonder, come along. Nothin' ain't goin' to happen that you can't get over. Meet us on the corner by the post office at half-past eight, and we'll be ready to pick you up and highball up the road."

"All right. I guess I'll go. What'll I wear?"

"The best you got, kid, and your dancin' shoes. And maybe you better not say anythin' 'round at the Broadens' to-morrow night. It ain't their stuff. But, believe me, it's got class of its own."

At the next corner Gardinia bid Lissa a breezy farewell and left her to continue on her way with a chaos of contending emotions as an accompaniment to her thoughts.

SATURDAY NIGHT found Lissa pacing slowly back and forth before the post office. All day she had vacillated between an overwhelming desire to go, and a deep premonitory fear that prompted her to stay with Mamba. When the late dark finally gathered she had dressed with a desperate speed and without telling her grandmother where she was going had kissed her passionately, then rushed out, leaving the old woman's questions unanswered.

After all, she had arrived at the rendezvous ahead of time, for she had been standing several minutes when St. Michael's chimed the half hour. About her the streets were quiet, and high over her head mellow tones of the old bells ran their double trill and left the air singing. Lissa caught the faintly throbbing note and held it until the last vibrations fluttered out and died. The corner on which the girl was waiting was one of the most beautiful and significant in the old town. Opposite her the church lifted its straight white spire out of the yellow glow of the street lamps into the cool faint glimmer of the early stars. Diagonally across the way the clusters of lamps were aglow on the City Hall steps, with the building darkling above them like frowning brows over watchful eyes. Behind the City Hall lay the dim quietude of the park, with its stained marble busts and shafts ghost-like under the spreading trees.

Under the spell of the familiar beauty the reckless mood that had finally decided Lissa to come commenced to pass. Her gaze followed the pointing finger of the steeple into the vast serenity of the summer night, and she gave an involuntary start. She was standing out at the pavement's edge, at the intersection of the two broad thoroughfares, and now, as she gazed up, she realised that they marked the sky off above her into a gigantic cross, its head and foot pointing north and south and its arms dipping east and west into the two rivers.

A fear that was neither superstition nor religion but a little of both assailed her, making her suddenly long to be safely at home with Mamba. What if she cut Gardinia and her crowd now and ran home? They were late, anyway, and that would give her a good excuse.

Then abruptly the moment of quiet was broken and with it the spell that it had woven upon the girl. Several automobiles approached the corner, sounding their claxons. Down the rails from the north a great double-truck trolley hummed and rattled, then passed with a series of deafening jars over the switch.

Two white men came out of the post office and passed close to her, smoking and talking together. One glanced at her curiously in the half light. They sauntered on, and she heard laughter and, very distinctly, the words "high yellow."

A moment later a dilapidated Ford came to an abrupt and noisy stop before her, and she heard Gardinia's husky, voluptuous voice.

"Here's th' lady friend—all dressed up and bells on, eh, Lissa? Good girl. Meet my friends. This here's Charlie, and that's Slim in the back seat. Boys, this is Lissa. No Miss and Mister in this gang. Hop in there with Slim. He's going to be your feller for to-night. Look him over and see if he ain't got class."

Charlie called "Hello, Lissa" from the driver's seat. Slim jumped out and shook hands. "Glad to know you," he said, and he held the door open for her to get in. Then they were seated. The machine seemed to crouch for a moment, took a spasmodic leap, then settled down into a brisk steady gait.

The couple on the front seat paid no further attention to their companions but sat close together talking in low voices that were absorbed in the rattle of the vehicle.

At first Lissa could think of nothing to say, and Slim seemed to experience the same difficulty, for he sat well over on his side of the car and let the moments pass in silence. When they drove under the arc lights Lissa took advantage of the transient illumination to appraise her partner. He was dark, a full-blooded negro, with a receding forehead, a broad flat nose, and a very large mouth. Once he looked up, met her scrutiny, and broke into a broad, friendly grin. She saw the whiteness of his teeth spring out against the black, and his eyes laughing shyly into her face. She was reassured and began to feel that they would get along together. There was nothing about him to make a girl afraid. Then the lights were behind them, and ahead the road, a broad grey band of concrete, plunged straight out between dense patches of woodland and nebulous distances of open field.

The car, like a wild creature that has broken long captivity, flung the city behind it and leaped for the open. Gardinia's voice came back with the whistling wind to the silent couple behind her.

"Hey, there, you two—what do you think this is—a funeral? What's the matter with you, Slim, you don't hold that gal in—don't you know she ain't use' to country ridin'?"

Thus encouraged, Slim allowed himself to be bounced over to Lissa's side of the car and put his arm around her shoulder. For a moment the girl's body remained rigid. Then, on another bounce, the man's arm fell lower and closed firmly about her waist. A tremor shook the girl. Then suddenly she relaxed into Slim's arms and closed her eyes.

"Don't you worry," he said in a low husky voice. "Ah ain't goin' to let you get thrown out."

For half an hour the car drove steadily northward; then from the dense shadows of massed live oaks a row of lights leaped out. Charlie jerked the machine hard over. It left the concrete for a rough side road, executed a series of jackrabbit bounds, and brought up short before the door of a dance hall. A rush of talk, laughter, song, and instrument-tuning greeted them, shattering the peace of the night and challenging the new arrivals with a mood of wild gaiety. Slim waited with the girls while Charlie parked the car.

The wide doorway was swarming like a hive; couples came and went between the tawdry brilliance of the room and the piled blackness of night under the live oaks. A group of young bucks lounged near the door, smoking and passing a flask from mouth to mouth.

Charlie rejoined the party just as the music flung its unifying rhythm into the discordant babel. They elbowed their way through the press and entered the hall. The room was a-flutter with tissue-paper streamers of every shade that depended from the rafters and responded with an agitated waving to the sound and motion beneath. There were eight men in the orchestra, and Lissa noted immediately with the colour snobbery of the Broaden set that they were all full-blooded negroes. There were two guitars, two banjos, a fiddle, a cornet, and trombone, and a man with drum and traps. The sound was unlike anything that the girl had ever heard. Strive as she might, she could not recognize the tune. As a matter of fact, it was not an orchestra in a strict interpretation of the term, but merely a collection of eight individuals who had taken some simple melody as a theme and were creating a rhythm and harmony around it as they played. Her immediate sensation was one of shock at the crude and almost deafening uproar. Then, as she stood listening, a strange excitement commenced to possess her. Music had never moved her like this before. It had made her cry—and it had shaken her with delight, but this seemed to be breaking something loose deep within her—something that seethed hot through her veins and set her muscles jumping.

The crowd came jamming into the room, black girls with short knappy hair, tall long-limbed negroes from the wharves, sailors from the Navy Yard, dark and heavy, with here and there the pallor and passivity of a Filipino. There were many couples out from town who, like themselves, had the mark of the city on them in their straightened hair and well-made clothes.

Slim caught Lissa closely to him. His shyness had vanished, but to the girl that did not matter, for she was no longer afraid. The music snatched them up, and they were off into the thick of it. It is unlikely that anywhere else in America at that moment there were more and different steps being trod on a dance floor. The old fundamental rhythm of the turkey trot prevailed, but the more sophisticated were dancing a one-step or fox trot. In a corner out of the jam a group of country negroes were dancing singly. The dance was a strange, fascinating, and wildly individual affair. They stood two and two, facing each other, as though dancing in competition rather than together, and the basic step consisted of rising on alternate feet while the free leg was hurled outward and backward, knees touching, and toes turned in, parrot fashion.[9]

Lissa made Slim stop with her to watch, and immediately the desire to dance it possessed her. Slim laughed. "Come along," he urged, pulling at her arm. "That's nothin' but a ole country nigger dance."

She would not listen. Presently she had the step and started in at the edge of the circle. When the music stopped she was angry. "Oh, I almost had it, Slim," she exclaimed. "One more try and I'll get it pat. Why did they have to stop just then?"

Her partner led her out of doors, then slipped his arm around her and guided her toward the automobile. Gardinia and Charlie were there already, and when the four of them were together, Gardinia handed Lissa a flask. "Hit her up, Sister," she invited.

Lissa hesitated. "What's it—whiskey?"

"Sure—go ahead, ain't goin' do you no harm."

The girl lifted the flask and took a swallow, with the result that she choked and coughed.

They all burst into laughter.

"My Gawd," Gardinia mocked, "can't you even take a drink o' hooch?"

Lissa snatched the bottle back from Slim. "Can't eh? I'll show you." She wasn't going to be laughed at by Gardinia, that was certain.

What a night! Life with a red lining. The orchestra was at it again. That new dance. Lissa must master that if she kicked the floor boards loose.

DURING AN INTERMISSION, when they crowded to the door for air, a wicked-looking stripped Ford, painted scarlet, jerked itself into the light and stopped. Gardinia grabbed Lissa by the arm. "Here's Prince," she cried. "You got to meet him. Hello, Prince, here's a lady friend I want you to know."

The new arrival was evidently a favourite, especially with women, for a number ran forward and crowded about the car. He got languidly out and, with casual greetings to right and left, came forward and joined the girls. They met where the shaft of light from the open door stabbed the darkness and splayed out on the gravel. "Lissa, this is the Prince I been tellin' you about," Gardinia introduced.

"Glad to know you," he said, and took her hand, while he slid his glance over her in deliberate and frank appraisal. Then he raised his eyes to her face, and the grip on her fingers tightened. He gave a low whistle and, still gripping Lissa's hand, addressed Gardinia—"Some class, baby; where'd you find her?"

A shudder of repulsion started under the man's hot, moist clasp, flashed up the girl's arm, and communicated itself to her whole being. The man sensed it with evident satisfaction, his loose sensuous lips parted, and he gave a low, confident laugh. He bent forward, and Lissa got an impression of a light muddy complexion, heavy-lidded eyes, and a long scar across the forehead close under the hair. The air was heavy with its warning of danger; she felt her skin creep under it. And yet, in spite of the repulsion that she felt at his touch, there was a compelling power that drew her toward him and made her pulses race. She summoned all her strength and snatched her hand away.

Prince laughed again and turned toward the hall. "Me an' yous goin' to be buddies," he said. "Come on in an' let's have a drink on it."

His glance included Lissa's party in the invitation, and the four of them followed him across the hall to the gaily decorated booth in the corner where soft drinks were being served.

"What'll you take?" he asked largely.

They made it "dopes," and when the glasses stood before them their host produced a silver flask and poured a generous drink in each tumbler.

Charlie exclaimed, "Hot damn! None of dat moonshine rot-gut for Prince. Nuttin' but de bes'."

Lissa noticed that Slim's bashfulness had descended upon him again and that he accepted the drink from Prince with reluctance.

The music crashed out, smiting the air with the flat impact of a blow, causing the fluid in the tumblers to quiver. They emptied their glasses in gulps.

Prince drew his hand across his mouth and said, "All right, girlie, le's go."

Slim seemed to have suffered a sort of paralysis. When Lissa looked toward him, he said nothing, but stood looking at her with wide mournful eyes. Prince put his arm around her, and she looked into his face with a shaken, reckless little laugh. "I'm on," she said, and was snatched from the corner into the maelstrom of the dance floor.

They danced three dances together. Prince looked older than the boys with whom they had come, but he could dance circles around them. Lissa was delighted to find that he was an expert in the step that she had just discovered, and she made him go to a corner near the band and teach it to her.

It was while they were there that the musicians broke into a medley of old jazz tunes, launching from their wild syncopated improvisations into that early ragtime classic of the Johnson brothers, "Under the Bamboo Tree."[10] In Lissa the music ceased to be a thing external, apart. It became a fire in her body taking her suddenly like sheeting flame about a sapling, cutting her off from the others, possessing her, swaying her irresistibly forward toward the players. She did not realise that she was singing until her gaze rested on the face of the leader, and over his fiddle she saw the white flash of his grin and the surprised delight in his eyes. He waved his bow in invitation and called, "Come up, Sistuh. Up here's whar yo' b'longs." Then she was among the swaying bodies, the smashing harmonies of the band. Her muscles twitched to the rhythm moving her feet and legs in the intricacies of the new dance, her arms were thrown wide with fingers snapping the time. She forgot that there would be a solo in church to-morrow and that her voice needed saving. She remembered nothing except the words and music that came in a rush out of an old forgotten memory, beating out from lungs and throat in a torrent of song.

> "If you lika me lika I lika you,
> An' we lika both the same,
> I'd lika say this very day
> I'd lika change your name . . ."

On the floor couples were still dancing, whirling more wildly under the added excitement of the song. The drive of the music through the girl wrought in her for the first time the almost miraculous duality which is the gift of only the true artist. It seemed mysteriously to divide her into two separate entities, one of which floated over the heads of the dancers through the wide doorway to go blundering inconsequently about among the soft summer stars. This part of her was concerned only with beauty—with far thrilling things—Mamba's love—the harbour at dawn—Battery gardens under summer moons—all of these things it must capture and prison in the music that she was making. The quest seemed suddenly more holy than her prayers. It lifted her up to the point of exaltation that trembles on the brink of tears. Then there was the other part of her that followed her gaze here and there across the dance floor, cool, deliberate, detached, arresting first one couple, then another, holding them tranced and gaping where they stood. This Lissa was egotistical, supremely self-confident. "I will make them all stop and listen," it boasted. "I shall possess them all before I let them go. I can. I will." It was the personification of this second self that stood there on the dais, clad in close-fitting red silk, her sinuous body a fluid medium through which the maddening reiteration of the rhythm beat out to the listeners and forced them to respond, her voice with its deep contralto beauty the very spirit of youth, yet shading the edges of laughter with a shadow of a sob.

When the song ended the leader merged it without an appreciable break into "Yip I aidy I ai I ai." The choice was an inspiration. Lissa had them all now. Out under the fluttering paper streamers the crowd stood motionless except for those who, while they held their eyes fixed upon the singer, swayed their bodies unconsciously in unison with her own. She had made good her boast. She had captured the last one. The new song with its devil-may-care note of triumph lifted over the weaving accompaniment of the band and beat against the flimsy walls like a living thing. It said: "You are all mine—mine." It flung it at them arrogantly with a trace of indulgent contempt, then it wavered, softened, and said it again in a torrent of passionate gratitude and love. Her very own—her first audience.

> "Sing of joy, sing of bliss,
> Home was never like this.
> Yip I aidy I ai . . ."

With an intoxicating thunder of applause sounding in her ears, Lissa stepped down from the platform. Charlie was waiting there for her, and before Prince could reach her side he slipped an arm about her and elbowed a way for her through the stamping, shouting crowd. When they were finally out of doors they were joined by Gardinia, who flung her arms about Lissa in a hug that left her breathless. "Where did you get it, kid?" she asked in wonder.

"Heaven knows! I guess I was as surprised as you."

Gardinia gave her a second embrace, then turning to Charlie dismissed him with: "Run along. I got something to say to this sister."

When he had passed out of earshot she said to the girl: "Look here, bright eyes, you want to watch your step with that feller they call Prince. Did he ask to drive you home?"

"Yes, he did say something about it."

"Well, I hope you told him no. After all, Slim's settin' you up to the party to-night, and he's got some rights coming to him."

"All right," Lissa replied obediently. "I'll turn Prince down."

"An' look here," the big girl said seriously, "don' you go losin' your head over that nigger. He's free with his money, and he's always good for a swell time, but the sky's his limit—watch your step. I ain't so sure you're his sort, anyhow. Now, me—that's a different matter."

Lissa gave a confident laugh. "Don't you let that worry you, Sister," she replied. "I'm a pretty good hand at taking care of myself."

Charlie and Slim came up and joined them.

"All right," Gardinia warned, "just watch your step—that's all."

It was well after midnight when the Ford bounced out onto the concrete road and headed south with the four revellers. Slim sat in his corner glum and silent. He evidently felt that he had been rather hardly used. Lissa made several attempts to draw him out and finally yielded to a growing exasperation. If he thought that she was going to apologise and eat humble pie, he had another think coming. Her anger rose. He ought to thank his stars that she had even gone with him, she, a member of the Reformed Church, a friend of the Broadens. She did not need to worry. There was Prince, now, ready to show her a good time. The premonition of danger that she had felt toward him at first had abated until it had left only an exciting element of mystery and adventure. She smiled at the memory of Gardinia's warning. As if she couldn't take care of herself. No. She was out on her own now, and she didn't have to ask favours of anybody.

When Lissa entered her room she found Mamba sitting just as she had left her; the lamp was turned low, and the old woman was slouched deep in her big chair, her gaze fixed beyond the open window to where the late fragment of a moon was climbing over the housetops. She did not scold as the girl had expected. Instead she turned her eyes, which had a slight film of weariness over them, in mute questioning toward the door.

Lissa exclaimed, "Why, you ought to be ashamed, Grandma, sitting up at this hour. How come you didn't go to bed?"

The old figure drew itself together in the chair and spoke. "Turn up dat lamp so Ah can see yo' an' come here."

Lissa did as she was bidden, and Mamba took her hand and drew her down upon her lap, then peered searchingly into her face.

She said, "Yo' been drinkin', chile."

"Oh, nothing much, Grandma, just a couple."

"Yo' ain't been bad?"

The girl laughed and patted the old face lightly.

"Not on your life, Grandma. You needn't worry about me. I had a swell time dancing, but I'm nobody's fool."

"Well, go 'long to bed, an' in de mornin' yo' got to tell me all 'bout it."

"Sure thing," Lissa replied, "but you musn't wait up for me like this. You need your sleep, you know. I got to take care of this old lady. I can't get along without her."

She caught the old woman for a moment in her strong young arms, then got to her feet and commenced to undress.

"Ain't no use to say dat, chile," Mamba replied. "When you gone out nights Ah all de time gots a feelin' you might need me, an' Ah ain't likes to take off my clo'es till yo' gets back home."

From Part V

[Lissa's Triumph]

[Lissa has made her New York operatic debut in a production that is eerily predictive of *Porgy and Bess* (Heyward wrote the scene in 1928, when the opera was still but a nebulous concept taking shape in Gershwin's mind). Saint Wentworth and his mother have come to New York to witness this "epoch-making" work of art, presented to a mixed-race audience. It is applauded by its viewers as something "new— different . . . something of our own. . . . Negro, if you will, yes, but first, American."]

SLOWLY THE LIGHT in the big auditorium commenced to ebb, dimming the modern decorations and endowing them with a mysterious beauty, then plunging the audience into interstellar night. The slow throb of music filled the dark, then the curtain of the final act drew up on a stage of swirling mists and vague half-lights. Instantly the mood of the play was re-established, fixing the watchers in attitudes of rigid expectancy.

Dawn again, but no longer the red of an old despair. A thin essential radiance breathed upward behind the massed towers of a metropolis. It gathered strength, spraying out like the corona of an aurora, gilding the towers, then dominating them. The music caught the mood of the sky. The arresting dissonances, the sharp syncopations of the early acts, were no longer individually evident but seemed to merge into a broader irresistible current of sound. The rhythm, too, was no longer a thing separate. It became a force as indistinguishable and pervasive as the life current. It was a fundamental law that moved light, music, the sway of the crowd, the passage of time, in a concerted and inevitable progression. The artificial declamations of operatic convention were gone. The cast was reduced to two elemental forces. The crowd with its heavy mass rhythms and reiterated choruses was the body, and the single transcendent mezzo-soprano that soared above it was the spirit, aspiring, daring, despairing, lifting again. The movement became faster. The voice commenced to lift the chorus from its inertia and carry it along on short, daring flights. Then, in a final acceleration, the scene soared toward its tremendous climax. The light, the movement, the music, merged into a sweeping crescendo, the chorus sprang from its lethargy, while the voice of the woman climbed triumphantly above it until it shook the air like a storm of beating wings. Then the curtain shot downward.

When Wentworth recovered from his trancelike absorption the house was applauding; the large negro chorus was taking a curtain call. The demands of the audience became deafening. Lissa's great hour! She advanced to the footlights and bowed. Now, in the full light she was plainly visible for the first time, a mulatto, a little above medium height, and of superb proportions. Wentworth noticed that she wore no make-up except a slight darkening of the lips that made them seem fuller, more deliberately negroid. This struck him as significant. From the light bronze of her face her eyes looked out, large, expressive, and extraordinarily brilliant—Mamba's eyes—yes, and Hagar's. Now, for the first time, he noticed that she appeared self-conscious, anxious to be away. She bowed for the second time, and without waiting for the curtain, withdrew among the chorus.

But the audience would not let it rest at that. They got to their feet and cheered. They kept the clamour going with a sort of mad persistence. After five minutes of it the curtain was seen to move, rising slowly on a bright vacant stage.

Lissa stepped from the wings, and the clamour plunged into silence. The trace of embarrassed self-consciousness was gone. She seemed detached, oblivious of both herself and her audience. The conductor rose and looked up to her for his cue. Apparently she did not see him, for she gave no sign. Instead she stopped where she was just out of the wings, and unaccompanied commenced to sing the National Anthem of the American Negro. Apparently most of the audience had never heard of it. Wentworth never had. From the first note he was aware of an absolutely new sensation. Against his perception beat the words of James Weldon Johnson's inspiring poem swept forward in the marching rhythm of Rosamund Johnson's music:

> "Lift every voice and sing
> Till earth and heaven ring,
> Ring with the harmonies of Liberty;
> Let our rejoicing rise
> High as the list'ning skies,
> Let it resound loud as the rolling sea.
> Sing a song full of faith that the dark past has taught us,
> Sing a song full of the hope that the present has brought us:
> Facing the rising sun of our new day begun,
> Let us march on till victory is won."

Wentworth, listening, felt suddenly the impact of something tremendously and self-consciously racial; something that had done with apologies for being itself, done with imitations, reaching back into its own origin, claiming its heritage of beauty from the past.

On the stage, as the song progressed toward its conclusion, the singer commenced to sway—sway as Mamba always did toward the end of a spiritual. Only in this young voice to which art had brought discipline there was a difference. It wasted nothing in hysteria, but released the full torrent of its pent emotion into the words and music. Now she was singing the final stanza:

"God of our weary years,
God of our silent tears,
Thou who hast brought us thus far on the way;
Thou who hast by Thy might
Led us into the light,
Keep us ever in the path we pray.
Lest our feet stray from the places, our God, where we met Thee,
Lest our hearts, drunk with the wine of the world, we forget Thee;
Shadowed beneath Thy hand,
May we forever stand.
True to our God,
True to our native land."

The song ceased, and the curtain descended. In the auditorium the audience paid it the tribute of a breathless silence. Then they rose quietly and filed out into the street.

IT IS A SATURDAY in late May, and Mamba, happy in the gifts that the gods have left her, sits upon the doorstep of her crumbling mansion and lets the new and altogether mad world go hurtling past. Beneath her feet the multi-coloured flagstones have given place to a cement pavement. Before her eyes the old cobbles have been superseded by an asphalt roadway from which the heat quivers visibly upward, shaking the geometric perfection of lines that converge toward vanishing points northward and southward. Upon the buildings to her right and left the restorers have been at work. It is now several years since this army of invasion appeared, determined and zealous, to restore the district to its ancient high estate. Strangely enough, Mamba recognises among the invaders faces of those who, earlier in the century, came to tear the cobbles from their century-old beds, to smash the flagstones to atoms and haul them away. But now they are bent upon a frenzied quest for the antique, buying the ruined mansions, banishing the negroes, and preparing the street for white occupancy. Only the great four-story structure where Mamba sits and suns herself, and which is said to contain some of the finest Georgian panelling and ironwork in the city, is impregnable, for its title stands in the

name of one Lissa Atkinson, and Saint Julien Wentworth, who manages the
property, states definitely that it is not for sale.

Unmindful of the direct rays of the morning sun, Mamba is sitting, as is
her custom, to watch the New York steamer put to sea. As though in mute
protest against the invasion of law and order, she is attired in an old wrap-
perlike garment, faded and far from immaculate. Her legs, thrust straight out
before her, are stockingless, and her feet disappear into disreputable-looking
men's shoes. An old clay pipe juts at a rakish angle from between her tooth-
less jaws, and from it smoke fumes in a lazy cloud about her face and drifts
away to offend the sensitive nostrils of the white passers-by, who are becoming more and more numerous as the houses fall one by one into the hands of
the restorers. Her age is a matter for speculation, as it is a subject upon which
there is no one left to speak with authority. Her body is shrunken with the
actual physical contraction of age. Under the tired flesh the bones are commencing to assume undue prominence, foreshadowing their grim survival.
Through gaps in the sparse grey hair the skull shows in sharp outline, and the
brows are ridges beneath which the eyes are lost when the head is lowered.
But this inevitable physical mutation which in another would denote senility
has, instead of diminishing the force of her personality, in some strange way
intensified it, so that those who speak to the old woman as she sits there feel
it in the air about her like an aura. The negro children who come and go sense
it and grin delightedly at her word of affectionate abuse. The cur now lying
beneath her knees with only his muzzle showing under the folds of the wrapper knows it, and has gone there for refuge from a world that has no pity
upon an unlicensed mongrel.

Mamba has at last accomplished what she believes to be her final adjustment to the changing exigencies of life, and she has no complaint with Fate.
The old room one flight up where Lissa was born, and from which Hagar was
led to her banishment, is again her stronghold. But now how different in appearance! Papered with pictures of Lissa—Lissa at a steamer's rail, off to Europe—Lissa smiling from the centre of a rotogravure page in the costume of
her latest opera—Lissa in a hundred poses, a hundred settings.

But Mamba, scorner of limitations, has at last learned the necessity of their
acceptance, for only by so doing can she project her memory back into a past
shared by her daughters. Across the way, where the muddy beach once lay,
where the mosquito fleet was wont to dock, and where the negroes would
swarm and chaffer; where the smacks, when they were sea-weary, would leave

their bones awash in the warm tides, all is now quiet—barren—orderly. If she moves her gaze ever so slightly to the north it encounters the long line of a modern pier; to the south, and her happiness is ambushed by the spectacle of a dozen gleaming yachts belonging to rich Yankees who have invaded her familiar precincts. And so she has schooled her eyes to span the distance and dwell unimpeded upon a rectangle of sunny harbour. Beautiful, familiar, unchangeable, it lies as always mirroring the first dim fires of dawn or sparkling in the bright windy afternoons. And across it, as they used to do when Lissa was a baby, the New York steamers come and go, bellowing their deep hails and farewells.

Over the hot roofs come the measured tones of St. Michael's chimes announcing the hour of ten. From behind the pier sound shouts and commands. Mamba sits forward, tense, expectant. Then, majestically, across her rectangle of harbour moves the lofty cut-water of the New York steamer, folding back the flat blue into a thin green line lipped with white, drawing after it the steep, black wall of the hull, the high, gleaming superstructure.

This is the moment for which Mamba has been waiting. Now that the vessel has drawn its full length into her sphere of vision she sees in it more than the form of a familiar friend out of a loved past. It is no longer a great and mysterious adventurer putting forth from her little world into a vast unknown. No. To-day she is watching a sure voyager of that fabulous distance which lies between the wish and the rainbow's end—between her first fantastic dream for Lissa and the consummation of that dream.

Now from the whistle a plume of steam is blown against the stark blue of the sky, and a hoarse, baying note wakes the echoes along the waterfront. Far below the crowded decks, the soaring funnel, on her own private doorstep, Mamba draws herself together, and her eyes light with a gleam of her old impudent spirit. "Git along, den," she says patronisingly. "Git along. Ah ain't holdin' yo'. An' when yo' get whar yo' is goin', 'member what Ah tol' you' an' gib my gal huddy fuh me."

THE END

FROM

Peter Ashley

Chapter IV

[Peter's Conflicted Identity]

[Peter Ashley has returned home to Charleston after study at Oxford to find the city gripped with secessionist fever. The young man has been raised by his uncle, Pierre Chardon, his guardian since Chardon's wife and children perished in a typhoid epidemic and the Ashley family allowed Chardon to raise Peter as a surrogate son. Chardon, in the true spirit of his Huguenot ancestors, is a philosopher and an aesthete. He is a nonconformist in a culture dominated by tradition. Chardon has raised Peter to be like him, and so when Peter arrives in Charleston as the Ordinance of Secession is being signed in December 1860, he is flung into a conflict for which he is unprepared. In his youth with Chardon and later in his studies at Oxford, Peter has come to question the accepted southern orthodoxies, especially the issues of slavery and the wisdom of separation from the Union. Peter manages to keep his artistic and political principles intact and distanced from the secessionist spirit of his hometown, particularly through a difficult stint of writing for the local newspaper, which forces him to pepper his articles with anti-Union sentiments, and in a duel with the vulgar Archie Holcombe, who has publicly called him an abolitionist. In these chapters, we follow him through his observation of a slave auction, of Race Week, and his participation in the St. Cecilia Ball—all emblems of Charleston's white aristocracy and its values. But eventually the force of tradition and the need to belong pull Peter back into the fold of family and society, and he joins a local regiment just in time for the artillery duel with the Union forces at Fort Sumter. He weds a local woman named Damaris Gordon, puts his objections to war aside, and goes off to fight.]

SOURCE: *Peter Ashley* (New York: Farrar and Rinehart, 1932), 52–89.

PETER PAUSED upon the threshold of the big Chardon drawing room and looked about him with that impersonal appraisal that only a protracted absence can render possible. He saw now in the familiar apartment with its Adam decorations, its mellow portraits, its dim, warm brocades, an intrinsic beauty that enhanced immeasurably his natural pleasure in the familiar setting. Grandfather Chardon was still an ancestor, but he was also a Romney; and the two stiff little girls who had looked down upon his adolescent wonderings with prim disapproval were not only great-aunts Katherine and Amanda, but also Thomas Sully at his best. The warm transparent loveliness of the flesh tones seemed to endow the wooden little figures with an incongruous and deathless vitality. It was strange, he thought, as he stood looking up at them, how much more alive they were, fixed there in paint, than they had been as the two wistful and virginal shadows that he dimly remembered, and that time had absorbed by so gentle a process that their final passing left not the slightest impression upon his mind. Their biographies and their epitaphs were complete in the sentence that his mother had spoken when he finally remarked upon their absence. "Your poor aunts, my dear, they were very unfortunate. They never married."

Caesar appeared with a julep, and unwilling to disappoint him, Peter yielded to local custom and accepted it. He wandered from object to object, smiling familiar greetings between drafts of the fragrant drink.

But when he arrived at one of the broad south windows he stood, arrested at last by the new and unfamiliar note. The old untroubled quiet of White Point Gardens was gone. Groups of people streamed constantly across the park toward the Battery wall, where a view of the harbor could be obtained. Upon the promenade itself a solid block of humanity was massed, and over their heads could be seen the constant march of funnels and mastheads as noisy, crowded dispatch and troop boats threshed their way to and from the harbor defenses that were being hurled up with feverish speed. The steady, blurred disconcerting sound of the crowd penetrated and disturbed the habitual tranquility of the room.

A slight sound caused Peter to turn, and he found that Chardon had entered and was sitting, watching him with quiet approval.

"Where do they all come from, Uncle Pierre?" Peter asked with a graphic gesture toward the window.

There was a vague resentment in Chardon's voice. "For the most part, rowdies from uptown, I suppose. War or no war, we are already ruined by an army of invasion. There is no such thing as privacy any more. They act as though the city belonged to them. Upon my word, Caesar has to spend half his time dislodging them from the front steps."

The smile that Peter gave his uncle was quick, amazed, tender. It was strange, but before that moment he had never thought of Chardon as being definitely of an older generation. "And these people," he thought suddenly, "whom Caesar is kept busy driving from the door, will presently be expected to die for the perpetuation of the status quo!" He wondered whether it was an invasion of his country, or his class, that represented the ultimate horror of war to the old aristocrat, and decided that it was probably the latter. He remembered his uncle's often repeated assertion that he was interested in the point of view of those of an inferior class. "Both sides of the question," he would say. This attitude of Chardon's had influenced his own outlook profoundly. He could not believe even now that it was merely sophistry. His uncle had sincerely believed himself to be a liberal, but when it came to a practical expression he had always reverted to type. There had been certain days when he had awakened in the morning and said: "Now I shall be one of the people." Race Week, for instance, when he always served on the committee that had in charge the public stands, and when he even exchanged modest bets with his barber. But there had always been the big house with the high iron fence to return to after Race Week was over.

While these thoughts were passing through his mind, Peter turned back to the window and let his gaze rest abstractedly upon the bustle of the street. He stood at right angles to Chardon, his glass poised lightly in his long sensitive fingers, with the clear winter sunlight beating directly in upon him.

Chardon, sitting deep in his armchair, took advantage of the opportunity to study his nephew. He told himself that even with the rush of pride that whelmed his senses when he looked at the boy, he was still philosopher enough to subject him to a cool and impersonal estimate. He had deliberately refrained from crossing during the four years that Peter had been abroad. He had wanted the boy to go it absolutely alone, and now he was being repaid by the discovery of an altogether new and highly individual Peter.

Across his mind flashed his statement to Thomas,[1] when he had won for the boy the right to choose his own way: "Life will have her claws in him, Thomas,—mark my words, and sooner or later she will tear him to pieces." Now he wondered about his pessimistic and rather hysterical prophecy. Physically he had come through rather well. That would have been the rowing at

Oxford, Chardon thought, and the riding, for which the boy's passion had never abated. He followed Peter's movements as he turned back to the window, the unconscious flow of resilient power that broke his inertia, swung the body around in a slow, suave, continuous movement and brought it to rest lightly on the balls of the feet. There was a nervous energy, a complete coordination that would realize the utter limit of muscular power. He noticed with pride that he was taller than his brother Wakefield, probably as tall as Thomas, and would tip the scales at a good twelve stone. His English homespun was well cut, and actually achieved the effect of studied casualness that was just missed by the local tailors. He wore a low, soft collar, and his loose scarf, God bless him, was not the conventional black, but a bright, hard blue.

But when Chardon shifted his gaze to Peter's face, his old misgivings returned. It was a face made to bear the wounds of singularly vulnerable emotions; to be scarred by a warfare between the heart of a romanticist and an intellect that would be relentless in its destruction of illusions. There was more than a suggestion of the sensual in the large, beautifully formed, mobile mouth and the wide nostrils, but the sternness of the ascetic in the straight brows and high, intellectual forehead. The eyes, large and of a deep brown, were unusually expressive. The nose, Chardon decided, was the feature that most pleased him. It had nothing to do with the Ashleys. It was high-bridged, long on the face, pure Huguenot. It rescued the face from a too pure, too feminine beauty. It gave it a definite male distinction, and it linked Peter inevitably with the successive Pierre Chardons who had stood where he was standing at that moment and had watched a century and a half march past under the wide windows.

Chardon, when he spoke, was surprised to find himself a little in awe of his strange nephew. It annoyed him to detect an almost timid note in his matter-of-fact inquiry. "You're glad to be at home, I hope, Peter?"

Peter turned with a swift, yet almost immediately arrested, impulsiveness. Chardon was to learn that this was his most striking characteristic of manner.

"Yes," he said warmly. "Yes, but I'd have liked to wait for the race with Cambridge. It will take place a week or ten days before Easter, you know, and Easter is early this year. I was only a substitute. If I had made the crew I would have had to stay. But it was wise of you to send, and I have been wanting to get seriously to work." He stopped speaking for a moment. "This"—he added, with a new wave of his hand toward the window—"it is all so new and unexpected. I was coming home to write, you know."

"I know, my boy. 'The best laid plans—'"

Peter said reassuringly: "It's nothing to worry about. I'll feel better when I get orientated. And then there's you, sir. It's splendid to see you and Mother and everything again. When I saw you two on the dock yesterday in the midst of all the hullabaloo, it was like—well, like finding a port in a storm."

The glances of the two met. There was a moment of self-conscious confusion. The old faculty of sharing an unvoiced emotion had survived the separation. They were both men now and there must be no sentimentality between them.

Chardon said: "You haven't told me yet how you liked yesterday's performance. Everybody is envying you your view of the encounter."

Peter dropped into a chair, drained his glass, and placed it on a table beside him.

"Another?"

He shook his head, and Chardon saw the old, puzzled, absorbed look come into his face. "That's something I've been trying to decide for myself, Uncle Pierre—my feeling about it all. Perhaps it will help me to talk. The whole business has thrown me into terrible confusion. You see, I hadn't expected war. From the other side it seemed utterly incredible. And while I was in England, without quite realizing it, things happened to me. I've sometimes wondered if you had that in mind when you sent me to Oxford. Whether I was one of your experiments. You're damned devious, you know, sir."

Pierre answered the wry smile that accompanied the accusation with a rather guilty grin.

"At any rate, it worked. Harvard made me more of a Carolinian than ever. I could have stood the usual jibes at slavery, and all of that. But their assumption of a monopoly of intellect was unendurable. You see, I knew what we had here. I knew that, given a little time, we'd have a Southern school of literature that would make them all stand and listen." His voice trailed off into silence and his eyes had an expression that Pierre remembered well. They had ceased to focus on the object before them, as though they were looking out into another dimension.

"Yes," Chardon prompted, "and what about England?"

"England was different. You see, they've never got over thinking of us all as their own raw provincials. They are beginning to read our books, but that doesn't mean anything. If they are good, it is because they taught us how to write. If they are bad, they are typically American. It gets your dander up, I can tell you, sir. North, South, are all one to them. We are all stewed in the same skillet. But it worked, Uncle Pierre, that experiment of yours. In the second semester of my first year I took a most awful mauling because I wouldn't admit that Tennyson was a better poet than Longfellow. It was funny, wasn't it?

"And once on a holiday the boys in my form went down to Plymouth. It's warmer, you know, and there's a legend that the sun shines there. I wanted to get the mildew out of my bones. We were down on the Hoe. And then we saw that something was in the air. There was an official stand with a band in it. And a lot of gold braid and bunting. And a steam frigate was rounding the mole into the inner harbor. As soon as I saw her I got a shiver down my spine and I knew where she came from even before she broke out the Stars and Stripes. And then—you won't believe me, sir, but the sun *did* come out. Then I saw a palm tree growing near. It must have had a most superior constitution, but anyhow, there it was—and it looked like home. And suddenly everybody started to cheer and the band struck up 'The Star-Spangled Banner.' I felt then the way you ought to feel when you're drunk—but somehow never do.

"Then that night Bobby Chavers, who just misses being a gentleman, thought he'd bait me. And he said that 'The Star-Spangled Banner' was a good song because, like pretty much everything else, we'd stolen the tune from the English. I answered that we were at least clever enough to disprove one of his good old proverbs, then, because we had made a silk purse out of a sow's ear. Of course, I pronounced it 'air'—I was still that much of a Charlestonian. Bobby was solemn and fuddled and a little more than tight. He shouted that we could steal the air for all he cared but that he'd be damned if any American was going to call England a sow.

"I hate fighting, you know, and the sight of blood still makes me sick. You remember my first and only fox hunt, when I got in at the death and disgraced the family by losing my breakfast at the sight of blood. The fight was fast and furious. I had rather the edge, I think, but his nose bled and I vomited. It was awfully humiliating. But anyhow I had fought over the flag and all that. And you'll be glad to know, sir, that I came out of it a nationalist."

Chardon said that if it was the result of an experiment on his part, and he wasn't admitting that it was, he was afraid that he had done the boy a poor service.

"I had those weeks at sea to get used to the idea of disunion," Peter replied. "Your letters calling me home hadn't left any doubt on that score. I thought

I had got it pretty well rationalized. Patriotism is only a broadened love of home, I said. Carry it to its farthest limit and you become an internationalist. Contract and intensify it and it narrows to your own hearthstone. And after all, I said, I'm going home. That's what counts.

"But you see, the idea of war had never occurred to me. It was too preposterous. And then suddenly, without warning, I was in the midst of it. And it wasn't at all as I had imagined. I saw Captain Ferguson and the men on the *Kiawah* go suddenly mad. And those boys on the troop ship—they were so damned young, Uncle Pierre—they were singing, and they had their servants with them as if they were bound to town for Race Week. And I wanted to break loose and whoop with them. I wanted to feel again as I had that day at Plymouth when I saw the flag, and took a thrashing. And instead of that I went as cold as a corpse. I had come home to my world—the one that I remembered, the old life, the crowd at Russell's Book Store. I was going to get down to work. I was going to capture all of this. And like that"—he made a graphic gesture—"my world was gone."

An impulsive movement took Peter to the window. He stood with his back to his uncle, his face turned toward the street.

"You jump to conclusions," Chardon told him. "Even after this there may be a peaceful adjustment. Even in the event of war, hostilities may be brief."

Peter turned and met the older man's eyes squarely. "Do you believe that?"

"No."

There was a silence, then Peter said: "What I can't understand is the suddenness of it all. From the other side, the idea of an armed resistance seemed absolutely incredible. Then by the time I arrived they were at it hammer and tongs. What brought it to a head so quickly?"

"Anderson's occupation of Sumter," Chardon told him. "A beautifully executed tour de force, but, I believe, a fatal blunder and one that will lead inevitably to war. It happened on Christmas Eve night. The holiday spirit was in the air. We have a way, you know, of forgetting our troubles when we go to a ball. Major Anderson very cleverly spent the early night in town, dining with friends. No one had the slightest suspicion that there was anything in the air. Then when we got up on Christmas morning we discovered that under cover of darkness the Yankees had spiked the guns at Fort Moultrie, and had moved over, lock, stock, and barrel, to Sumter. It unquestionably put them in a better position to defend themselves in the event of an attack, but the secret nature of the evacuation, and the dismantling of armament at

Moultrie, came perilously near to being an act of war. At least, the Secessionists interpreted it in that light, and the fat was in the fire."

After a moment Peter asked, "What's the book store crowd doing?"

"It no longer exists," Chardon answered. "Simms has developed into a military engineer. It is said that the plan for the ironclad battery on Morris Island is his idea as well as Stevens'.[2] He was a rabid Secessionist, you know. Timrod has done a war poem or two, but he told me that he was enlisting. He is probably in uniform by now. Hayne has been commissioned on the Governor's staff. With his gallantry and charm, and his new gold braid, it will be a miracle if the women don't ruin him. No, it is all gone. You might as well make up your mind to it. You'll hear of nothing but war."

Peter said, "They'll all be expecting me to rush in. On the wharf yesterday, everybody assumed that I had come home to fight."

Chardon looked up sharply. Now they were upon the moment that he had been dreading. "Yes?"

"I can't, Uncle Pierre. I've got to have time to think it out. To get my bearings. Ever since I returned I have felt that I was looking on from another star. Yesterday when the crowd cheered, for a moment I seemed one of them. Then something perverse took possession of me and I was back outside of it all again. I've got to be a part of it. I've got to feel it here inside of me. It isn't a question of the Union. I haven't even that excuse. It is just that if I went in now, feeling as I do, I'd be an alien in either army. I'd be breaking faith with myself!"

Chardon said, "I'm to blame for that. I have taught you to think, and that is fatal in time of war."

After a moment he got to his feet. "Your position will not be altogether pleasant," he said. "You must be prepared for that. But you'll not be hurried, and you'll not be coerced by the family. Thomas has promised me that. But if you do not enlist at once he will probably suspect me of practicing Unionist black magic upon you. You will have to exonerate me."

Peter smiled and assured him that he would.

"And now," consulting his watch, Chardon said, "I've an appointment for you. Is the carriage at the gate?"

Peter replied in the affirmative, and presently they stepped together out into the unwonted bustle of the street. The barouche[3] rounded the corner into East Bay Street and headed north. Now they were in the thick of it. The crowds had preempted the roadway and impeded their progress. Perched

above them on the high box, Caesar had difficulty in controlling the restive
and high-stepping bays. Peter leaned back against the cushions, feeling conspicuous and a little ridiculous. Whatever his uncle's mysterious engagement
was, the distance could not be great. They could much better have walked.
He eyed Chardon sitting beside him, his body held very erect, his hands resting on top of the other upon the gold head of his stick, his gaze fixed upon
the two brass buttons in the small of Caesar's back. It was that fastidious
horror of the multitude, Peter thought. But he was mistaken, for presently
Chardon said:

"You're not enjoying this, Peter. Well, neither am I. But we are sure to
meet friends on Broad Street, and in here we are at least free from embar-
rassing questions. When your plans are made it will be different."

Peter said, "Thank you, sir." Then, tentatively, "Plans?"

"I haven't told you. You have a dangerous way of jumping to conclusions,
and I want you to be in full possession of the facts before you decide. But if
you want to write, you shall have a chance. My friend Willington of the *Daily
Courier* and I have been plotting together and he has promised to see us this
morning."

Peter had to be content with that meager intimation of his prospects, and
presently even the conjectures that it aroused were crowded from his mind
by the drama of the morning streets. He was amazed at the temper of the
crowd. There was an infectious and gay excitement in the air. He had conceived of yesterday's incident as a preface to the grim business of civil war.
But here it seemed as though the whole population were engaged in some new
and thrilling game. The atmosphere was more comparable to that of Race
Week than to the prospect of imminent death. He had always thought of his
native city as being predominantly English in temperament and tradition. But
now, fresh from England, he saw it suddenly as Latin in its moods.

At Broad Street the carriage was caught in a jam of other vehicles and pedestrians. Across the babble of voices came the high-pitched, thrilling music of
fifes. A company of soldiers swung into view. The uniforms fresh from the tailors made a brave show—gray peajackets trimmed with red, gray pants, and
on their heads smart kepis with the initials Ae. G. in gilt. The familiar insignia
started Peter wondering—then he remembered. This was the old Aetna Fire
Company metamorphosed into the military. The Aetnas passed and were followed by a company of Zouaves[4] bound for the debarkation docks. The high,
colorless January sunlight fell full from the noon sky and the street seemed to

split it into all of the colors of the spectrum. The red of the baggy breeches, the snapping blue of the flag, the ocher, orange, yellow, of the stuccoed buildings, and the tiers of bayonets that flung ripples of light up into the windows to play upon animated faces under secession bonnets.

"By God," thought Peter, momentarily swept out of himself, "we're not even European. We're tropic—Morocco—Egypt!" The crowd burst into wild cheering. About Chardon's carriage the confusion was noisy, continuous, ecstatic. A group of young women in hoops became hopelessly involved with a rear guard of shouting pickaninnies that trailed after the Zouaves. Two youths in uniform rescued them, cuffed the ears of the small negroes soundly, and ordered them to go home before they were sent to the jail-house for a thrashing. Everywhere there was excitement, color, sound.

A wave of cheering broke over them. It caught at something that was young and boyish in Peter, and lifted him to his feet in the carriage. Then the cheers swept past him down the street. For a moment or two they came back to him in brief bright gusts like foam snatched from a receding breaker. Then the parade turned a corner toward the wharves and the street dropped swiftly back into the commonplace. For a moment Peter had almost lost himself, had almost been one of them; but now the spell was broken, leaving him to wonder. This strange and apparently carefree exuberance! Was it all forced gaiety, covering the hideous premonition of war? Or was it the voice of a people still living in a happy dream which they had endowed with an illusion of imperishable reality, and of which this bright pageantry was merely a part?

Chardon directed Caesar to the newspaper office on East Bay, and presently the vehicle drew in to the curb and stopped before a handsome building with an imposing marble front. They were received by Mr. Willington, the owner and senior editor of the *Courier.* Mr. Willington was eighty years of age, and a cataract had deprived him of the sight of one eye; but he conveyed an impression of mental vigor that was extraordinary, and he seemed to possess that intuitive faculty which is given in compensation to those with impaired vision, for his face was quick to answer and even to anticipate the moods of his visitors.

Upon their entrance he emerged from beneath a deep drift of foreign papers that had accumulated upon his desk, and held out his hand. His hearty greeting put Peter immediately at his ease.

"I am delighted to meet you, Mr. Ashley," he said. "Your uncle and I are old friends, although I am sure I cannot explain why, since I was born a Yankee and am now an ardent Secessionist, while he is a native Carolinian and is suspected of Unionist tendencies."

Without waiting for comment from his visitors, he hurried on to details which had been arranged in conference with Chardon, and Peter gathered that he was to start in to work at once, under the direction of a Mr. Tattenham, an assistant editor. His new chief was summoned and introduced; Chardon departed, and presently Peter found himself being shown over the plant under the enthusiastic guidance of Tattenham.

His conductor, Peter decided, was a man of about fifty, the possessor of an impressive mustache, linen that could have been cleaner, an untidy black string cravat, a suit of black broadcloth well shined at shoulder blades and elbows, and a hobby. This last asset became immediately evident on their tour of inspection. Mr. Tattenham proclaimed that the contention that the South was dependent upon outside sources for its manufactured supplies was all rubbish, and he proceeded to demonstrate his point. Passing lightly over the big new type racks upon which Peter was indiscreet enough to notice the name "L. Johnson & Co., Philadelphia, Pa.," Mr. Tattenham directed his charge's attention to the great rolls of print paper. "Manufactured in South Carolina, my boy, and at Greenville, the thriving metropolis of our own Piedmont." And later, when they arrived before the steam engine that drove the presses, he led Peter cunningly with the question, "I suppose you think that we are indebted to the Yankee manufacturers for our power?"

Peter obligingly admitted that he would have thought so.

"Not at all, young man, not at all. If you are going to succeed as a newspaper man you must know your own community." He dropped an affectionate hand on the machine. "From the foundry of William Lebby, no farther away than Hayne Street. You have much to learn, young fellow, much to learn."

Peter meekly conceded the point and followed his chief back to the offices for his first assignment.

Chapter V

[The Slave Market]

PETER TURNED into Chalmers Street and directed his steps toward the slave mart. The city lay under a bleak rain that slanted out of the northeast.

It was, he thought, like London at its worst. It had blown up during the night, and so pervasive had been its dispiriting presence that he had been aware of it even before he had quite awakened that morning.

He did not particularly relish his assignment for the day. Mr. Tattenham had evolved a theory which it was his humble reportorial duty to put into practice. While others were watching the markets on state and municipal bonds for indications of public confidence in the independent state of South Carolina, Mr. Tattenham had decided that the slave markets were logically the most accurate barometers of public confidence. If the prices of slaves held up in the face of a threatening and abolitionist North, it would amount to a popular vote of confidence in the future of the State. It was, therefore, Peter's duty to attend all sales and keep accurate records.

But he hated the work. England had been very upsetting to his theories. He had heard John Bright[5] inveigh against the institution. The air was thick with abolitionist propaganda. And most galling of all had been the attitude of his college mates, who, conscious of England's superior position on the question, invariably pointed to slavery as a confirmation of their contention that the States continued to exist in a state of barbarism. When he returned home, it was with the conviction that the system was, to say the least, outmoded; that while it continued to work in fact, it was wrong in theory, and that sooner or later it was doomed.

But now, on the other hand, here it was under his eyes. And it worked. Even the term "slave" was seldom used among his associates; the occupants of the quarters at Wakefields were always referred to as "our people," and the domestics as "the servants." Personified, the institution presented itself to him in the form of Caesar and the fourteen members of his household who occupied the brick range in the kitchen yard of the Chardon residence, and who were reprimanded by the big house only when their noise transgressed all bounds and disturbed the peace of the neighborhood.

And as for the plantation: It had been generations since a slave had been sold from Wakefields, the natural procreation which took place in the negro yard having been accompanied by an equal increase in the successive families in the big house. Land was cheap. It had been the custom in the plantation country, as the boys attained manhood and returned from college, to extend the domain and present a certain number of families to each son. So that as time passed and the process was repeated, the negroes became as indigenous to the locality as the masters themselves.

Of course Peter knew that the negroes were whipped. That in the country, when this was necessary, it was attended to out of earshot of the big house by the overseer. And that in town they would be sent to the jailhouse on Magazine Street with a written order for the number of lashes to be delivered by the jailer. It was not uncommon in the vicinity of the jail to see a negro proceeding alone with a paper clutched in his hand, while behind him stalked the invisible terror of a still greater evil if he failed, that propelled his dragging feet toward the high iron gates. As the negroes approached, they would sometimes burst into loud, anticipatory wailing. Then the gatekeeper would open the gate and let them in. Later they would emerge, bent under the burden of pain, and still clutching the paper, which had been certified by the jailer. It was all admirably arranged for the protection of refined sensibilities. The servant returned chastened, was given a day to recuperate, and life proceeded upon the even tenor of its way.

Chardon had never sent a servant to the jail, as Caesar was a sufficiently strict disciplinarian for his own household. In fact, during his periods of intensive training of some black boy, the unrestrained howls that emanated from the yard were so disturbing that the master had been forced to intercede, for fear the neighbors would think that he kept a "driver" on the premises.

That the slaves of the planters in the Carolina Low Country were well treated, he knew. He had seen his own negroes at Wakefields. He knew the reputation of Gilmore Simms and others of his friends for pampering their negro yards. And on the other hand, he had heard of the horrors of the cane fields in the deeper South. The threat of selling a negro into that servitude was more efficacious than a dozen whippings.

What standard, he had often wondered, could be so elastic in its application? Property value: to a certain extent, yes. But it was warmer, more human, than that. A moral code, perhaps; but within his own class there was a wide range of personal morality. Then one day he had hit upon a possible explanation. Good form. About the treatment of the negroes in his locality there had grown up as intricate a code of good form as that which surrounded the institution of dueling, or behavior upon a ballroom floor. In the interrelationship that had developed between master and slave during their generations together, there were certain decencies to be observed. A gentleman, confronted by a certain situation, would conduct himself in accordance with the unwritten code. If he failed—well, there were deflections in every social order; it was unfortunate, but the transgressor was no longer quite a gentleman.

That the conventions of his particular locality and class had crystallized from the attitude of individuals of high moral character was a matter for gratitude, Peter thought. It made it easier in the present crisis to reconcile conscience and necessity. It buttressed the threatened edifice with certain Christian virtues and endowed the impending conflict with the indispensable elements of a crusade.

This theory, once accepted, explained much to Peter that had been obscure. The historic case of old Dr. Montague, for instance. The doctor had sent his houseboy to the jail for a whipping. The negro had commenced to blubber when he neared the place of punishment, and, blind with grief and terror, had collided with the choleric and overbearing person of Major Radleigh. The moment was that unfortunate one which lay between the major's aperitif at his club and the dinner to which he was hastening. His morning had been fatiguing. The August sun dogged his footsteps down the mournful and naked street that led past the jail, and bathed his body in tepid perspiration. He was writhing under this last gratuitous indignity when the doctor's boy walked blindly into his stomach and well nigh carried him from his feet. The major had promptly anticipated the action of the jailer by giving the boy a thorough caning on the public street.

The doctor had demanded an apology. The major would be damned if he would. There was a significant meeting at the Washington Race Course at the hour of sunrise. Thereafter the negro boy continued to polish a now meaningless brass plate beside the doctor's front door. The major continued upon his choleric way. Dr. Montague, with half an ounce of lead in his brain, retired to the long quiet of a cemetery on the banks of the Cooper. But he had been a great gentleman. There was no doubt of that. And his martyrdom to the code had been a shining example to the succeeding generation.

Now Peter saw all of this in its true perspective. The hasty cane that had brought about the trouble had fallen most grievously, not upon the skin of the boy, but upon the prerogatives of his master. Major Radleigh, an old man now, and still under a cloud, had laid his hands upon another man's negro, and between gentlemen it wasn't done.

And here, in the slave mart, good form was the criterion, covering the bald fact with the garment of an almost too assertive and self-conscious respectability. The days of the trade, when naked negroes were knocked down to the lowest bidder at the ship's side, were a conveniently forgotten page out of a long past. The mart had much the aspect of an employment agency. An open fire blazed on a hearth at one side of the long, low, bare room. Near the fireplace, ten or a dozen gentlemen were sitting. They all stopped their talk and looked around as he entered, regarding him with what he felt was not hostility, but a speculative and intense curiosity that was almost as painful to endure. It was the attitude that he encountered everywhere and in every gathering, or even a casual meeting with one of his relatives or boyhood friends.

His highly sensitive perceptions were immediately and painfully conscious of it. These men were so extraordinarily alike, he reflected, that any variation from type in one of their own people upset all the customary standards of evaluation. They did not know exactly how to take him, and their attitude of tolerant, often even indulgent, watchfulness afflicted him with the feeling of embarrassment and frustration that had tortured him as a boy on the plantation. In spite of his height and his Oxford rowing record, it made him feel in some oblique way physically inept and inadequate.

The moment of embarrassed silence was broken by one of the group, who rose and thrust his chair back noisily as he stepped forward with hand extended.

"Why, it's Peter Ashley!" he exclaimed. "You won't remember me, but I'm Bert Lawrence of Oak Hall. You were usually buried in the library while I was hunting with your brother Wake, but I remember you distinctly."

His manner was charming, gracious; but there was the old difference again—a difference that implied the inferiority of one who sat by the fire while the men were afield. It left Peter for the moment without anything to say.

Lawrence sensed it and blurted enthusiastically: "But you were a great rider. My father always said that you had a better seat than any of us."

He led Peter to the fire and introduced him to the others. "You should remember Charles Gilbraith," he concluded, indicating a man of his own age with an expression of boyish gravity upon his face. "He is from our parish, and we're down together to fight it out for the boy over there. He belongs to Archie Holcombe, and Archie's in a chronic state of bankruptcy. At present he's selling out, lock, stock and barrel, and outfitting his own company. He's had to let his negroes go, of course. And as he's from our neighborhood he asked us to come down and see that his stablemen didn't get into bad hands. He's a prime hand, too, so I suppose we can make use of him."

They were a thoroughbred lot, Peter thought, as he surveyed his new acquaintances. But he had to control a fastidious distaste for the volleys of tobacco juice that were being continuously directed towards the fire. While he had been in England, he had forgotten that gentlemen chewed.

A desk stood at the farther end of the room, and beside it, upon a bench set against the wall, were ranged the negroes who were presently to be offered for sale. With but one exception, they were evidently house servants. A man of about thirty, a strong finely made woman a few years younger, and a boy of about eight sat close together and were obviously a family. Next on the bench sat a man, tall and intelligent looking, who, Peter speculated, must be about sixty-five, and beyond him, two young women completed the group. At the end of the settee sat the negro to whom Lawrence had referred. He was magnificently proportioned and in the full prime of manhood. His clean jeans and broad, free movements indicated the yard or field hand rather than the house servant. The negroes sat composed but alert, studying with deep and speculative interest each new arrival at the fire.

The door opened and a man of middle age bustled in, accompanied by a clerk who placed several papers on the desk. The official was well dressed and had a manner which, while it took cognizance of the dignity of his own position, conveyed just the proper shade of deference when he addressed the group of gentlemen who had risen upon his entrance and were standing with their backs to the blaze.

"Good morning, gentlemen," he said in a hearty voice. "An unpleasant morning outside, but I hope that our transactions here may prove to be agreeable. At any rate," he added, as he recognized several faces, "I feel that our business will be brief and to the point."

The agent wasted no time over his preliminaries. The house servants were assets of an estate. The order for sale was read. "I am instructed," the agent supplemented, "to offer the first lot as a family. It is the earnest hope of the administrator that purchasers will cooperate with this humane desire, and offer a satisfactory bid for the lot. I presume that all of you were acquainted with the late Mr. Barstow, and so when I say that they were trained in his yard, I can offer no higher recommendation. The man, Adam, is a competent butler and personal servant; the woman, Rachel, is skilled in chamber work and is an excellent seamstress; and the boy, I am informed, is of good character and quick to learn."

He turned toward the bench. "Stand up," he directed.

The three negroes rose to their feet. Their faces were dark curtains behind which their emotions beat invisibly, but they drew together as though the command had shot a magnetic current through their bodies. The agent cleared his throat and transferred his gaze to the group of gentlemen.

"My clients vouch for the fact that these people are of sound health, but if anyone wishes to make an examination it may be done before we proceed with the bidding."

An elderly man with a myopic squint advanced, and leaning on his cane, ordered the man briefly to open his mouth. A shudder ran through the three negroes. The child's eyes grew huge in their sooty black setting. The face of the woman quivered. She raised her eyes and, across the width of the room, her gaze went clear and sharp as a cry to a young man standing before the fireplace. He turned deliberately and spat into the fire. The sudden hiss was the only sound in the room. Then he turned back and smiled, suddenly, warmly, and nodded his head encouragingly.

The tension at the bench went slack again. The examination consisted merely of looking at teeth, eyes and feet. It was soon over. But the other bidders were plainly impatient at the delay.

The young man who had smiled said, "Let us get ahead, sir, if you please. We are all acquainted with the negroes and are anxious to have it over with."

The auction was a tame affair, Peter thought. With the exception of the man who had made the examination, and who soon became irritated at the concerted action of the others and departed, all seemed to be relatives or friends of the deceased and their bidding was not highly competitive.

First the family went at fourteen hundred dollars, then the two women at five hundred fifty and five hundred. The older man, who proved to be a coachman, on account of his age fetched only two hundred fifty dollars. Prices which, Peter concluded as he made his notes, indicated a normal condition of the market.

When the farm hand was put up, something happened that disturbed the harmony of the occasion. During the sale of the house servants a man had been waiting at the door. From time to time he had looked in, but at the inhospitable glances that he received from the bidders, he had withdrawn. Now he entered with an air of bravado, shouldered his way to the fire and spat noisily. Then he walked over to where the negro was standing and measured him with appraising eyes.

Bert Lawrence and his friend drew together in a hasty conference. The man was a trader named Magrew, they told Peter, who bought up gangs of prime negroes and shipped them to the cane fields. He was also what was known as a "nigger splitter," buying up families at a reduced price upon the understanding that they were to be kept together, then splitting them and selling at high prices singly. He was always willing to bid high as he made huge profits on his shipments. There was an understanding among the planters that wherever possible they would keep the local negroes out of his hands. A sale to the cane plantations was considered only as a last resort in the case of an incorrigible.

"The devil take the damned vulture," Lawrence grumbled. "He's going to cost us a pretty penny."

To the inquiry as to whether anyone wished to make an examination, the trader replied succinctly, "Strip him."

The agent's clerk conducted the negro to the far end of the room where a screen was placed for the purpose, and instructed him to undress.

The two planters regarded this performance in silence, but when Magrew went toward the screen they exchanged quick glances and followed him. Several of the bystanders, sensing possible excitement, joined them, and Peter, repelled yet under the influence of a strong and morbid attraction, brought up the rear. It was an experience that was destined still further to confuse him upon the issues with which he was grappling. But it was a memorable moment, big with a certain dark and tortured beauty.

Against the clean blank whitewash of the wall, the negro stood erect and naked. Above him a large high window showed a square of bleak sky from which the light fell neutral and indecisive, assuming character only when it limned the hard clean arc of a breast or shoulder muscle, or brought out planes in the flat straight back, and the cheek, taut from jaw to cheek bone. Between the fullness of the lips, the man's mouth was a hard straight line. The lids were lowered slightly over eyes that were focused upon a point remote in space. Peter had never seen such a physique on any human being. Over six feet in height and perfectly proportioned, it possessed that indefinable added beauty that transcends perfection of form, and springs from that inner harmony which, when repose gives way to movement, becomes suddenly lyric.

Magrew stood before the man, his short heavy legs wide apart, his massive shoulders hunched forward. His face was covered with a beard grizzled at the sides, foul and brown from tobacco under the mouth. Under bristling brows, his eyes were cold, absorbed, impersonal like those of a chess player.

He first made the man turn around, and examined his back for scars.

When his blunt fingers touched the skin it moved under them in a swift involuntary shudder of repulsion, then lay still over taut muscle. The unblemished back was Washington's certificate of good conduct. Magrew gave a grunt of satisfaction and said, "Turn around."

The man obeyed.

The inert bulk of Magrew's body surged forward on its short heavy legs. A fist shot out, and delivered a terrific blow to the man's groin. There had been no warning. The muscles of the stomach were slack and unprepared. A spasm drew the negro almost double, but he made no sound. In a moment he was again erect. His gaze was still remote, but under the lowered lids it had the sullen luminousness of molten ore. The line of the jaw leapt out hard as iron.

Peter looked at Magrew's face. The eyes were the same as before—cool, calculating, preoccupied. There was no personal animus. He had nothing against the negro. He was doing his job. That was all. "Good!" he exclaimed. "No hernia." He turned to the small group of gentlemen. He had forgotten that they despised him. He said, with an air of pride in his professional acumen, "You'd be surprised how many of these bucks are ruptured."

The emotions of the several individuals who stood there congealed into an atmosphere of frigid and menacing hatred. Magrew was a more dangerous enemy than an abolitionist, for he held their peace of mind in deadly jeopardy. His existence in the flesh before them imperiled the beliefs by which they lived, in the support of which they were prepared to die. They would have torn him to pieces with pleasure. But they were gentlemen. All that they could give him was a silence that seemed to thud in the room like the blows of a club.

But Magrew for the moment was oblivious. He was engrossed in the technique of his atrocious trade. He had never yet been guilty of buying an unsound negro. He had a reputation to sustain. He chuckled in his beard with a loathsome self-appreciation, and turned back to his examination. Eyes, teeth, feet. The rest of it was soon over. The negro was allowed to dress and resume his seat on the bench.

Back in the auction room, the trader seemed to become aware of the hostility of others. They were waiting, massed solidly before the fire. They looked remarkably alike, bearing as they did the marks of their class. Clean cut, high bred, erect. Movements free, easy, assured. Eyes direct and candid. Not the eyes of analysts, but of a people with an enormous capacity for faith in its accepted beliefs. Faces singularly free from the marks of mental conflict, hale and ruddy from good whiskey, offset by hard riding under a semi-tropical sun.

Magrew, standing across the room, lowered his head and looked out at them through his heavy brows like a charging bull.

The agent put the question.

Instantly Magrew hurled his attack. "One thousand dollars."

As an opening bid it was preposterous. Bidders, especially in times of political disquiet, started at a few hundred at most and worked slowly, eliminating rivals as they advanced. One thousand dollars would not have been an unreasonable final figure. No, this was not a bid. It was a challenge. A challenge from all that Magrew stood for. If the precious gentry with their fine ideals wanted this negro, they were going to have to pay for him.

But this action was a tactical blunder, for it immediately eliminated all competitive bidding among the planters and consolidated his opposition. All except Bert Lawrence and Charles Gilbraith withdrew, leaving the field to them. The two young men consulted together, then Lawrence took the floor. He was evidently a shrewd trader, and was not going to be stampeded into extravagant bidding that would imply a determination to get the man at any price. He mentioned the sum of a thousand and twenty-five.

Magrew promptly lifted it a hundred.

After a conference, Lawrence added another twenty-five.

It was not until the price of fifteen hundred had been reached that Magrew hesitated. At that figure there would be no possible profit in the transaction, and he was beginning to wonder how much more the gentlemen would be willing to pay for their scruples.

Peter joined Lawrence and Gilbraith in their next conference. He found that they had joined forces and were actually bidding together, each planning to use the negro for six months of the year. Suddenly to his own surprise he found himself saying, "Look here, if Father or Wake were here, they'd be in on this. There is no reason why you two should have to carry the parish. I'll answer for Wakefields and take a third interest, if you say so."

They looked at him in surprise. Then Lawrence smiled. "I thought you were a Unionist," he said, "and it's rumored you are even for emancipation. But I am glad to see that you are still one of us."

And Gilbraith warned him, "Your father already has more negroes than he knows what to do with. Of course, you know that."

Peter looked across the room at the negro. He was sitting passively, his huge frame relaxed, his eyes lowered. By his very attitude of withdrawal, in his failure to plead by word or sign, he implied a confidence in their class that could not be violated. "I know," Peter answered, "we're all in the same boat. But if you want to count Wakefields in, go ahead."

A moment later, when Magrew's tentative sixteen hundred was topped by Lawrence's sixteen twenty-five, the trader turned abruptly on his heel and strode out of the mart.

If Peter had expected a melodramatic scene of gratitude, he was destined to be disappointed. The negro got to his feet and looked in their direction with the same cryptic impassivity that he had exhibited during the gruelling twenty minutes of the auction. Peter had the somewhat let-down feeling that he had taken the whole thing as a matter of course, that he had thrown the burden of responsibility upon them and had not for a moment doubted the result. The negro said simply, "T'ank yo', Mas' Bert. Whar yo' want me tuh go now?"

Lawrence looked at him a moment, then he laughed ruefully. "You damned worthless rascal," he said, "I don't know what the hell we'll find for you to do, but you can go down to Adger's wharf and wait at the boat for me. We'll go up the river after dinner."

The negro grinned under the familiar and reassuring words of abuse. For a moment the massive shoulders filled the doorway. A gust of raw air cut through the close room, then the door slammed and a snatch of song came back to them, muffled by the heavy brick walls.

To HIS DISMAY Peter found that it was already noon and he would be late for his second assignment. He hastily completed his transaction by giving the agent a draft on his father, and Lawrence promised to call at Wakefields immediately upon his return and explain the situation. The two young planters regarded him quizzically. Peter felt that they were amused at his expense. They stood looking at each other for a moment, then quite spontaneously they all laughed aloud.

"You've been pretty reckless with Mr. Ashley's money," Lawrence said, "but I wager when he hears the story he'll think it was well spent, eh, Charles?"

Gilbraith nodded an amused affirmative and held out his hand. "Ride over and look me up the next time you're at Wakefields. I've heard you like horses. I have a two-year-old I am thinking of running in the meet next month that I'd like you to try."

"And don't delay," advised Lawrence. "We'll all be in the army in a week or two and we must make the most of our time."

In the street again, with his ulster buttoned about his throat and the raw salty wind in his face, Peter was conscious of a pleasant inward glow. His action had been unpremeditated. It had been prompted by some imperative impulse and he had been swept forward by it into action before his fatal habit of reasoning it out had arrested him. The sensation of having been understood, approved, even liked was exhilarating.

Continuing on his way, Peter traversed a small park, crossed Meeting Street and elbowed his way through a scattered crowd that waited in the cold before the courthouse steps. He was shockingly late and the sale was practically over. It was, however, an unimportant event, and he could get the figures from the office of the sheriff when the crowd had dispersed.

The character of the crowd with whom he was now rubbing elbows differed greatly from that from which he had just come. They were for the most part idlers who were there to enjoy themselves at the expense of a group of free negroes who were being sold into slavery. Everybody distrusted a free negro. They were the tools of the abolitionists. They were dangerous to have on a plantation associating with obedient and contented negroes. Ever since the insurrection of eighteen-twenty-two, in which many of them were implicated, every man's hand was against them. This sale consisted of a group who had failed to leave the state under an order of expulsion from the court, and their persons had been promptly seized and placed upon the auction block.

As Peter arrived the auctioneer called for a bid on the last negro of the lot. It was evidently an occasion for mirth. The auctioneer wore a manner of mock gravity. "Come, my good people," he cried, "what am I offered for this likely girl?"

The crowd laughed.

From where he stood Peter could see no one on the step but the stout red-faced auctioneer. He pressed forward, and as he did so the crowd milled and opened, and he saw seated on the step at the feet of the man, the form of a woman, incredibly aged and bent. He noticed first that she was not a full black; probably half white, he thought. And then that she was immaculately clean. Someone had evidently helped her prepare for the occasion, so that, where words were not permitted, her appearance might offer a mute plea to some tender-hearted passer-by. In the cold wind her knees shook under the clean faded calico of her frock. She wore a "headkerchief" of black and white plaid. And under it her gaze was fixed unseeing upon the crowd, somber and remote. From time to time her lips moved inaudibly. Peter wondered whether the words of the auctioneer and the laughter of the crowd had any meaning for her, or whether her thoughts had retreated to that frontier which lies between the known and the unknown and that offers sanctuary to the very old.

The auctioneer was at it again. A fresh witticism reached Peter's ears, and a burst of coarse laughter. A wave of anger swept over him. His muscles tensed and he started forward. Then almost instantly his hatred of the spectacular, his diffidence in the face of the crowds, arrested him. He cursed himself for a coward. Something must be done to stop it—but what?

Someone was poking him rudely in the back. It added to his anger, his feeling of impotence. He moved his position. Then he was tapped smartly on the shoulder. He swung around angrily and his confusion became overwhelming. It had been bad enough to find himself in this position, but to have his plight witnessed was infinitely worse. A carriage was drawn up at the curb, and in it sat a young woman. Peter was conscious only of indignant eyes that flashed at him from under a secession bonnet. And the sudden abrupt interrogation,

"Aren't you Mr. Peter Ashley?"

"Why, yes," he stammered.

"Then," she demanded, "are you going to stand there all morning and allow those rowdies to bait her like that? Oh, it's shameful!"

Over the heads of the rabble came the voice of the auctioneer, distinct for a moment, then drowned in a fresh burst of laughter.

The young woman tapped her foot angrily. "Well," she said, "aren't you going to do anything about it?"

Peter's embarrassment became so acute that it affected him with a sort of physical paralysis. His fingers opened and dropped his hat, which he had been clutching, to the pavement. He stooped automatically to retrieve it, but when he straightened up, what he saw frightened him into desperate action.

The young lady had laid hold upon her hoops and was gathering together her voluminous ruffles, preparatory to quitting her carriage. She flashed upon him a look of mingled contempt and anger. "Men are absolutely hopeless," she announced.

Peter extended a restraining hand. "Please, please stay there," he begged. "Tell me what to do."

The agitation in the carriage ceased abruptly. And the eyes under the bonnet met his with a distinct propulsive impact.

"You'll have to buy her. You can't possibly leave her to their tender mercies."

"Buy her!" ejaculated Peter, aghast. "Do you mean acquire her—possess her—for my own?"

Under the bonnet the lines of the face suddenly wavered. There was a be-wildering flash of laughter and a full lip caught under white teeth. Then her head dropped and the bonnet fell like a curtain between them.

Peter stood looking foolishly at the black and white cotton ruffles, the co-quettish streamers, flaunting their little palmetto trees. Then he blurted des-perately, "You'll wait here—you'll tell me what to do when I get back?"

The top of the bonnet nodded an affirmation, and he turned blindly into the crowd. In his pocket his fingers closed upon a paper bill. He drew it out and saw that it was ten dollars. He elbowed his way toward the steps. The auctioneer paused in his travesty and looked up. Immediately his manner changed. His attitude became obsequious. "Are you interested in this woman, sir?" he asked.

Peter said, "I bid ten dollars for her." In the sudden curious silence that had fallen, his words boomed ridiculously in his own ears.

"The gentleman has bid ten dollars. Are there any further bids?"

There was a moment of silence—then, "Going, going, gone to the gentle-man for the sum of ten dollars."

The sharp finality of the hammer. The crowd thinning and drifting off in silence. St. Michael's bell across the way rolling out its quarter hours inter-minably, then capping them with a single deep note. And the auctioneer ask-ing Peter to whom the deed should be executed.

That brought him to his senses. He looked desperately toward the car-riage. Yes, she was still there. More than that, she was laughing into her hand-kerchief. From the box, her coachman was regarding him with a wide grin that he swallowed hastily when he saw that he was observed. A sudden idea flashed across the confusion of Peter's thoughts. He turned from the auc-tioneer and the woman who was still sitting on the step, and presented him-self at the carriage. The humor of the situation came home to him, and with it his complete self-possession.

He bowed formally. "You have an unfair advantage," he said. "You know my name and I am still in complete ignorance of yours."

She controlled her laughter and held out her hand. "I am Damaris Gor-don," she told him. "I believe that you and your uncle are having tea with us tomorrow evening, and—"

But Peter excused himself and left her sentence unfinished. She saw him speak to the auctioneer, who gathered his papers and entered the courthouse. Then he spoke to the old negress. She had some trouble getting to her feet, and he assisted her to the pavement's edge.

"Permit me, Mistress Damaris," he said, with deep gravity, "to present you with this memento of our first meeting. Her name, I am informed, is Virginia, and like her humble donor, she is already eager to be of service to so charming a mistress."

Damaris emitted a stifled scream. "But I can't possibly. We live in town, and our quarters are already overflowing."

But Peter paid no attention to her protests. "Virginia," he said, turning to the woman, "this is Miss Damaris Gordon, your new mistress."

The old woman looked hazily from one to the other, then dropped a curtsey to the carriage.

"And now," Peter went on, taking command of the situation, "if your coachman will make room on the box, I will give her a hand up."

The driver shifted the reins nervously and rolled his eyes toward his mistress.

"Move over and lend me a hand," Peter commanded. And at the note of authority the bewildered negro at once complied. Virginia was hoisted to a precarious seat.

Peter turned to the speechless girl. His eyes were mocking, triumphant, but his voice was deferential. "Until tomorrow," he said, "at tea," and with a low bow, turned and walked briskly away.

Emendations in the Copy-Texts

HEYWARD was not a very good speller or grammarian; neither did he retain much control over his texts once he delivered the manuscript to his editor or publisher. Some demonstrable errors—misspellings and compositorial errors—have been identified by the editor and corrected for this volume. In a small number of cases, some words have also been regularized to conform to the first usage in the text. Also, words generally italicized, such as book titles, that Heyward encloses in quotation marks have been silently emended to italics. Occasional archaisms (e.g., *prison* for *imprison*) and Anglicized spellings (e.g., *centre*) have been retained as expressive features of the author.

All editorial emendations in this volume are listed below. The first column identifies the page and line number. The second column shows the word or words as they appear in this edition, followed by the angle bracket, which should be read as "emended from"; the final column gives the original reading.

"Poetry South"

3.7	constructive	]	construction
5.11	Laurence	]	Lawrence

Preface to *Carolina Chansons*

11.8	has	]	had

"And Once Again—the Negro"

13.1	reading	]	reaidng

Foreword to the *Year Book of the Poetry Society of South Carolina* (1923)

18.4	Lindsey	]	Lindsay
18.18	Feidelson	]	Fiedelson
21.13	Gibbon	]	Gibbons

"The New Note in Southern Literature"

25.8   Hinsdell   ]   Hinsdale

"The American Negro in Art"

31.19   McClendon   ]   MacClendon
33.7   McClendon   ]   MacClendon
33.8   "Roseanne"   ]   "Rosanne"

"The Negro in the Low-Country"

36.18   suggest   ]   suggests
36.35   no   ]   Noe

"Porgy and Bess Return on Wings of Song"

47.1   Theatre Guild   ]   Guild Theatre
47.15   with   ]   by
47.19   entrusted   ]   intrusted

"Dock Street Theatre"

53.18   Planter's   ]   Planters
54.17   notables   ]   notable
54.30   Planter's   ]   Planters
56.7   Burnet   ]   Burnett

"Silences"

76.2   Philip's   ]   Phillip's

Note on "The Pirates"

84.29   pirates";   ]   pirates;"

"The Last Crew"

91.29   Many   ]   Man

Note to "The Last Crew"

93.22   Hunley   ]   Hundley

"The Brute"

126.2   down."   ]   down.
126.14   Greybeard   ]   Graybeard
126.29   later   ]   late

From *Porgy*

151.16	focused	]	focussed
153.30	envelops	]	envelopes

The Half Pint Flask

186.23	retorted,	]	retorted
189.30	arrange	]	arranged
191.8	jasmine	]	jamine

From *Mamba's Daughters: A Novel of Charleston*

226.28	let's	]	lets
227.24	Then she was	]	Then was
234.16	grey	]	gray

Notes

Introduction

1. The fullest biographical treatment of Heyward is James M. Hutchisson, *DuBose Heyward: A Charleston Gentleman and the World of Porgy and Bess* (Jackson: Univ. Press of Mississippi, 2000). An earlier biography is Frank Durham, *DuBose Heyward: The Man Who Wrote "Porgy"* (Columbia: Univ. of South Carolina Press, 1954). For analyses of specific works, see William Slavick, *DuBose Heyward* (Boston: Twayne, 1981).

2. Jane Screven Heyward, "Journal," in the Jane Screven Heyward Papers, South Carolina Historical Society (SCHS). For a fuller treatment of this journal see Harlan Greene, "Charleston Childhood: The First Years of DuBose Heyward," *South Carolina Historical Magazine* 83 (1982): 154–67.

3. The DuBose Heyward Papers at SCHS, the main repository for the author's papers, contain these unpublished/unproduced efforts. Although some contain a gem or two of insight, they are by and large plodding and predictable, written to formula for the mass-circulation magazines. Heyward's one notable story, "The Brute," is reprinted in this collection.

4. A full history of this organization is found in Headley Morris Cox Jr., "The Charleston Poetic Renascence, 1920–1930," Ph.D. diss., Univ. of Pennsylvania, 1958.

5. See Martha R. Severens, "South Carolina and the American Scene," in *The American Scene and the South: Paintings and Works on Paper, 1930–1946*, ed. Patricia Phagan (Athens: Georgia Museum of Art, 1996), 135–67; "Charleston in the Age of *Porgy and Bess*," *Southern Quarterly* 38 (1989): 5–23; and her comprehensive *The Charleston Renaissance* (Spartanburg, S.C.: Saraland Press, 1998) for more on the visual arts during the Charleston Renaissance.

6. Scholarship on the Charleston Renaissance has been advancing rapidly. On Bragg, see Louise Anderson Allen, *A Bluestocking in Charleston: The Life and Career of Laura Bragg* (Columbia: Univ. of South Carolina Press, 2001). On John Bennett (below), see Harlan Greene, *Mr. Skylark: John Bennett and the Charleston Renaissance* (Athens: Univ. of Georgia Press, 2001). Susan Pringle Frost has been treated by Sidney Bland in *Preserving Charleston's Past, Shaping Its Future: The Life and Times of Susan Pringle Frost* (Columbia: Univ. of South Carolina Press, 1999). A biography of Josephine Pinckney is

currently being written by Barbara L. Bellows. And all of these figures are treated in the forthcoming essay collection, *Renaissance in Charleston: Art and Life in the Carolina Low Country, 1900–1940*, ed. James M. Hutchisson and Harlan Greene (Athens: Univ. of Georgia Press, 2003).

7. See his appreciative essay "The MacDowell Colony," *Southwest Review* 11 (Jan. 1926), 162–68.

8. Nina Purdy, "Love at Dawn Hill," [*True Love Magazine?*] 66 (ca. 1930). A clipping in the Yates Snowden Papers, Caroliniana Library, Univ. of South Carolina.

9. DBH to DKH, 6 October 1922, DKH Papers, SCHS.

10. DBH to Hervey Allen, 13 May 1924, Hervey Allen Papers, Hillman Library, Univ. of Pittsburgh.

11. See JB to DBH, 26 October 1925, JB Papers, SCHS.

12. DBH to Brickell, 2 December 1928, Herschel Brickell Papers, John Davis Williams Library, Univ. of Mississippi.

13. DBH to JB, 11 April 1925, JB Papers, SCHS.

14. DBH to Laura Bragg, 30 June 1925, Laura Bragg Papers, SCHS.

15. At least this is the popularly held theory first espoused by Louis D. Rubin Jr., who argues in part that coastal southern communities are handicapped by certain cultural limitations, among them the absence of major universities, and thus that all great southern art originates in the piedmont areas. See "Southern Literature: A Piedmont Art," in *William Elliott Shoots a Bear: Essays on the Southern Literary Imagination* (Baton Rouge: Louisiana State Univ. Press, 1975), 195–212.

16. DBH to JSH, 21 September 1927, DBH Papers, SCHS.

17. Qtd. in James Haskins, *Black Theatre in America* (New York: Crowell, 1982), 61.

18. For more on this topic, see in particular Ann Douglas, *Terrible Honesty: Mongrel Manhattan in the 1920s* (New York: Farrar, Straus and Giroux, 1995); and Michael Kammen, *The Lively Arts: Gilbert Seldes and the Transformation of Cultural Criticism in America* (New York: Oxford Univ. Press, 1996).

19. The manuscript is preserved among Heyward's papers at SCHS. It exists, however, in an extremely fragmentary and disordered state.

20. Most prominently, Michael O'Brien, "'The South Considers Her Most Peculiar': Charleston and Modern Southern Thought," *South Carolina Historical Magazine* 94 (1993): 119–33. Also interesting is Heyward's technique in this novel—not the standard archivistic or diaristic technique of the historical writer, but one purposefully limited in scope. See his brief note, "New Theory of Historical Fiction," *Publishers Weekly* 122 (13 Aug. 1932), 511.

21. Undated typescript in Heyward Papers, SCHS.

22. Letter of Harriette Kershaw Leiding to Laura Bragg, 16 Feb. 1932, Laura Bragg Papers, SCHS.

23. A good analysis of liberal southerners' thinking about race and reform in the

pre–Civil Rights era is in John T. Kneebone, *Southern Liberal Journalists and the Issue of Race, 1920–1944* (Chapel Hill: Univ. of North Carolina Press, 1985).

24. "I always hated the publicity of the platform," he later told Jessie Rittenhouse, and also thought that "only by saving my energy in every possible way could I meet the demands of my writing" (DBH to Jessie Rittenhouse, 29 May 1939, Jessie Rittenhouse Papers, Olin Library, Rollins College).

25. Interview with *Literary Guild Magazine,* spring 1931, a typescript draft in DBH Papers, SCHS.

26. Letter of Heyward to Hervey Allen, dated "June 4th" [ca. 1931], Hervey Allen Papers, Hillman Library, Univ. of Pittsburgh.

27. Ibid.

28. DBH to Stein, 6 April 1935, Stein Papers, Beinecke Library, Yale Collection of American Literature, Yale Univ.

29. William Lewis and Max J. Herzberg, interview with DBH, rpt. in *The Emperor Jones, with a Study Guide for the Screen Version of the Play,* Student ed. (New York: Appleton, 1949).

30. See Slavick, *DuBose Heyward,* 96–97.

31. He was even unclear as to why he got the assignment in the first place. He figured the spurious reasoning ran: "Negroes were not a Caucasian people. Neither were Chinamen. I wrote understandingly of Negroes.... Then I would understand the Chinese." See "Porgy and Bess Return" (pp. 46–51).

32. Qtd. in Kammen, *The Lively Arts,* 199.

"Poetry South"

1. All writers who might be said to have presented the Negro in stereotype, although that is not Heyward and Allen's meaning here. They laud these figures as pioneers in southern writing for having captured their subject at the eleventh hour of an era. One sees here the animating impulse in Heyward's first works—to preserve in art a way of life that was quickly slipping away.

Page (1853–1922), local-color writer of romances about the Civil War and Reconstruction, best known for *Marse Chan* (1884), *The Old South* (1892), and *Red Rock* (1898). He was American ambassador to Italy under Woodrow Wilson; Edwards (1855–1938), of Macon, was notable for *Eneas Africanus* (1919); Harris (1848–1908), originally from Eatonton, worked after 1876 as a journalist on the *Atlanta Constitution,* when he famously wrote *Uncle Remus: His Songs and His Sayings* (1880) and subsequently many dialect stories that drew on African American folk tales; Heyward (1864–1939), Heyward's mother, who by the 1920s had established a lucrative career as a performer of Gullah folktales and folk songs, collected in *Songs of the Charleston Darkey* (1912) and *Brown Jackets* (1923). Her poetry collections were *Wild Roses* (1905) and *Daffodils and Other Lyrics* (1921).

2. Dunbar (1872–1906), born in Ohio of parents who had once been slaves, was the earliest major African American poet to use folk materials and plantation lore in his largely dialect poetry about the South. He became a frequent figure on the lecture circuit in the U.S. and England. Henry Ossawa Tanner (1859–1937), depicter of African American scenes in a realist manner, studied at the Philadelphia Academy of Art under Thomas Eakins and in Paris under Jean-Paul Laurens.

3. A description that fits Heyward's poems in *Skylines and Horizons* (1924), highly compressed verses that depict the hardscrabble life of isolated, unsocialized mountain people.

4. See "Porgy and Bess Return on Wings of Song" (pp. 46–51), where Heyward describes how Gershwin put these emotional religious spectacles to use in some scenes in the opera.

5. Heyward himself was among the earliest modern southern writers to reject the nineteenth-century image of the author as dilettante and literature as gentlemanly avocation. For more on this topic, see James M. Hutchisson, "Professional Authorship in the Charleston Renaissance: The Career of DuBose Heyward," in *Renaissance in Charleston: Art and Life in the Carolina Low Country, 1900–1940*, ed. James M. Hutchisson and Harlan Greene (Athens: Univ. of Georgia Press, 2003). His comments here on the education of a Charleston gentleman are telling, a portrait more fully fleshed out in the title character of *Peter Ashley* (1932).

6. Pike (1809–91), originally from Boston, migrated to Arkansas in 1833, was a lawyer and a Freemason, served in the Mexican War, and authored *Prose Sketches and Poems, Written in the Western Country* (1834). He is best known, however, for his poem "Dixie," collected in *Hymns to the Gods* (1872). During the Civil War he commanded Native American troops in the Confederate army. Simms (1806–70), Charleston author and arguably the most famous nineteenth-century Southern literary figure, wrote scores of romances drawing on South Carolina history and edited such magazines as *The Southern Quarterly Review* (1856–57) and *The Southern and Western Monthly Magazine* (1845). Simms also produced a *History* (1845) and a *Geography* (1843) of the state, and biographies of some of its most notable figures.

7. *Russell's* was one of several antebellum literary magazines devoted to advancing the cause of southern literature. It was conceived in the best Johnsonian coffeehouse tradition in 1856 in John Russell's bookstore on King Street in Charleston, where a group of the city's keenest intellects gathered for spirited literary, political, and philosophical discussion. The magazine was edited by Paul Hamilton Hayne. Contributors included William Gilmore Simms, Henry Timrod, and others.

8. From a 30 March 1866 letter of Timrod to Hayne that begins, "You ask me to tell you my story for the last year," rpt. in *The Last Years of Henry Timrod*, ed. Jay B. Hubbell (Durham, N.C.: Duke Univ. Press, 1941), 59.

9. J. Gordon Coogler (1865–1901), forever made infamous as the target of H. L.

Mencken's unrestrained attack on the puerility and aridity of southern art in "The Sahara of the Bozart" (1917). Heyward does not quote the lines that Mencken attributed to Coogler: "Alas, for the South! Her books have grown fewer— / She never was much given to literature." A printer in Columbia, South Carolina, Coogler used to have a sign outside his shop which read "Poems Written While You Wait," and published *Purely Original Verse* (1891).

10. The opening lines of Lanier's "The Symphony." Heyward was probably quoting from the 1906 Scribner selected edition of Lanier's verse, edited by his wife (60). Heyward much admired Lanier, of Macon, one of the younger generation of southern writers after the Civil War, who had served in the Confederate army and spent time in a Union prison camp, an experience which much weakened his health; he was later a flautist with the Peabody Orchestra in Baltimore, as well as a lecturer on English literature for the Peabody Institute and (after 1879) the new Johns Hopkins University. Heyward seems to have been inspired by the man's drive to create art in the face of poverty, ill health, and intellectual estrangement. A passage from Lanier—"A man does not reach any stature of manhood until, like Moses, he kills an Egyptian (i.e., murders some oppressive prejudice of the all crushing Tyrant Society, or Custom, or Orthodoxy) and flies into the desert of his own soul"—is pasted on the inside cover of an early writing journal. Heyward reprinted this passage at the beginning of a late novel, *Lost Morning* (1937), which concerns a southern artist's struggle to create the art he feels driven to create and renounce the commercial forces that have pressured him into sacrificing his artistic principles.

11. Louisville native Cawein (1865–1914), a poet who stressed locale in traditional forms, under the heavy influence of nineteenth-century British lyricists.

Preface to *Carolina Chansons*

1. Robert Frost, of course, needs no introduction, but Edwin Arlington Robinson (1869–1935), the poet and playwright, is now less well known. He was from Maine, which provided much of his subject matter; his *Collected Poems* (1921) won the Pulitzer Prize.

2. A probable reference to Walt Whitman's self-descriptive phrase in "Song of Myself": "I too am not a bit tamed, I too am untranslatable, / I sound my barbaric yawp over the roofs of the world" (section 52).

Foreword to the *Year Book of the Poetry Society of South Carolina* (1923)

1. Therese Kayser Lindsey (b. 1870 in Chapel Hill, Tex.) was educated at Chicago and Harvard. Her poems were published in *Voices*, *Kaleidograph*, and *Bookman*

and in such anthologies as *A Century with Texas Poets and Poetry* (1934). Throughout her long and prolific career as poet and teacher of creative writing, Lindsey also financially supported arts activities in Texas. In 1978 the English department of Southwest Texas State University established an endowed chair in her name; Karle Wilson Baker (1878–1960), poet, novelist, essayist, and children's book author whose early work appeared under the pen name Charlotte Wilson. Baker held degrees from Chicago, Columbia, and California and was awarded an honorary doctorate from Southern Methodist University in 1924. She served as an officer in the Poetry Society of Texas and was briefly an English professor (1925–37) at Stephen F. Austin State Teachers College; Hilton Ross Greer (1879–1949), born in Hawkins, Tex., was a journalist working in various capacities on newspapers throughout Texas and the Southwest. His verse appeared in *Cosmopolitan, Smart Set, Lippincott's* and numerous other periodicals. Collections included *A Prairie Prayer, and Other Poems* (1912) and *Ten and Twenty Aprils* (1925).

2. Sally Bruce Kinsolving (1876–1962), founder of the Poetry Society of Maryland in 1923, civic leader in Baltimore, and author of three collections of verse: *Depths and Shallows* (1921), *Grey Heather* (1930), and *Many Waters* (1942).

3. Marie Conway Oemler (1879–1932), Savannah-born writer best known for *Slippy McGee* (1917), a moderately successful novel about a likable gangster.

4. Feidelson, former newspaper editor and judge of the juvenile court in Savannah, Georgia, taught journalism at William and Mary in the early 1920s. The Poetry Society of Virginia was organized in May 1923 on the William and Mary campus; writers from around the state attended, and Feidelson was elected president.

5. Ransom (1888–1974), Tennessee-born poet and critic, editor of the *Kenyon Review*, and professor at Vanderbilt and Kenyon College. The Southern Prize went to Ransom's poem "Armageddon."

6. Davidson (1893–1968), poet and professor at Vanderbilt University who with Ransom and Allen Tate led the Fugitives and contributed to the group's symposia; wrote essays opposing centralization of political and economic power in the North and reflections on southern literature; probably best known for *Lee in the Mountains* (Boston: Houghton Mifflin, 1938), short narrative poems on Southern heroes. Davidson received honorable mention for "Avalon" and William Alexander Percy for "A Fragment."

7. Rosenthal, editor and underwriter of *The Nomad*, published from January 1922 through the summer of 1924; Frasier, Alabama poet and author of *Things That Are Mine* (1922) and *Guest's Prayer* (1923).

8. Henderson (1877–1963), professor of mathematics at the University of North Carolina at Chapel Hill who developed interests in literature, especially the work of Shaw, whose biography he went on to write, as he did also of Mark Twain. He also published several books that popularized literary topics, historical figures, and con-

temporary developments in scientific theory. A friend to the Charleston writers, he used his forums in metropolitan newspapers to propagandize for the revolution in southern literature.

9. Koch (1877–1944) was professor of drama at the University of North Carolina at Chapel Hill and founder of the Carolina Playmakers in 1918.

10. Reed (1892?–1978), American actor, director, author, and founder of the Town Theatre in Columbia, South Carolina. He produced there one of Dorothy Heyward's early plays as well as the stage version of Julia Peterkin's *Scarlet Sister Mary.*

11. *Deirdre of the Sorrows* (1910), by the Irish playwright John Millington Synge (1871–1909), a verse drama and his last work, published posthumously.

12. Clelia Peronneau Mathewes McGowan (1865–1956), known primarily for her forays into politics: a suffragette, she became the first woman appointed to public office in South Carolina (on the city council) and even ran for mayor.

13. Grimball, wife of the distinguished South Carolina jurist William Heyward Grimball (1886–1964); Sass, the former Marion Hutson who in 1919 married Herbert Ravenel Sass Jr., Charleston author of the Civil War novel *Look Back to Glory* (1933) and numerous stories and articles (many concerning Native Americans in the low country) in popular magazines.

14. Ambrose Elliott Gonzales (1857–1956), of Cuban descent, was a newspaper publisher and writer of Negro dialect stories. He was born on a plantation in Colleton County, S.C., that was soon to fall victim to Sherman's army. After public school in Beaufort, S.C., and one year at a private school in Virginia, at sixteen Gonzales learned telegraphy and worked for four years in Grahamville, S.C., at a small station on the Charleston & Savannah Railway. While there he and his brother, N. G. Gonzales, "printed" with pen and ink a small "newspaper," the *Palmetto.* After working several years as a telegraph operator in New York City and a few months in New Orleans, Gonzales returned to South Carolina and served (with his brother) as a traveling correspondent on the *Charleston News and Courier.* Both took an interest in politics, and found the racist views of Ben "Pitchfork" Tillman, elected governor in 1890, repugnant. Gonzales and his brother began in 1891 to publish the *State,* at Columbia, S.C. The paper's outspoken opposition to lynching, its plea for child-labor laws, better schools, compulsory-education laws, and its fight for wholesome politics won for it a high esteem among liberal people, but made many bitter enemies for its editors. Enlarging on stories that he had contributed over the years to newspapers, Gonzales produced four volumes of stories (all published by The State Company) in the unusual dialect of the low-country or Gullah Negroes: *The Black Border: Gullah Stories of the Carolina Coast* (1922), *With Aesop along the Black Border* (1924), *The Captain* (1924), and *Laguerre, a Gascon of the Black Border* (1924). The stories portray the humor and the pathos of the Gullahs. Gonzales also compiled a glossary and philological

commentary, appended to his first book, which constitute one of the few accurate studies of the Gullah dialect.

15. Artist who specialized in miniatures and dioramas, usually of a historical nature. He came to Charleston in 1923 for a convention of the American Association of Museums and became friendly with the Charleston group, especially Heyward, John Bennett, and Laura Bragg. In 1934 Heyward met Franklin again in Hollywood, where he was a set designer for MGM.

16. Allen (1889–1949), American author born in Pittsburgh, Pennsylvania, and best known for the historical novel *Anthony Adverse*, a runaway best-seller of 1933. Wounded in France during World War I, Allen returned to the States and began his studies at Harvard. Upon graduation he accepted a teaching assignment at Porter Military Academy in Charleston. There, with Heyward and John Bennett, he cofounded the Poetry Society of South Carolina. Early on, Allen published slim volumes of verse that received solid critical acclaim (notably *Wampum and Old Gold* [New Haven: Yale Univ. Press, 1921] and *Earth Moods* [New York: Harper & Row, 1925], in addition to *Carolina Chansons* [New York: Macmillan, 1922], coauthored with Heyward). He then went on to write *Israfel* (New York: George H. Doran, 1926), a melodramatic although highly vivid and thorough two-volume biography of Edgar Allan Poe, as well as numerous historical novels, such as *Action at Aquila* (New York: Farrar and Rinehart, 1938) and *It Was Like This: Two Stories of the Great War* (New York: Farrar and Rinehart, 1940). An ambitious five-novel cycle, to be known collectively as "The Disinherited," was to revive colonial America through the adventures of a hero named Salathiel Albine, but Allen was able to complete only three of these five novels (*Bedford Village* [New York: Farrar & Rinehart, 1944], *Toward the Morning* [New York: Rinehart, 1948], and *The City in the Dawn*, published posthumously by Rinehart in 1950) before his death in 1949 at the age of sixty.

17. Bennett (1856–1965), another cofounder with Heyward of the Poetry Society, was an author and illustrator born in Chillicothe, Ohio, who married into a prominent Charleston family and settled in the city in 1898. At the time Bennett had just published *Master Skylark* (1897), a popular children's tale set in Elizabethan England that remains a best-seller today. An avid investigator into the history and culture of the Gullahs, Bennett produced three books in which Gullah folktales figure prominently: *The Treasure of Peyre Gaillard* (1906), *Madame Margot: A Grotesque Legend of Old Charleston* (1921), and *The Doctor to the Dead: Grotesque Legends and Folk Tales of Old Charleston* (1946).

18. Hutty (1877–1954), one of the premier etchers of the twentieth century. Born in Michigan in 1877, he was trained in stained glass work in St. Louis and then went on to Woodstock, New York, an important artists' colony. In 1919 he moved to Charleston to winter and ended up staying as a permanent resident. He established

an art school for the Carolina Art Association (the Gibbes Museum of Art) and adopted the Gullahs as one of his trademark subjects—sympathetic, realistic etchings that are now in collections the world over, notably the Metropolitan and Cleveland art museums, the British Museum, and the New York Public Library. Hutty was a consummate draughtsman, whose line alone suggested spatial relationships and values. Critics generally agree that his paintings reveal little of this linear aptitude, although he produced many fine oils and watercolors in his time.

19. Maud Winthrop Gibbon, local music teacher who organized the Charleston Music Society in 1919. Gibbon was much sought after as an expert on the care and repair of violins; Ella Isabel Hyams (1877–1932), founder of the Musical Art Club (forerunner of the Charleston Music Society), who also formed and directed a chorus at the Charleston Orphan House; Addie Howell, cofounder with Hyams of the Musical Art Club and patron of the Gibbes Art Gallery, the Charleston Museum, and the Library Society.

20. Laura Mary Bragg (1881–1978), first full-time director of the Charleston Museum and organizer and first librarian of the Charleston County Library. Bragg was influential in guiding arts development in the city. She left the museum in 1931 to join the staff of the Berkshire Museum in Pittsfield, Mass., and later was director of the museum at Highlands, N.C., but returned to Charleston in 1940. Thereafter, each Sunday afternoon she held a salon in her home for the creative artists of the community.

21. Ellen Milliken FitzSimons (1862–1953), librarian of the Charleston Library Society for fifty years.

"The New Note in Southern Literature"

1. Born in New Orleans, George Cable (1844–1925) made established southern society uneasy with his 1880 novel, *The Grandissmes*, in which he treated the races as equals. His fiction and polemical essays drew fire from both old Confederates and New South supporters for his suggestions that mutual education was necessary for both races, and that the future fate of the former slave was not best managed by his former master.

2. "The Literary Lantern," a syndicated book-review column by Addison Hibbard Jr. (1887–1945), a professor of English at the University of North Carolina from 1918 to 1921, then at Northwestern until his retirement in 1942, noted critic and anthologizer of American literature. Influential publications included *The Lyric South* (New York: Macmillan, 1928) and *A Handbook to Literature*, coauthored with William Flint Thrall (Garden City, N.Y.: Doubleday, Doran, 1936).

3. "The South and Literature," by Burton, an English professor at the University of Minnesota, in *The Bookman* for February 1925.

4. Vollmer (1898–1955) was born in North Carolina to a traveling lumberman and his wife, and spent her summers among the mountaineers. Her numerous regional folk plays focused sympathetically on the mountain families as an inarticulate segment of American society cut off from the rest of the world. *Sun Up,* her most successful play, opened off Broadway on 24 May 1923, and became the surprise hit of the season. *The Shame Woman,* less critically successful, opened off Broadway on 16 October 1923, and also enjoyed a long run.

5. North Carolinian Hatcher Hughes (1883–1945), a professor at Columbia and Pulitzer Prize winner, authored the drama *Hell-Bent Fer Heaven* (1923). The play, set in the Blue Ridge Mountains of Kentucky, focused on the religious fervor of the inhabitants, as well as their clan feuds.

6. *Roseanne,* Stephens's first play, related the story of a black laundress who exposes the fraudulence of her beloved pastor. It played forty-one performances after its opening night on 29 December 1923, at the Greenwich Village Theatre, and ignited a controversy over the casting of white actors in black roles. The play was subsequently closed down and later redone by a black company. Heyward's knowledge of Stephens's difficulties makes all the more courageous his and Dorothy's insistence in 1926 that their play version of *Porgy* be cast with black actors.

7. Stallings (1894–1968), born in Macon, Georgia, an author, dramatist, and screenwriter best known for his realistic depictions of war, most stemming from his own experience as an honored soldier in World War I. His collaboration with Maxwell Anderson (1888–1959), *What Price Glory?,* was produced in 1924 and achieved critical acclaim and a finalist position for the Pulitzer Prize. The antiwar play was an unglamorous view of war, focusing on ordinary American soldiers in France during World War I.

8. Green (1894–1981), Koch's student and successor, best known for the outdoor historical drama *The Lost Colony* (1937). Born in North Carolina, both his drama and novels reflect his rural southern roots. He was also the author of *White Dresses* (1923), which dealt with the controversial issue of interracial love. The play was to be produced at the University of North Carolina, but university officials canceled it during rehearsals. Soon after Heyward's article was published, Green won the 1926 Pulitzer for *In Abraham's Bosom,* another realistic play about southern black life.

9. The second annual Little Theatre Tournament took place 6 May through 10 May 1924, at the Belasco Theatre in New York City. *Judge Lynch,* written by newspaperman J. William Rogers Jr., dealt with the mob lynching of an innocent black man. In 1925 it was performed by The Little Theatre of Dallas under the direction of Oliver Hinsdell, dramatic editor of the *Dallas News.*

10. Peterkin (1880–1961), born in Laurens County, S.C., and reared by her black nurse after her mother died shortly after her birth. From her nurse she learned the

dialect, customs, and superstitions of the Gullah blacks. When she married William George Peterkin in 1903 and became mistress of his family plantation, Lang Syne, in the farming community of Fort Motte, S.C., she oversaw an operation that employed between four hundred and five hundred Gullah blacks, whom she portrayed in a series of vivid novels: her first book, *Green Thursday* (1924), a collection of sketches and short stories; her first novel, *Black April* (1927), which won wide acclaim and made Peterkin a leader in the southern literary renaissance; and her widely popular *Scarlet Sister Mary* (1928), which won a Pulitzer Prize.

11. White (1893–1955), born in Atlanta, Georgia, comrade-in-arms of James Weldon Johnson and W. E. B. Du Bois in the executive leadership of the National Association for the Advancement of Colored People from 1918 until his death. White was Caucasian in skin color and physique, yet he vigorously asserted his Negro ancestry and spent most of his life as a leader in the campaign against lynching. *The Fire in the Flint* (New York: Knopf, 1924) showed how the lynching of his brother rouses a complacent black doctor to active opposition of racism.

12. The collection *Chills and Fever* was published by Knopf in 1924 and marked the beginning of Ransom's most critically acclaimed period of verse writing. Heyward most likely drew the Morley quote from his friend Herbert Gorman's review of *Chills and Fever* in the *New York Times Book Review* of September 1924.

"The American Negro in Art"

1. Throckmorton (1897–1965) was a pioneer in stage set design whose most notable work was done for Eugene O'Neill's plays in the 1920s.

2. Mamoulian (1897–1987), born in Russia, had emigrated to London and gained experience working in the West End theatres. He went on to establish the American Opera Company in Rochester, New York, where Lawrence Langner of the Theatre Guild spotted him and offered him a job. He later became one of Hollywood's most innovative directors, in such films as the 1931 *Dr. Jekyll and Mr. Hyde* and the first Technicolor feature, *Becky Sharp*. Mamoulian also directed the opera *Porgy and Bess* (see "Porgy and Bess Return on Wings of Song," pp. 46–51). In August 1927, he and Throckmorton visited Heyward's old mentor, John Bennett, in Charleston, to soak up the atmosphere of the city and learn something about Gullah culture. On this trip Mamoulian "discovered" the Jenkins Orphanage Band and signed them to lead the procession, "Sons and Daughters of Repent Ye Saith the Lord," to "Kittawah Island" in act 2. Throckmorton based his set on what he observed of the Negro tenements in Charleston, and by all accounts, it was astonishingly realistic.

3. Casting the play required herculean efforts from Heyward and Mamoulian. Actors had to be selected from productions quite unlike *Porgy*—vaudeville shows,

revues, and cabarets—in venues quite unlike the legitimate stage. Trained in such environments, these actors found it difficult to offer realistic readings of character; moreover, they were refined and sophisticated, unlike the gaunt, tragic figures that Heyward had seen on the waterfront in his youth. So few black actors were available that Mamoulian went so far as to stop likely-looking prospects on the street and ask them to come to an audition. Heyward later admitted that with so few actors from which to choose, casting pretty much resolved itself into giving the roles to whoever was available.

4. Evelyn Ellis (1894–1958) was an American actress whom Mamoulian discovered in a Harlem stock theatrical company. Ellis performed in several important African American plays, notably as Lucy Bell Dorsey in the 1927 revival of *Goat Alley*, Ernest Howard Culbertson's 1921 drama about black life in the Washington, D.C., slums. She also appeared with Charles Gilpin in Nan Bagby Stephens's *Roseanne* (*q.v.*). In the 1930s Ellis became a director in the federal government's Negro Theatre Project through the WPA and in 1941 played Hannah Thomas in Orson Welles's highly acclaimed staging of Richard Wright and Paul Green's drama, *Native Son.*

5. Wilson was the star of Paul Green's recent *In Abraham's Bosom* (1926), a southern drama of miscegenation and racial violence. Heyward greatly admired the play, telling Green that "my hat is off to you for your courage and your art" (Letter of DBH to Green, 2 Feb. 1927, Paul Green Papers, Southern Historical Collection, Wilson Library, Univ. of North Carolina at Chapel Hill), but though he was not quite as disappointed in the choice of Wilson as he was in the choice of Ellis, he still felt that Wilson had not delved deeply enough into his character's psyche and had presented a thin, attenuated rendering.

6. Georgette Harvey (1883–1952) began her career as a nightclub performer, achieving her greatest renown abroad, in night spots in St. Petersburg and, after the Russian Revolution, in major cities in Japan. She portrayed "Black Maria" in two different productions of the play *Porgy* and again in a revival of the opera, fresh from appearing in the title role of the Heyward play version of *Mamba's Daughters* (1939).

7. Rosalie Virginia Scott McClendon (1884–1936) was a leading dramatic actress of her day. She had appeared with Wilson in *In Abraham's Bosom* and on Broadway in the supporting role that made her a legend: an aging mulatto in Laurence Stallings and Frank Harlin's 1926 "native opera," *Deep River* (see p. 33). She had also performed in Stephens's *Roseanne* (*q.v.*). A co-head of the Negro Theatre Project, McClendon's greatest role may have been one she never was able to perform due to her untimely death in 1936: the title role of Euripides' *Medea*, with additional text by Countee Cullen and direction by John Houseman, who had reset the play to an African American environment.

8. R. J. Huey had also appeared in *In Abraham's Bosom* in 1926–27 and had ten shows to his credit before retiring in 1944. Dorothy Paul first appeared in *Goat Alley*

in April 1927; her last appearance was in the Heyward stage version of *Mamba's Daughters* in 1939.

9. Mamoulian's method was to time the action and speeches in a play according to a rhythm similar to that in music. Activity on stage would be done to a count: first one-two time, then faster times and faster times. Spirituals provided other rhythms, as did the tolling of the bells of St. Michael's Church. The sound of these bells and their rhythmic properties were actually imported from Charleston; Heyward knew a member of the church, who faithfully recorded the exact number of beats per minute and sent the data to him in New York.

10. Whipper (1876–1975) was one of America's best-known character actors, born in Charleston to a father who was a circuit court judge and a mother who was a physician. Whipper joined the theater after graduating from Howard University Law School. His long and varied career spanned more than sixty-five years, including an Academy Award nomination for his part in *The Ox Bow Incident* (1943). He was the first black member of Actors Equity Association and a founding member of the Negro Actors Guild.

11. Act 2, scene 1; Hill was born in Baltimore, Md. (birth date unknown), and died December 1930 in Bronx, New York.

12. *Shuffle Along* (1921), score by Noble Sissle and Eubie Blake; *Runnin' Wild* (1922) introduced audiences to the high-spirited dance known as "The Charleston." Both were typical examples of the vaudeville roles that were usually the only opportunities available to black actors.

"The Negro in the Low-Country"

1. For this essay, Heyward drew heavily on Ulrich B. Phillips's then-authoritative study, *Life and Labor in the Old South* (Boston: Little, Brown, 1929). To convey the information (and prejudices) upon which Heyward was relying, some of his source material is reprinted in the notes that follow. Slave coast: "But from the middle zone, the Slave Coast, where the Niger threads its delta to the sea, where in the fetid ports of Bonny and Begin, Lagos and Calabar, a stream of slaving ships met converging streams of slave coffles and bartered their firearms and fire water, goods and gewgaws, there came the main supply of living 'ebony'" (Phillips 190); Calabar: city port in western Nigeria, near the eastern border of Cameroon, on the Gulf of Guinea along the Slave Coast. It is now the capital city of the state of Cross River and still a principal port; Angola: presently a state in southwestern Africa, on its western coast. By the early seventeenth century, 5,000–10,000 slaves were exported from Luanda, Angola, in a year's time. Phillips notes, "From another extreme, the far south, came Congoes and Angolas, slender and sightly, mild and honest, but as a rule, notoriously stupid" (190).

2. Corramantees: a Sudanese tribe from the Gold Coast region of western Africa, also referred to by Phillips as "Fantyns" (*Life and Labor* 189).

3. Governor General of this section of the West Indies from 1698 to 1704.

4. From a letter dated 30 December 1701, from then Governor Christopher Codrington III to the Council of Trade and Plantations. See *Calendar of State Papers: Colonial Series, America and West Indies, 1701*, ed. Cecil Headlam (1910; Vaduz: Kraus Reprint, 1964), 720–21.

5. From a region referred to now as The Gambia, a narrow enclave along the Gambia River within the country of Senegal. The river was used extensively by the Portuguese, French, and British for slave trading. Mandingo slave merchants traded there, selling their own slaves; Mandingos were a tribe within Gambia. (See Phillips, *American Negro Slavery* 44).

6. Senegalese: from Senegal, now the westernmost republic on Africa's bulge. A trading post at the mouth of the Senegal River served Europeans in their exportation of slaves throughout the seventeenth and eighteenth centuries. "The Senegalese, who had a strong Arabic strain in their ancestry, were considered the most intelligent of Africans and were especially esteemed for domestic service, the handicrafts and responsible positions" (Phillips 42); Mandangoes (or Mandingos): another name for the Malinke tribe, originating from the Gambia River valley; Whydahs (or Ouidah, as the Benin city is spelled currently): people originating from present-day Benin, on the Slave Coast in the Bight of Benin. A sophisticated people, accustomed to trading. The Portuguese especially prized this tribe's slaves for what was believed to be extraordinary skill at finding gold; Nagoes: another tribe from along the Slave Coast; Pow Pows (or Po Pos): another tribe originating from present-day Benin. The coastal city of Grand Po Po sits slightly east of Ouidah; Congoes: the tribes situated around the Congo River, which reaches into the interior of West Africa; Gaboons: natives of present-day Gabon, on West Africa's coast, straddling the equator; Eboes: "As to the Eboes or Mocoes, described as having a sickly or yellow tinge in their complection, jaundiced eyes, and prognathous faces like baboons, the women were said to be diligent but the men lazy, despondent and prone to suicide" (Phillips 43).

7. Randolph movement: namely, the suggestion made by Thomas J. Randolph before the Virginia General Assembly on 10 January 1832, that slaves born after 4 July 1840, be gradually emancipated and colonized. Randolph, Thomas Jefferson's favorite grandson, thus launched the first open debate on emancipation within the Virginia legislature; news of the unprecedented discussion soon spread and the legislature's galleries were crowded throughout the ensuing two weeks. The expediency of the plan and property-rights issues were debated, and the motion was eventually defeated 73-58.

8. Phillips gives slightly different figures in *American Negro Slavery*, but lists as his source the Annals of Congress for 8 December 1820, in which South Carolinian William Smith presents Congress with figures from Charleston's custom-house officer. Heyward's total (39,075) and British/French figures (21,027) match the Congressional records, as do the total for Rhode Island (8,238); however, if the Annals were indeed Heyward's "authoritative" source, his figures for slave and nonslave states do not seem to be substantiated, except that together with Rhode Island's 8,238 they combine to match a figure in Phillips's account of the *Annals* (138).

9. For example, forbidding slaves from learning to read or write, preaching or assembling outside their home without a white person present, trading, hiring themselves out, keeping liquor or weapons.

10. In 1791 in the region now known as Haiti, slaves working the coffee and spice plantations rose in rebellion, inspired by the ideals espoused in the concurrent French Revolution. The nearly 500,000 slaves overthrew their French masters with much destruction and bloodshed, setting up their own government and sending waves of fear throughout the American South.

11. Thomas Parker and Lionel H. Kennedy, presiding justices in the trial of Denmark Vesey, published what they asserted was a full account of the trial and sentencing in *An Official Report of the Trials of Sundry Negroes, Charged with an Attempt to Raise an Insurrection in the State of South Carolina* (Charleston: James R. Schenck, 1822).

12. William Drayton (1776–1846), Charleston attorney and judge, Representative in the South Carolina and U.S. legislatures; Robert J. Turnbull (1775–1833), Charleston attorney, best known for publishing, under the pseudonym of "Brutus," *The Crisis, or, Essays on the Usurpations of the Federal Government* (Charleston: A. E. Miller, 1827); James Legare (1762–1830), planter and South Carolina Representative; James R. Pringle (1782–1840), South Carolina Representative and Senator; Nathaniel Heyward (1766–1851), owner of Whitehall rice plantation in Charleston, South Carolina Representative. All of these men were prominent Charleston citizens, selected by city council to preside over the special court headed by magistrates Kennedy and Parker.

13. New legislation passed in South Carolina after the averted Vesey insurrection included the following: No free Negroes who left the state could return, those free males between fifteen and fifty that had not lived in the state for five years were required to pay an annual tax of fifty dollars, no slaves could hire themselves out, and any persons (white or black) aiding in insurrection were subject to execution. Of particular controversy was the Negro Seaman Act, requiring free Negro employees on ships arriving in any South Carolina Port to be imprisoned until their ship sailed out, with the expense of imprisonment to be paid by the ship's captain.

14. The breeding of slaves explicitly for sale was of course prevalent on Virginia

tobacco plantations from the seventeenth century onward, and was a practice that gained new popularity with U.S. prohibition of the international slave trade in 1807.

15. The plantation of Heyward's mother's family.

"Porgy and Bess Return on Wings of Song"

1. Sometime in the early summer of 1926. See "On the Genesis of a Folk-Opera," *New York Times*, sec. 11 (Oct. 6, 1935): 3.

2. Formed in 1915 to present plays of American origin. The theatre was a professional offshoot of the Washington Square Players, entering the ranks of Broadway in 1919. The group was dedicated to artistic and experimental theatre.

3. Heyward refers here to the nonmusical stage version of *Porgy*, produced by the Theatre Guild in New York in October 1927. At about this time, Heyward also entertained an offer by Al Jolson, who wanted to produce and star (in blackface) in a musical version of the play, with music by Jerome Kern and book by Oscar Hammerstein II. That project, however, never materialized. Gershwin did not think that any musical version of the play would spoil his operatic designs for it. He told Heyward that what he had in mind was "more a labor of love than anything else" (qtd. in Hollis Alpert, *The Life and Times of Porgy and Bess* [New York: Knopf, 1989], 75).

4. *Rhapsody in Blue* was published 4 January 1924.

5. Heyward refers to the shadow effect in the group prayer scene (act 2, scene 4), which was actually created by accident—when a stagehand left a footlight on during rehearsal. Crown's line occurs in the same place.

6. Philip Moeller (1880–1958), director and playwright, was one of the six members of the Board of Managers of the Theatre Guild. Moeller was best known as the author of *Madame Sand* (1917), a biographical dramatization, and similar plays in that vein. Heyward describes Alexander Woolcott, legendary New York drama critic, below.

7. *Porgy* ran for 217 performances in New York before going on a profitable road tour; it returned to Broadway in April 1928 for another 150 performances; then, the following spring the company drew sizable crowds at London's Pavilion Theatre, where it ran through June. There was talk of further Continental engagements, though none materialized.

8. Around 1926.

9. Schillinger (1895–1943), innovative Russian-born composer and ethnomusicologist among whose early work was the preservation of folk music of some of the Georgian tribes and the establishment of the first jazz orchestra in Russia. Later radical theories, emanating from his dissatisfaction with the tempered scale, led him to apply strict mathematical principles and formulae to musical composition.

10. François Villon (1431–63?), one of the great medieval poets known for his alternately compassionate, ironic, ribald, and penitent verses celebrating his life among

a band of thieves; "King of Bavaria" (Ludwig II), Richard Wagner's patron, who rescued him from debtors' prison and brought him to Munich with a lifelong carte blanche for creative work. Ludwig's generosity made possible the first festival performances of the *Ring* in Bayreuth in 1876.

11. Caius Maecenas (d. 8 B.C.), Roman statesman and patron of letters under Augustus, a symbol of one who is a benefactor of the arts.

12. Sportin' Life sings "It Ain't Necessarily So" and "There's a Boat Dat's Leavin' Soon for New York."

13. Heyward had purchased his "Folly shack," as he called it, in the early 1930s, in order to reestablish himself partly in Charleston without living in the city proper and thus being subject to those pressures of celebrity—and of social obligations, the reason he had fled the city in the first place after the success of *Porgy* in 1925. Heyward's house still exists today; the ocean-side cottage in which Gershwin worked, however, was destroyed by a hurricane a few years later.

14. Act 3, scene 2—the storm scene. Actually Gershwin wrote none of the prayers. Heyward wrote one and Ira Gershwin the other five. The prayers were cut from the opera after the Boston tryout in September 1935, however, in service to shortening the production.

15. 17 October 1933.

16. *Four Saints in Three Acts*, which premiered in New York in 1935, with book by Gertrude Stein and music by Virgil Thomson, was an esoteric opera that allegorized the development of modernist art in Paris in the 1920s. Heyward worried that it might steal thunder in advance from *Porgy and Bess*, because it employed an all-black cast, but the subject matter of the two works was so dissimilar that this did not happen; Smallens (1889–1972), Russian-born composer who held several landmark conducting positions, including the Boston Opera (1911–14), Chicago Opera (1919–23), and Philadelphia Civic Opera (1924–31). He later moved toward a lighter repertoire, conducting the premiere of Gershwin's *Porgy and Bess* and its European tour in 1952. From 1947 to 1950 he was director of Radio City Music Hall.

17. Alexander Lang Steinert (1900–1982), pianist, conductor of the Russian Opera Company, composer of numerous scores for film and television.

18. By Claude Debussy, Camille Saint-Saëns, and Wagner, respectively.

"Dock Street Theatre"

1. The funneling of this federal money to Charleston was engineered by its mayor at the time, Burnet R. Maybank (see below), who was fast friends with Harry Hopkins and a pioneer in the use of federal funds to preserve historic buildings.

2. Located near the corner of present-day Queen and Church Streets. In 1736 Dock Street had recently been renamed Queen Street.

3. The fire that destroyed the theater was in 1740. The name of the playhouse that succeeded Dock Street was referred to as "The Theater."

4. Early nineteenth century.

5. Douglas D. Ellington (1886–1960), North Carolina–born architect who studied at Drexel and the University of Pennsylvania. He practiced in Pittsburgh in the early 1920s; when in 1926 he was given a commission to design the First Baptist Church in Asheville, N.C., he moved there with his family and went on to attain several architectural commissions of great variety and scope, including an S&W cafeteria in Pritchard Park, which is considered one of the finest Art Deco structures in the state, and the "model community" of Greenbelt, Md., in the suburbs of Washington, D.C.

6. Albert Simons and Samuel Lapham, architects in Charleston responsible for the renovation of many historic buildings, most notably the Fireproof Building at the corner of Chalmers and Meeting Streets. It houses the South Carolina Historical Society. Simons wrote *An Architectural Guide to Charleston, S.C., 1700–1900* and co-authored with Lapham the volume on Charleston in the Octagon Library of American Architecture, a projected series on historic American buildings, although only this one volume was published.

7. Built between 1800 and 1806, the house occupied two lots in the center of the peninsula. It became the Charleston High School in 1917 and is today the gymnasium of the College of Charleston. Mitchell King (1783–1862) came originally from Fifeshire; he migrated to Charleston in 1805, where he became a judge, a trustee of the College of Charleston, and the main convenor of the city's Conversation Club; he possessed one of the larger private libraries in the South; with others, he helped to found *Russell's Magazine.*

8. See "Poetry South," p. 268, note 7.

9. William Melton Halsey (1915–99), a native Charlestonian and professor of art at the College of Charleston, was a pioneer of abstract painting in the South. He studied under Elizabeth O'Neill Verner and directed art classes at the Gibbes Museum.

10. Burnet Rhett Maybank (1899–1954), mayor of Charleston from 1931 until 1938, when he was elected governor. An affable, well-connected politico from one of Charleston's most aristocratic families, Maybank (later elected United States senator) was a highly successful chief executive. In the midst of the Depression, he brought in a new paper mill and built several public housing projects. One of the crown jewels of his administration was the restoration of the Dock Street Theatre.

11. Robert Newton Spry Whitelaw (1905–74), first full-time professional director of the Gibbes Art Gallery and architecture preservation pioneer. An accomplished artist, Whitelaw excelled at miniature dioramas (he trained with Dwight Franklin [q.v.] in New York) and under the sponsorship of the Carolina Art Associ-

ation made a survey of the architectural heritage of Charleston in *This is Charleston* (1944).

12. In 1937.

13. *The Recruiting Officer* (1706) by the Irish playwright George Farquhar (1678–1707) concerns the humorous follies of recruiting soldiers and love in a country town.

"Charleston: Where Mellow Past and Present Meet"

1. What is today known as Charles Towne Landing.

2. In 1564 Fort Carolina was established at the mouth of the St. Johns River. The settlement was destroyed by Spanish invaders under the leadership of Pedro Menendez.

3. Also called "hackbut," the first gun (rifle-like) that was fired from the shoulder; invented in Spain in the mid-fifteenth century.

4. Yeamans (ca. 1610–74) had emigrated to Barbados in 1650, when the Commonwealth was in the ascendancy. When the Lords Proprietors were granted Carolina in 1663, Yeamans, seeing an opportunity for himself and other ambitious Barbadians, successfully negotiated through his son, Maj. William Yeamans, for the right to establish a colony there with himself as governor. After a failed first expedition, in 1671 Yeamans arrived to establish a permanent residence, built a home, and introduced the first negro slaves. He claimed the governorship on the ground that a provision in the charter stipulated that a proprietor or a landgrave must be governor, and he alone met the requirement.

5. Anthony Ashley Cooper, first baron Ashley and first earl of Shaftesbury (1621–83), was initially a Royalist during the English Civil War and then a Parliamentarian, though in opposition to Oliver Cromwell; after the Restoration, which he helped to arrange, he became Chancellor of the Exchequer (1661–72), but subsequently fell out of favor and was obliged to flee to Amsterdam, where he died.

6. See "The Negro in the Low-Country" (pp. 34–45), for another discussion of the economics of the slavery/plantation system.

7. As a boy, Heyward worked for a time as a cotton checker on the docks of Charleston harbor (see part 1 [pp. 17–18] of the semiautobiographical novel *Mamba's Daughters*).

8. Truck-gardening or truck-farming, as opposed to market-gardening, is the production of green vegetables on tracts remote from market.

9. Drafted in 1699 by Lord Shaftesbury and John Locke, this was the original frame of government for the Carolinas. It was abandoned in 1693 and replaced by a frame of government diminishing the power of the proprietors and increasing the rights of the provincial assembly, thus eliminating the feudal nature of the original frame.

10. In the Carolinas, "cassiques" and "landgraves" were similar, the rough equivalent of Lords and Earls. Cassique (also "cassock"): obsolete form of "cacique"—originally, a native chief or "prince" of the aborigines in the West Indies and adjacent parts of America (cf. William Gilmore Simms's *The Cassique of Kiawah* [1859]). More generally, someone who owes his ascendancy to his power or influence.

11. Henry Wager Halleck (1815–72) of New York, formerly commander of the Department of the Mississippi, until he became chief of staff under Ulysses S. Grant.

12. Joseph Eggleston Johnston (1807–91) of Virginia commanded the Army of Northern Virginia in the Peninsular campaign in 1862, was wounded, and upon recovery was reassigned to the western theater, where he was blamed for the fall of Vicksburg; subsequently, he was appointed commander of the Army of the Tennessee, in which capacity he conducted the retreat into Georgia.

13. The "single house," so named because it consisted of a wooden frame that was one room wide.

14. St. Andrew's Society: founded 1792, the oldest of the Charleston societies. Members were made up of the Scottish community in Charleston; Hibernian Society: founded 1799, an informal gathering of Charleston Irishmen who were dedicated to social enjoyment and helping the Irish needy; German Friendly Society: established in Germany in 1766 by Michael Kalteisen. It arrived in Charleston in the early eighteenth century, providing a place for members of the German community in Charleston to meet and discuss their future; St. Cecilia Society: founded early eighteenth century and, by all accounts, the first society to support a paid orchestra—for its elaborate and socially exclusive balls, admission to which was by subscription only and was quite expensive. The society still flourishes today.

15. See also "The American Negro in Art" (pp. 27–33). The Jenkins Negro Orphanage was organized in 1895 as a municipally funded home for young black children. In the 1910s the Reverend Daniel Jenkins, its founder, formed a band from among the children. The first black instrumental group in South Carolina, this collection of amazingly talented musicians performed up and down the East Coast to rave reviews. The orphanage eventually became known in the jazz world as the cradle of musical genius, as many of its residents grew up and went on to play with Duke Ellington, "Jelly Roll" Morton, Count Basie, and Lionel Hampton.

16. First residence of the American branch of the Drayton Family, located alongside the Ashley River. Ownership of the plantation extended some 320 years.

17. Eighteenth-century plantation along the Ashley River. Home of the Middleton family, beginning with Henry Middleton, president of the First Continental Congress.

18. A three-thousand-acre estate, originally part of Dean Hall, along the Cooper River. The gardens that exist today were created by Benjamin Kittredge in the late 1920s.

19. Brookgreen comprises four rice plantations. George Washington spent the night there, as did Julia Peterkin, who used the plantation as a backdrop for several of her novels; Belle Isle: one of three Winyah Bay plantations in Georgetowne, S.C., formed in 1801 by General Peter Horry, one of the state's prominent figures during the American Revolution.

20. Stede Bonnet (1688?–1718), called the "Gentleman Pirate." A plantation owner in Barbados who turned to piracy, looting ships off the coast of Virginia, New York, and South Carolina. Imprisoned in Charleston, escaped, and pursued by William Rhett, he was captured and hanged at White Point Gardens, on the Battery at Charleston Harbor. See Heyward's poem "The Pirates" (pp. 77–85).

21. See Heyward's poem "The Last Crew" (pp. 85–93). The *Hunley* was a Confederate submarine, built in 1863, that sunk the federal *Housatonic* before itself sinking on 16 February 1864, killing all nine crew members on board. The wreck was located in 1995 and brought to the surface on 8 August 2000. Preservation efforts are now under way.

22. See Heyward's "Dock Street Theatre" essay (pp. 52–56).

23. Heyward was baptized here, 22 November 1895.

24. Thomas Heyward Jr. (1746–1809), who long served in South Carolina's colonial assemblies, was a coauthor of the South Carolina constitution of 1776, as well as of the Articles of Confederation; he was in the Continental Congress from 1776 to 1778. He was DuBose Heyward's great-great-great-grandfather.

25. Society for the Preservation of Old Dwelling Houses, founded 1920 by Susan Frost and Mr. and Mrs. Ernest Pringle, to prevent the destruction of architecturally or historically significant homes, among them the Heyward-Washington house and the Joseph Manigault mansion. A Board of Architectural Review was created, still in existence today, to approve any exterior changes to historic dwellings. The Historic Charleston Foundation (1940 to the present) subsumed the earlier organization with the express purpose of raising funds to accomplish its mission.

26. Now home to the South Carolina Historical Society.

27. Robert Mills (1781–1855), who was born in Charleston, was active in designing buildings in the city, including the Independent (Congregational) Church (1822) and the First Baptist Church (1822). He designed a Washington Monument (1814) for Baltimore. From 1836 to 1842 he was the "federal architect" of the District of Columbia and of federal buildings nationally; his notable work included the Treasury Building, the Patent Office, and various modifications to the U.S. Capitol. In 1846 he offered a design for the Washington Monument, but it was not completed in a revised version until 1884.

28. Site of the first Church of England in Charleston, 1670, then moved to a different location in the city. The cornerstone of the present St. Michael's was laid on 17 February 1752, and the church opened for services on 1 February 1761.

29. Sir Henry Clinton (1738?–95), born in Newfoundland, entered the Coldstream Guards in 1751, served in Germany (1760–63), fought at Bunker's Hill in 1775, and became British commander-in-chief in America in 1778. He resigned in 1781, after quarreling with his second-in-command, Lord Cornwallis.

"The Pirates"

1. A warship that had been converted to a merchant ship by removing its upper deck and thus reducing it in height.

2. In 1562 Jean Ribault had established fleetingly a French Huguenot settlement at Port Royal; in 1564 Fort Caroline on the St. John's River in Florida was established as an extension of French colonization, but it lasted little over a year.

3. William Sayle (d. 1671) had earlier been governor of the Bermudas; he died in office, being well into his eighties when appointed.

4. Alexander Spotswood (1676–1740), who had fought at Blenheim under the Duke of Marlborough, was governor of Virginia from 1710 to 1722; he remained in the colony after his displacement; Edward Teach (d. 1718), known as Blackbeard, thought to have born in Bristol, became a privateer during the Spanish War of Succession, then a pirate in the West Indies and off Virginia and the Carolinas; he was wrecked off Topsail Inlet, obliged to surrender, and was executed; Stede Bonnet (1688?–1718) was a retired major in the King's Guards, who came to own a plantation in Barbados. It is said that the impulse to escape a nagging wife led him to buy a sloop, called *The Revenge*, which he used ineptly for piracy, in company with Teach. Bonnet was hanged at White Point, Charleston, in 1718.

5. William Rhett (1666–1723) arrived in South Carolina in 1694 and, through the influence of Richard Shelton, the secretary to the Lords Proprietors, became one of the most powerful men in the colony. A merchant–sea captain, Rhett earned a profitable living by not being particular with whom he traded or how the goods that he sold were acquired. He held numerous public offices from 1703 on and rose swiftly in the state militia from lieutenant colonel in 1706 to lieutenant general in 1719. Rhett died of apoplexy on 12 January 1723, in the midst of several intrigues related to his business improprieties and his failed attempts to curry favor with the new governor, James Moore.

"New England Landscape"

1. Mountain in southwest New Hampshire, isolated on a peneplain, featured in several Edwin Arlington Robinson poems.

The Half Pint Flask

1. A light vehicle, usually built by slinging a plank on top of two sets of wheels.

From *Mamba's Daughters: A Novel of Charleston*

1. "Truck," that is, garden-truck—crops that had been harvested in the country then transported to the city for sale. See "Charleston: Where Mellow Past and Present Meet," p. 283, note 8.

2. Hagar's "white folks"—the white family that she determinedly attached herself to as house servant. In other parts of the novel, Heyward mocks the parvenu intentions of the Atkinsons, wealthy northerners who try to buy their way into the deeply rooted Charleston society.

3. Both Eurasian herbs of the family *Rubiaceae* (the madder family) with whorled leaves and small, yellowish panicled flowers succeeded by berries.

4. A figure probably modeled on Edwin A. Harleston (1882–1931), African American portrait painter and Charleston native who was active in the Black community, serving as the first president of the Charleston chapter of the NAACP.

5. Harry Thacker Burleigh (1866–1949), American baritone and composer singled out by Carl Van Vechten and other observers of the Harlem Renaissance as a noted preserver and arranger (to most African Americans, "formalizer") of Negro spirituals.

6. The Avery Normal Institute, founded in 1865 by the American Missionary Association, to train black teachers. The Institute closed in 1954, but in 1978 Avery graduates reopened it as the Avery Institute of African-American History and Culture, a community-based historical society affiliated with the University of Charleston.

7. Hayes (1887–1977), the first African American male to win acclaim in America and Europe as a concert artist. He obtained his basic music training in Chattanooga with Arthur Calhoun and at Fisk University and toured with the Fisk Jubilee Singers.

8. The novel opens with a farcical episode in which Mamba is present at the Wentworth guest house on Sullivan's Island (the Wentworths are her first employer). One of the visitors, Judge Harkness, loses his dentures in the surf while swimming; Mamba recovers the teeth when they wash ashore and takes them to a dentist to be fitted for herself

9. I.e., "The Charleston," the dance step made popular by Black Broadway revues of the time.

10. One of the more famous of the many tunes composed by Bob Cole, John Rosamund Johnson, and his brother, James Weldon Johnson—"Cole and John-

son Brothers." Rosamund and James also penned "Lift Every Voice and Sing," which came to be called the Negro National Anthem. A leading figure of the Harlem Renaissance and admirer of Heyward's work, James (1871–1938) authored the famous black "passing" novel *The Autobiography of an Ex-Colored Man* (1912) and was for ten years the general secretary of the NAACP. Rosamund followed a lifelong career in music and played Lawyer Frazier in *Porgy and Bess.* (See the headnote to part V.)

From *Peter Ashley*

1. Peter's father.

2. Brig. Gen. Clement Hoffman Stevens, an official of the Planters and Mechanics bank who in January 1861 presented to Gen. David F. Jamison, South Carolina's secretary of war, a design he had prepared for an armored battery (built of pine timber and covered with bars of railroad iron) of two guns on Cummings Point, known as the Stevens iron battery. It was of great service in the bombardment of Fort Sumter.

3. A covered carriage.

4. Well-drilled military unit in bright uniform patterning itself after the French infantry company originally composed of Algerians.

5. Bright (1811–89), English politician, orator, and M.P. (almost continuously from 1843 to 1889) who engaged in free-trade agitation and in movements for financial reform, electoral reform, and religious freedom.

Index

Italicized page numbers refer to works that appear in the book.